Media Law in Bulgaria

Media Law in Bulgaria

Third Edition

Boris E. Kolev
Tzvetelina Petkova

This book was originally published as a monograph in the International Encyclopaedia of Laws/Media Law.

Founding Editor: Roger Blanpain
General Editor: Frank Hendrickx
Volume Editors: Peggy Valcke & Eva Lievens

Wolters Kluwer

Published by:
Kluwer Law International B.V.
PO Box 316
2400 AH Alphen aan den Rijn
The Netherlands
E-mail: lrs-sales@wolterskluwer.com
Website: www.wolterskluwer.com/en/solutions/kluwerlawinternational

Sold and distributed by:
Wolters Kluwer Legal & Regulatory U.S.
920 Links Avenue
Landisville, PA 17538
United States of America
E-mail: customer.service@wolterskluwer.com

ISBN 978-94-035-4668-1

e-Book: ISBN 978-94-035-4678-0
web-PDF: ISBN 978-94-035-4688-9

The Authors

Boris E. Kolev holds an LLM in International Business Law from the Central European University (Budapest, Hungary, 2004) and a Magister Juris degree from the University of National and World Economics (Sofia, Bulgaria, 2002). He completed a post graduate research project in 2006 at ASSER College Europe titled 'Harmonization of the Legal Status of Professional Football Players Within the European Union: Lex Sportiva and Lex Mercatoria'. Boris Kolev has extensive practice as a corporate lawyer specializing in general corporate and intellectual property law, which he initially gained with leading Bulgarian law firms. Currently, he is the General Manager of the Consultancy Company Decaleges, which runs various projects in the field of sports and media law. He is a member of the Advisory Board of the *International Sports Law Journal* issued by the International Sports Law Centre of the ASSER Institute in Hague. Boris Kolev has numerous publications on sports and media law issues, including the article 'TV Rights in Bulgarian Football' in the *International Sports Law Journal* and the country chapter on Bulgaria (together with Anton Petrov) from the book '*TV Rights and Sport: Legal Aspects*', issued by T.M.C. ASSER Press in 2009. Together with Tzvetelin Simov, Boris Kolev wrote the book '*Sports Law in Bulgaria*' originally published as a monograph in the International Encyclopaedia of Laws/Sports Law, which covered also issues related to the legal regulation of sports events' broadcasting.

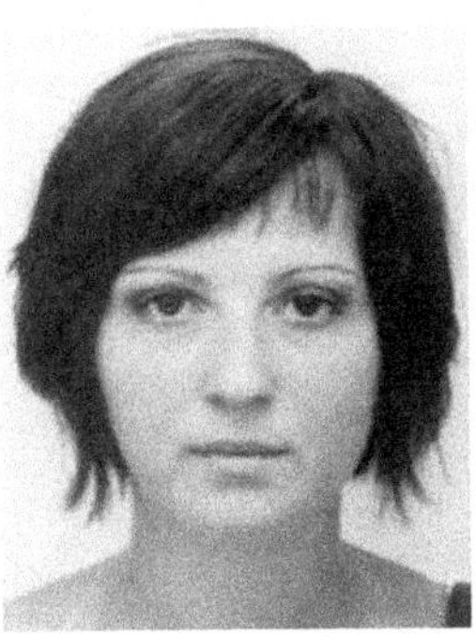

Tzvetelina Petkova studied business administration, economics and law at the universities of Bordeaux and Paris in France. She received her master's degree in European and International Public Law from the University of Paris 11 – Jean Monnet in 2008. After a traineeship at the Council of the European Union (Legal Service ECOFIN/Agriculture and Fisheries) in Brussels, Belgium, she joined the Administration of the Council of Ministers of the Republic of Bulgaria in 2011 as an European Union (EU) law expert. Located in Sofia, Bulgaria, she worked in the Directorate for Coordination of EU affairs which is responsible for the coherent policy conduct of Bulgaria in the decision-making process in the EU, and it was also part of the SOLVIT network that handles complaints submitted by EU citizens and/or companies and related to the application of the internal market rules by the public authorities of the EU Member States. Tzvetelina moved back to France in early 2015 and worked at the European Securities and Markets Authority (ESMA), an independent EU authority aiming at safeguarding the stability of the EU's financial system. Since 2016, Tzvetelina has worked as a legal advisor in the private banking sector. She is responsible for negotiating various financial contracts, e.g., master agreements related to derivatives, repurchase and securities lending agreements and other financial markets documentation.

Table of Contents

List of Abbreviations

ABBRO	Association of Bulgarian Broadcasters
ABCO	Association of Bulgarian Cable Operators
AEJ	Association of European Journalists
AIPF	Access to Information Programme Foundation
AVMSD	Audiovisual Media Service Directive
BDA	Bulgarian Drug Agency
BMU	Bulgarian Media Union
BNR	Bulgarian National Radio
BNT	Bulgarian National Television
BTC	Bulgarian Telecommunications Company
CEC	Central Election Commission
CEM	Council for Electronic Media
CEME	Central European Media Enterprises
CFC	Commission for Film Classification
CPC	Commission on Protection of Competition
CPT	Committee on Telecommunications
CRC	Communication Regulatory Commission
DESI	Digital Economy and Society Index
DTT	Digital Terrestrial Television
EBU	European Broadcasting Union
ECEM	Ethics Commission for Electronic Media
ECHR	European Convention on Human Rights
ECMB	Eurocom Cable Management Bulgaria
ECPM	Ethics Commission for Print Media
EEA	European Economic Area
EMC	Electromagnetic Compatibility
EMI	Electromagnetic Interference
EU	European Union
HBO	Home Box Office
ISOC	Internet Society Bulgaria

List of Abbreviations

ISP	Internet Service Providers
LAPI	Law on Access to Public Information
LCP	Law for Consumer Protection
LChP	Law for Child Protection
LCR	Law on Commercial Register
LEC	Law on Electronic Communications
LFI	Law on Film Industry
LMRHU	Law on Medicinal Products for Human
LOC	Law on Obligations and Contracts
LPC	Law on Protection of Competition
LPCI	Law on the Protection of Classified Information
LPDP	Law on Personal Data Protection
LPP	Law for the Protection of Competition
LRT	Law on Radio and Television
MPs	Members of Parliament
MTITC	Ministry of Transport, Information Technology and Communications
NCJE	National Council for Journalistic Ethics
NCRT	National Council on Radio and Television
NFC	National Film Centre
NURTS	National Unit Radio and TV Stations
PPC	Penal Procedure Code
RTTE	Radio and Telecommunications Terminal Equipment
RWB	Reporters Without Borders
SAC	Supreme Administrative Court
TL	Telecommunications Law
TWF	Television Without Frontiers Directive
UBJ	Union of Bulgarian Journalists
UPB	Union of Publishers in Bulgaria
WAZ	Westdeutsche Allgemeine Zeitung

General Introduction

§1. General Background of the Country

I. Political and Legal System of the Country

1. Founded in 681, Bulgaria is one of the oldest countries in Europe. Its contemporary legal system, which is influenced by Germanic and Roman law systems, dates from the second half of the nineteenth century when Bulgaria became an independent state after its liberation from the Ottoman dominance on 3 March 1878. On 16 April 1879, Bulgaria adopted its first monarchist constitution, the Tarnovo Constitution, defining it as a Principality and a vassal to the Ottoman Empire. On 22 September 1908, the Principality of Bulgaria proclaimed itself independent and became internationally recognized as a Kingdom with a constitutional monarchy. The Tarnovo Constitution remained the fundamental law of Bulgaria until 4 December 1947.

2. After the coup d'état of 9 September 1944, large political, social and economic changes occurred. In 1946, the monarchy was abolished and, in December 1947, a new Constitution, the Dimitrov Constitution, was adopted, declaring Bulgaria a People's Republic. In 1971, Bulgaria approved a new Constitution once more, the Zhivkov Constitution, also defining Bulgaria as a socialist state.

3. In 1989, massive opposition demonstrations demanded political reforms, as well as the resignation of the leader Todor Zhivkov. Bulgaria was on the road to democracy. The democratization process included, among other things, a new constitution, freedom of opinion, speech and people's will. On 12 July 1991, Bulgaria adopted its current Constitution. It defines the country as a unitary parliamentary Republic[1] and guarantees equal rights before the law for all Bulgarian citizens.

4. Article 8 of the Bulgarian Constitution proclaims a clear division between the legislative, executive and judicial powers.

5. The *legislative power* belongs to the one-chamber National Assembly. It is composed of 240 members who are directly elected for a four-year term on the basis of proportional and majority representation. Parties and political coalitions need 4% of the popular vote to qualify.

1. Articles 1 and 2 of the Bulgarian Constitution, promulgated in State Gazette, issue 56 of 13 Jul. 1991.

6. The *executive power* is in the hands of the Council of Ministers, which consists of a Prime Minister, Deputy Prime Ministers and regular Ministers. A decision taken by one of the ministers engages the responsibility of the whole government. Furthermore, the president represents the country in its international relations. He is directly elected and has a five-year term. Being the Supreme commander-in-chief of the Armed Forces, he has large prerogatives concerning national defence and security.

7. The *judicial power* is independent and has to protect the rights and legitimate interests of all citizens, legal entities and the state. It is composed of judges, prosecutors and investigating magistrates who are appointed, promoted, demoted and dismissed by a twenty-five-member Supreme Judicial Council.[2] Currently, the Supreme Judicial Council is charged with the financial and organizational management of the judicial system.

8. The Bulgarian legal system is divided into First Instance courts, Second Instance Courts and last instance courts which are part of a decentralized system. The First Instance Courts are regional and district Courts, and the Courts of Appeal are the Second Instance Courts. The highest level and last instance are composed of the Supreme Court of Cassation for civil and criminal matters and the Supreme Administrative Court (SAC) for appeals of government decisions, as well as other acts established by law. Bulgaria also has a system of Military Courts.

9. In addition, Bulgaria has a Constitutional Court, competences of which are described in a separate chapter of the Constitution.[3] Its main duties consist of reviewing the constitutionality of laws and statutes brought before it and verifying the compliance of these laws with international treaties that the government has signed. It is also its duty to provide binding interpretations of the Constitution. As a result, the decisions of the Constitutional Court are binding for all public authorities, legal entities and persons, including the Court itself. It should be noted that its interpretative power cannot, in any case, supplement or amend the Constitution.[4] The Bulgarian legal theory maintains that the interpretative decisions of the Constitutional Court are subsidiary sources of law.

10. Finally, the judicial branch is administered by the Supreme Judicial Council which is the highest administrative authority and is responsible for managing the judiciary and ensuring the independence of its bodies – the Supreme Court of Cassation, the SAC, Courts of Appeal, regional Courts, Military Courts and district Courts. Specialized Courts may be set up by virtue of law.[5]

---

2. Article 130 of the Constitution.
3. Articles 147–152 of the Constitution.
4. K. Stoychev, *Constitutional Justice in Bulgaria: Rules and Tendencies*, 1–7.
5. Article 19 of the Constitution.

II. Geography and Population

11. Bulgaria is situated on the Balkan Peninsula in south-eastern Europe, with Romania to the north, Greece and Turkey to the south, the Black Sea coast to the east and Serbia and the Republic of Macedonia to the west.

12. The official and spoken language in Bulgaria is Bulgarian, which is written using the Cyrillic alphabet.

13. The Republic of Bulgaria covers a territory of 110,993 square kilometres. Its territory is divided into 28 regions and 264 municipalities. Each region is headed by a provincial governor appointed by the government. The region is defined as an administrative-territorial unit, which conducts regional policy, implementing at the same time the policy of the state at the local level and providing for the balance between the local and state interests.[6]

14. Bulgaria has a population of 7,351,234 (in July 2011)[7] inhabitants, corresponding to an average density of 64 inhabitants/square kilometre. Most of the Bulgarian population lives in the cities. The urban population is about 70% of the total population and about 1.5 million people live in the capital city of Sofia. The population is rather homogeneous, even if various ethnic groups live in Bulgaria – Turks (the largest ethnic group), Gypsies, Russians, Armenians, Vlachs, Jews, Greeks, Romanians and Macedonians.

15. Bulgaria has faced serious demographic problems since the 1980s. With a population of 8.8 million in 1986, 8.3 million in 1992, 7.9 million in 2001 and 7.7 million in 2004, the population is expected to fall to 6.9 million by the year 2020.[8] The main reason for this decrease in population is not the migration rate, but the low fertility rate which is 1.42 children per woman.

III. Social and Cultural Values

16. Between 1944 and 1989, Bulgaria was a communist country. This came with permanent intervention and control from the state in the cultural and intellectual sphere of the country. Initially, the measures taken by the Bulgarian Communist Party were focused on the activity of the opposition, and any will to criticize the party was not tolerated.

17. Nevertheless, there was not, initially, total control over the media. The situation actually got more serious with the adoption of laws in 1947 and 1948, which

6. Article 142 of the Constitution.
7. *See* http://www.nsi.bg/census2011/index.php, population 7,364,570.
8. R. Vassilev, 'Bulgaria's Demographic Crisis: Underlying Causes and Some Short-Term Implications', 6 *S.E. European Pol.* 14 (2005).

imposed general control over literature, art, science, movie import and movie making.[9] As a result, the media was not serving the public interest anymore, but the interest of the communist party.

18. Radio broadcasting was established in Bulgaria in 1935 and was monopolized and state-owned. Television was introduced in Bulgaria in 1959, with its first emission dedicated to the Bolshevik revolution started by Lenin in Russia in 1917. As television appeared in Bulgaria during the communist era, this new form of media never had the possibility to operate in a free way. But television and radio were not the only media to be controlled – the press was also state-owned. The state had a monopoly on the content of all information. This remained the media reality for the Bulgarian society for about forty years.

19. Bulgaria had to wait until 1991 for the new Constitution to abolish the state monopoly on the audiovisual sector and affirm the freedom of opinion and expression. With the fall of the communist regime in November 1989, freedom of opinion and expression, as well as media independence became possible.

20. Bulgaria had to get familiar with the new situation and regulate its media market in order to guarantee its independence. One should stress that finding freedom, independence and objectiveness is not an easy task for a former communist country where everything was subordinate to the party. The media, often considered the 'fourth power', also had to gain its independence. The new Bulgarian democratic society had to build the necessary, accurate and true information system so that people could make the right choices. The media should take into account all opinions on an event, provide analysis and debate on important issues.[10]

§2. The Media Landscape

I. Overview of Media Markets and Main Actors

A. Introduction

21. Since the beginning of its transition period from a socialist, centrally planned, economy to a free-market economy, Bulgaria opened up to capitalism. These socio-economical changes, accompanied by technological progress, have strongly modified the media landscape.

9. V. Chichkova, *The Political Censure in Bulgaria* 118 (University Chernorizec Hrabar 2003).
10. Access to information is essential to the health of democracy for at least two reasons. First, it ensures that citizens make responsible, informed choices rather than acting out of ignorance or misinformation. Second, information serves a 'checking function' by ensuring that elected representatives uphold their oaths of office and carry out the wishes of those who elected them, from 'The Role of Media in Democracy: A Strategic Approach', U.S. Agency for International Development, *see* https://gsdrc.org/document-library/the-role-of-media-in-democracy-a-strategic-approach/.

22. The economic transition in Bulgaria allowed the emergence of private, market-oriented television and radio channels. Once the state monopoly on electronic media was abolished,[11] the public channels had to coexist with the new, private, ones. The creation of commercial radio and television channels allowed for the diversification of the programmes, which now benefit from a diversity of styles, formats and standards.[12]

B. Television

23. Television is the most popular media in Bulgaria, with as much as 98.2% of Bulgarian households having direct access to it.[13] Television is also considered to maintain a higher degree of credibility than other media.

24. Until 1994, the Bulgarian National Television (BNT) and the Bulgarian National Radio (BNR) were the only electronic broadcasters in the country. Nova Television was the first private television station to start broadcasting in 1994. At its beginning, the financial, technological and human resources were limited, which led to modest programmes of movies and sports and some imported entertainment programmes. Nova was mainly owned by the Serbian Darko Taminjic. However, due to bearer shares, the ownership structure was rather unclear.

25. In 1999, bTV became the first TV station to broadcast at the national level, effectively becoming the first private national operator.[14] The News Corporation was considered the owner of bTV. Here again, however, there was a doubt on who was the real owner of the channel. Later, it became clear that the Balkan News Corporation was financed by the media tycoon Rupert Murdoch and his company, News Corporation.

26. Since 2000, the media market in Bulgaria developed itself and became more dynamic, thanks to foreign investments. New international media groups entered the Bulgarian market: Antena Group, Emmis Communications, Communicorp Group, Apace Media group (owner of Television MM and Diema Vision, which runs the

---

11. The first legislative act that abolished the party-state monopoly in the electronic media was the new Constitution of 1991.
12. L. Raycheva, 'The Dynamics of the Electronic Mass Media System in Bulgaria (1989–1999)', 13 *The Global Network* 50 (2000).
13. http://www.kas.de/wf/en/33.14855/ (accessed 24 May 2011).
14. *National broadcaster* is an operator which builds, maintains and uses a telecommunications network that provides coverage with quality TV signals at least 85% of the territory of country and broadcasts their own programme, as recommended by the International Broadcasting Union, on how to do frequency planning and provide quality signal. *Regional broadcaster* is an operator which builds, maintains and uses a telecommunications network, providing coverage with quality television signals of one or several regions and emits its own programme, according to the International Telecommunication Union recommendations and on how to do frequency planning and provide quality signal. The same goes for *the local broadcaster* who provides coverage with quality television signal for one location. *See* CEM, *Report for the Development of the Radio and Television Activity in Bulgaria (2001–2006)*, 34 and 37.

TV cable channels Diema+, Diema 2, Diema Family and Diema Extra), SBS Broadcasting Group (acquired by ProSieben in 2008).[15] Since 2000, Nova Television has been entirely owned by the Greek company Antena Group. In 2003, Nova Television received a national television licence. Thus it became the third national television in Bulgaria, after bTV and Kanal 1, and the second private national media.

27. In 2010, the bTV Media group, which was a part of Rupert Murdoch's News Corporation, was bought by the Central European Media Enterprises (CEME),[16] a company owned by Ronald Lauder.[17] Today, bTV occupies a leading position in the media market. Already, in 2008, the CEME acquired two television channels (*Ring TV* and *TV2*) and the radio station *Mila.* The country's second-leading television broadcaster, *Nova Television*, was sold by the Greek Antena to the Swedish Modern Times Group.[18]

28. The Bulgarian Telecommunications Company (BTC), which recently became VIVACOM, wanted to extend its activity and offer not only landline phone, mobile connection and Internet access (as it did until now) but also satellite television. VIVACOM signed a contract with Intelsat Network, a leading provider of fixed satellite services. VIVACOM's new offer will include more than seventy channels of news, entertainment and sports.[19] The National Unit Radio and TV Stations Bulgaria (NURTS Bulgaria) inherited the only network transmitting the programmes of national television and radio broadcasters through a system of relay facilities covering the country's entire territory, which procured it a monopolist position.[20] In 2008, BTC decided to sell its broadcasting division NURTS to the Austrian Österreichische Rundfunksender. But the deal was fumbled by the Communications Regulation Commission, a Bulgarian regulatory body. Finally, in 2010, NURTS was sold to the Cyprus-based international financial investor Mancelord Limited.[21]

29. Today in Bulgaria only two state channels operate at the national level, namely Kanal 1 and TV Bulgaria (a satellite channel). The BNT, as a national public television provider, holds licences for regional programmes: BNT Sea, BNT Pirin, Television Plovdiv, North BNT and BNT Sofia.[22]

---

15. N. Daskalova, *The Bulgarian Media System after 1989: Restructuring in Three Directions* 7 (East-Bound 2010).
16. As well as the channels bTV Comedy, bTV Cinema, PRO.BG and RING.BG.
17. G. Lozanov & O. Spassov, *Media and Politics* 175 (Found. Media Democracy 2001).
18. Daskalova, *The Bulgarian Media System after 1989: Restructuring in Three Directions*, 7, *supra* n. 15.
19. https://investors.intelsat.com/news-releases/news-release-details/vivacom-launches-media-platform-bulgaria-intelsat-network/ (accessed 4 May 2011).
20. Lozanov & Spassov, *Media and Politics*, *supra* n. 17, 177.
21. https://www.novinite.com/articles/119356/Bulgaria+Wraps+Up+Tower+Company+Sale+for+EUR+57+M (accessed 4 May 2011).
22. CEM, *Report about the Activity of the CEM for the Period 01.07.2010–31.12.2010*, 5.

C. Radio

30. On 15 October 1992, the first private radio FM+ obtained a licence for radio frequency by the Temporary Council for Radio and TV Frequencies. The *state monopoly* that lasted since 1935 was symbolically put to an end with the Queen song 'Radio Gaga', which was played on that day in the air of Sofia. However, the first private radio station able to broadcast at the national level was Darik Radio. Its first programme was on air on 21 January 1993 with a mainly news-related programme.

31. At that time, apart from the state radio stations, the signal of five foreign radio stations financed by foreign governments could be received: Voice of America, BBC World Service, Free Europe, Radio France International, and Deutsche Welle. These stations were selected due to their sensitivity to the democratization process in Bulgaria.[23] During the period 1993 to 1996, eight more private radio stations started broadcasting in the air of Sofia, i.e., sixteen radio stations appeared in a city of 1,500,000 inhabitants. In that period seventy private radio stations were licensed for the whole country and approximately half of them had regular transmissions.

32. On 19 December 1993, seven legal entities and fourteen municipal directions obtained licences for organization and transmission of TV programmes. Private televisions, however, launched only in Sofia and several of the biggest Bulgarian cities. Despite the initial growth in the number of private radio broadcasters, this process inevitably stopped due to the small size of the advertising market which turned out to be insufficient to sustain the existence of all licensed operators. Consequently, a reversed process of mergers and consolidation started.

33. Under the then-existing rules, only regional radio stations could be licensed, and they united themselves into networks in order to decrease production costs. This way some networks of radio stations at the moment were able to cover half of the territory of the country by one programme. For instance, ten years after the first radio emission of radio FM+ it grew into a network of radio stations in twelve cities. The total number of radio stations in 2002 was 270.

34. All this development was not supported by legal norms, instead, it actually used the lack of legal regulation or the contradictions and omissions in the then-effective legal acts. The failure of the State Telecommunication Commission to license effectively stimulated the emergence of unlicensed radio stations, although the Law on Telecommunications of 1998 required the issuance of permits for operators interested in pursuing such activity. In 2000, the licensing process of new radio operators by allocation of free frequencies started, as well as the relicensing of those who operated on the ground of temporary licences. The legalization of the market attracted the interest of foreign radio groups. At that time the foreign participation

23. L. Raycheva, *Mass Media Developments in Bulgaria*, in *Press Freedom and Pluralism in Europe: Concepts and Conditions* 165–176 (Andrea Czepek, et al., (eds), Intellect Books 2009).

thereon (apart from the local radio stations of Deutsche Welle, Radio France Internacional, BBC, Free Europe and radio Vitosha, which was an offspring of the US Voice of America) was presented by the English company GWR holding at that time shares in FM+ through its Bulgarian subsidiary Balkan Broadcasting as well as the Belgian Contact, which owned Radio 99.

35. The emergence of private radios was followed by the introduction of new types of programmes on economy and business, as well as pragmatic information such as job announcements, entrepreneurship, health promotion and road safety. But the most remarkable change was the appearance of radio talk shows dedicated to various subjects such as lifestyle, love or discussions on the latest headlines. The state-owned radio programmes during the weekend as well were oriented towards entertainment, culture and leisure.[24]

36. On 3 March 2001, the National Holiday, a radio station with a unique format for Bulgaria commenced its broadcasting in Sofia. The programme of BG Radio, which was owned by the US Company Metromedia International Inc. via its local subsidiary Metroradio EOOD, included only Bulgarian music. Gradually, the signal of the new media also reached other parts of Bulgaria as it was transmitted by satellite. Meanwhile, Metromedia International acquired 75% of the registered capital of Radio TNN OOD.

37. In 2004, Metromedia International obtained control over Radio 1, started development on the radio chain NRJ and launched another radio station – NOVA. At the same time, it was sold to the Irish Communicorp Group Limited against USD 14.25 million, as reported by the press. As a result of the transaction, the Irish group took on the management of four radio stations in Bulgaria: BG Radio, Radio 1, NOVA and NRJ. Shortly thereafter, Communicorp Group added two more radio stations to its portfolio, namely RETRO and the sports radio GONG. The six radio stations under its control ensured the leading position of Communicorp. Group on the Bulgarian radio market.

38. In 2006, the ongoing process of consolidation of the market was said to have been over because most of the radio stations already belonged to either local or foreign groups. Twenty of thirty of the radio stations in Sofia were divided between four big foreign groups, having a constant interest in pursuing radio activity in Bulgaria due to the expected increasing revenues from the growing advertising market. In addition to the already mentioned Communicorp. Group, the Swedish SBS Broadcasting Group managed the radio and television station Vesselina, renamed later to the Voice, as well as the radio stations Vitosha, Atlantic, Ritmo (Plovdiv) and Express. The US Emmis Communications had the majority of the shares in the radio chains FM+ and Fresh.

39. The fourth big group was that of Balkan News Corporation, which owned the TV market leader bTV. It controlled the radio stations N-Joy, Z-Rock, Jazz FM

24. Raycheva, *The Dynamics of the Electronic Mass Media*, *supra* n. 12, 40.

and HOT FM through its affiliate company Radio Company CJ. In 2010 News Corporation was replaced by a new actor on the Bulgarian media market – CEME. Ronald Lauder's media company became the sole owner of the capital of bTV Media Group EAD and indirectly a holder of 74% of the interests in Radiocompany CJ OOD. Later in that year, bTV Media Group presented their new brand – bTV Radio Group, which united six radio stations: N-Joy, Z-Rock, Melody, 101.1 Pro FM, Jazz FM and Classic FM. In the autumn of 2011, the place of Pro FM radio was taken by bTV Radio. The platform of this new radio includes a mix of musical content, news emissions and the most popular television shows broadcasted on the television channels of bTV Media Group.

40. The withdrawal of Rupert Murdoch's News Corporation from the Bulgarian media market was not the last significant change of main media actors. The radio market underwent another remarkable change in 2011 when the Swedish SBS Broadcasting sold their shares of Vitosha FM EOOD to the Bulgarian company A.E. Best Success Services Bulgaria EOOD, registered by a Cyprian company with the same firm. Thus the company took control over the radio and television the Voice and three other radio stations: Vesselina, Vitosha and Magic FM (formerly known as Atlantic).

41. The consolidation of the radio market also had the effect of unification of the radio formats. The new owners changed the programme schemes by including almost 100% musical content as only part of them retained the short news broadcast hourly. It is worth mentioning that the single radio specialized in sport GONG was closed down by the new owners and replaced by the musical station Veronica.

42. In 2007 Communicorp. Group acquired 68% of the shares in the registered capital of Radio City OOD, which held the licence for the frequency of Radio City as well as the broadcasting permit for the cable music channel of the same brand. Radio City was considered to be the biggest media investment of the Swedish company Warner Music Scandinavia in Bulgaria. By establishing its control over Radio City OOD, Communicorp. Group fortified its leading positions in the radio market. Soon after that the US media company Emmis International announced its intentions to acquire one of the last stations which had remained independent from the big four radio groups – Info Radio. This acquisition, in fact, heralded the final victory of the music formats against information radio stations. Shortly before that radio Nova Evropa, which had a political information profile and played a very significant historical role, was replaced by the new owners of its frequency – music Z-Rock.

43. Nevertheless, it should be noted that all three national radio stations have information-based formats. The stations presented at the national level are the two programmes of BNR Horizont and Hristo Botev and the single private national radio station Darik. The latter obtained its national licence in 2000. The BNR, as a national public service provider, also created regional programmes – Radio Varna, Vidin Radio, Radio Blagoevgrad, Plovdiv Radio, Radio Sofia, Radio Stara Zagora, Radio Shumen and Radio Burgas.[25]

44. The consolidation of the radio market and the programme unification questioned the need for programme licensing, which up until then had been done by the Council for Electronic Media (CEM). Some programmes registered under social or information licences were actually not proposing such formats. This was the case, for instance, of radio Signal+ which was largely known in Bulgaria for proposing 'pop folk' music programmes and was registered as a social radio. Due to existing market forces, music formats were thus introduced.

45. One of the main problems of the radio market as identified by its main actors is the absence of a system for measurement of the advertising investments in the sector. The Managing Director of SBS for Bulgaria opined that the biggest competitors in the radio market should unite to create a Radio Advertising Bureau with the purpose of auditing the sector on an annual basis and introducing an instrument for uniform measurement of the radio audience. However, the situation remains unchanged.

46. In 2011, seventy-six radio stations operated in Bulgaria.[26] Radio broadcasting in Bulgaria was however not homogenous: it differed in the small villages as compared to cities, as well as in the different regions in the country. Situations of over-concentration or underdevelopment existed. For example, in Sofia, twenty-seven private radio stations broadcasted, while in Plovdiv and Varna, nineteen and seventeen stations broadcasted, respectively. In 2016, eighty-four radio stations operated in Bulgaria with forty-one stations in the south-west region of the country[27] compared to four for the north-east region.

D. *Cable Operators Market*

1. History and Development of Cable Operators Market

47. The scenario for the development of the radio and TV market with respect to programmes broadcast on air differed significantly from the one on cable TV. The reason was that the necessary facilities for transmissions as well as the shortage of radio frequencies urged the candidates to seek cooperation and reach agreements with representatives of the state, mostly those of the Committee on Posts and Telecommunications. Such cooperation was not necessary with respect to provision of TV content via cable.

25. CEM, *Report about the Activity of the CEM for the Period 01.07.2010–31.12.2010*, 4.
26. Media sustainability index 2011, *see* https://www.irex.org/sites/default/files/pdf/media-sustainability-index-europe-eurasia-2011-bulgaria.pdf.
27. *See* http://www.nsi.bg/en/content/4627/radio-operators-statistical-regions.

48. In the first years following the liberalization of the market after the change of the political regime and prior to the adoption of the Law on Radio and Television (LRT), the market of cable operators emerged almost in the absence of legal regulation. The scarce legislative basis in the period between 1992 and 1997 made for the development of a black media market. While at the political level the issue of terrestrial electronic media was predominantly on the agenda, cable operators experienced, in the words of Radomir Tcholakov, a quiet TV revolution.

49. Shortly after providing cables to residential buildings in the biggest Bulgarian cities at the beginning of the 1990s, cable operators started unlawfully broadcasting foreign TV channels without concluding any contracts for this purpose with the respective right holders. At a certain moment, they were tempted to create Bulgarian versions of the most popular film channels such as TV 1000 and Film Net. Many economic structures with unknown investment origins were attracted by the excellent revenue perspectives promised by the business of cable networks.

50. From 1991–1992, cable networks reached a lot of households in the major cities without any sanction or attempted regulation of the process on the part of the responsible authorities. Such an attempt was made for the first time in 1993 with the adoption of the Ordinance on the Cable Distributing Systems by the Committee on Posts and Telecommunications, which aimed to regulate the chaotic development of cable networks and put the existing market in some legal order. The ordinance specified technical requirements for the construction of cable networks and provided for a system of registration and licensing of such activity. Cable networks encompassing more than eight households or located in hotels and public buildings were subject to registration. Cable operators, willing to extend their networks over a larger territory, needed to also obtain a licence issued by the Committee on Posts and Telecommunications. The issuance of licences was made conditional on approval, to be given by the Committee as regards the technical characteristics of the network, and by the Temporary Council on the Radio Frequencies and Cable Networks as far as programme plans of the operators, i.e., the list of channels contemplated to be broadcast, were concerned. The above-described attempt for legal intervention in the cable operators' market remained merely an attempt because only a few cable operators applied for licensing, while a large number of them preferred not to do that and were labelled as cable pirates.

51. In the absence of licensing many of the cable operators allowed themselves to illegally broadcast programmes, which could have been received via satellite, without paying or having any agreement with the holders of the respective broadcasting rights. This conduct constituted a breach of the Law on Copyright and the Neighbouring Rights which was effective as of 1993. However, the practical withdrawal of the state from control over the market and the lack of competence on the part of the Temporary Council on Radio and Television to intervene made that conduct possible and safe for a long period of time. The Temporary Council had the power to sanction only licensed operators, and the others did not exist from a legal point of view. On top of that, in 1995, the Temporary Council seized to function, and, this way, the future development of that market lost any other alternative but continued growing illegally.

52. In 1996, a decree issued by the Council of Ministers obliged each company, which had acquired rights with respect to audiovisual carriers, to have them registered at the Copyright Department with the Ministry of Culture. In 1998, the decree was amended by adding the requirement for TV operators to submit the contracts for broadcasting the respective TV channels for registration with the said department of the Ministry of Culture.

53. In 1996–1997, cable operators started investing part of their enormous profits into the development of their own TV programmes. The operation of their own programmes turned out to be a question of prestige for every cable operator. The concrete figures for the cable operators' turnovers at that time were completely unknown. According to observers of the market, around 200 independent cable networks provided services to between 500,000 and 700,000 households. The concealment of the real number of subscribers and real income from that business and the laxity of financial authorities or, sometimes, practical impossibility to establish them and tax, accordingly, caused damages to the state fiscal system and the copyright and broadcasting rights holders.

54. The first contracts for broadcasting right grants were concluded in 1997 with respect to the programming of CNN, represented at that time in Bulgaria by the company Triada Communications.

55. In the summer of 1999, an agreement for simultaneous retransmission via cable of the programmes of thirty-seven public and private televisions from Germany, France, Italy, Spain, Greece (among which RTL, PRO 7, SAT 1, VOX, RAI and ARTE) was concluded between the cable operators and the holders of the rights (AGICOA, European Broadcasting Union (EBU), the Association of the German Private TV Channels (VRPT) and the collective societies Musicauthor, Filmauthor and Theatreauthor). The term of validity of the agreement was three years. Special prices were offered by the European partners, taking into account the state of economic development in Bulgaria at that time. The agreement provided, however, for gradual increase of the price in each of the three years of its validity. Within one year, 258 cable operators signed the agreement. Each operator was entitled to choose the respective channels preferred, and the price was also made dependent on the number of channels broadcast and the number of subscribers.

56. The broadcasting rights for the commercial channels not covered by the so-called global agreement of 1999 were held by several companies such as TV+, Zone Vision, Varna Cable Engineering and Media Link. For instance, TV+ represented Eurosport Sales Organization (Eurosport channel), SOEMIE (Euronews), CNBC Europe Limited and BBC World Service (BBC prime) for Bulgaria. The broadcasting agreements were entered into at the headquarters of the represented companies, as the Bulgarian company acted as an intermediary. Next to the above-mentioned channels, TV+ enjoyed exclusive rights for the retransmission of MCM. The company's portfolio included also Fashion TV and the erotic programme of XXL TV.

57. Zone Vision, a UK company, represented the following channels for Bulgaria: Discovery, MTV, VH-1, Animal Planet, Hallmark, Romantica, Reality, Private Blue, TV5, Landscape and, after the expiry of the contract of Triada Communications, CNN, Cartoon Network and TMC. Similarly to TV+, Zone Vision acted as an intermediary, and contracts were concluded directly between the respective televisions. The first of these contracts was executed in 1997 when the programme of MTV was offered for USD 0.03 per subscriber.

58. Media Link represented Fox Kids Europe, Fox Sports, Sky News and National Geographic. Varna Cable Engineering offered some Russian channels.

59. As of the year 2000, most of the channels have been lawfully broadcast in Bulgaria, and most cable operators have offered packages consisting of more than fifty channels. There have been only a few individual cases of smaller-in-size operators that broadcasted about one-fourth of the channels without duly acquiring the respective broadcasting rights.

60. In 1999, the process for licensing both existing and new cable operators began. Each owner of a cable network was obliged to obtain a telecommunication licence. In case such a cable operator produced its own TV programme, it was further obliged to obtain a licence for radio and TV activities. The operators which did not comply with the deadlines for providing technical plans and fulfil other requirements set by the State Telecommunication Commission were threatened with penalties on the grounds of Article 127 of the then-effective Law on Telecommunications. This law set forth that the exercise of a telecommunication activity, subject to licensing, without a licence shall be punished by fines ranging between EUR 5,000 and EUR 25,000 as well as immediate termination of that activity. Some of the biggest actors in this market as of 2000 were Sofia Cable, Eurocom, Cable Bulgaria, Centrum Group and M-Sat.

61. In 2000, the National Council on Radio and Television (NCRT) approved the first programme concepts for Bulgarian TV channels to be broadcasted through cable and satellite. Pursuant to the procedure approved by the media council, licences were to be granted following the conduct of an interview with the candidates. Unlike the procedure for national television's broadcast on air, in this case, the organization of a special competition was deemed to be unnecessary because there was no limitation regarding the number of TV programmes capable of being transmitted through cable or satellite. This way, the broadcasting activity of TV channels such as the first Bulgarian TV channel having a musical format (MM) and the first Bulgarian sports channel (Ring Plus) were legalized. The same happened also with the film channel Alexandra TV. Apart from these channels having specific formats, the NCRT gave licences also to some multi-thematic channels such as

Nova TV (which later in 2003 became the third national television transmitted on air), the channel of the cable operator Eurocom Corporation and SKAT (the channel broadcast on the territory of the city of Burgas).

62. By the end of 2000, the US cable channel Home Box Office (HBO) announced the commencement of its broadcasting activity via cable in the Bulgarian language. This was the first pay TV entering the Bulgarian cable TV market. HBO's representative explained the company's growing interest in the Bulgarian cable market as a result of increased measures against cable piracy, enhanced copyright protection, and the initiation of a licensing process. These efforts have effectively ended the illegal cable transmission of channels that directly compete with HBO, such as TV 1000 and Premiere. Another observation of the HBO representative in favour of the Bulgarian cable market was its (pending at that time) consolidation as a result of which some bigger operators were able to take a larger market share in the major cities and significantly increase their subscription numbers.

63. Upon obtaining licences for transmission by cable and satellite in the whole country, some small regional TV channels such as MSAT and Diema+ significantly increased their national audience and became important actors in that market.

64. Shortly after its establishment, the cable network was of poor quality, and cable operators were relying on foreign investments for the improvement of existing cable infrastructure. The legalization of cable operators, however, lured interest in their acquisition by foreign companies. In 2000, cable operators started offering the Internet for the first time. This was a very serious breakthrough in the market of Internet providers because up to that moment, the main access to the Internet was provided by the monopolist on the telecommunication market BTC on a dial-up basis. Cable access to the global network was preferred due to the advantages it offered such as higher speed, independence from fixed lines and the possibility for constant online availability.

a. The Ambitious Project of Cable Bulgaria

65. As of the year 2000, the market was highly segmented, and a significant number of small cable operators competed for 700,000 to 1.2 million households, who at that time had cable television subscriptions. Driven by the ambition to consolidate the market and to become the first company to offer new services via cable such as digital high-speed access to the Internet, digital and interactive television, video on demand, pay-per-view channels, e-commerce and various Internet services, the company Cable Bulgaria came to the fore in 2000. Potential successful implementation of Cable Bulgaria, a project aiming to encompass the whole country in a fibre-optic ring, would inevitably procure them a big advantage vis-à-vis the other cable operators. Considering the average monthly fee of around BGN 7 (EUR 3.5), the size of the market promised significant perspectives for the future development of Cable Bulgaria in case it would overcome the market splitting among a large number of small-sized cable operators. The idea of turning Cable Bulgaria into a company operating a national network was quite attractive and challenging.

66. Cable Bulgaria AD was set up as a local joint stock company having 100% foreign participation. At that time both the offshore companies of 'Clearway Investments' and 'Foresthill Holdings and Investments', which were registered in Cyprus, and two newly formed companies 'New Bulgarian Advisers' and 'Narizma Holdings', which were owned by the Irish corporation Ganley Group and the US Investment Fund Catamount Partners, held all shares in Cable Bulgaria AD. Ganley Group and the US Investment Fund Catamount Partners, having Commodities Corp. as a major shareholder, have been presented as the owners of Cable Bulgaria. Ganley Group was an investment holding having its seat in the Republic of Ireland. Commodities Corp. was owned by Goldman Sachs Group based in New York. This was the reason for the media observers in Bulgaria to conclude that Cable Bulgaria was acquired by Irish people investing American money.

67. The management of Cable Bulgaria announced the plan of the company to invest USD 50 million in the course of the next three years.

68. Cable Bulgaria entered the market by acquiring first the cable operators Union Television, Globo, TV Mix and City Cable. The acquisition of Union Television resulted in the acquisition of ten other cable operators. Thanks to the purchase of Globo, Cable Bulgaria ensured its control over some other cable operators in various Bulgarian cities. The ultimate goal declared by Cable Bulgaria was the establishment of a national cable network, which implied future acquisitions as well. By the first two acquisitions, the company gained positions on the market in twenty-two Bulgarian cities.

69. In 2000, the Council of Ministers of the Republic of Bulgaria decided to provide institutional support to the investment project of Cable Bulgaria. The project of Cable Bulgaria contemplated replacing the cable networks, which were owned at that time by the company, by building up a new fibre-optic network. Pursuant to the then-effective provision of Article 21 of the Law on Foreign Investments, and upon the initiative of an investor, the Agency on Foreign Investments was entitled to propose to the Council of Ministers to form a group having members representing different ministries and other institutions for provision of institutional support with respect to certain investment projects, in which such ministers and institutions might have been interested and which might have been declared by the Council of Ministers to have priority. The arguments, on the basis of which the government decided to support the project of Cable Bulgaria, were the intention of that company to invest EUR 100 million in the course of the next three years and the contemplated opening of 2,000 working places for highly qualified employees. The institutional support was necessary in the view of facilitating the administrative procedure, involving bodies of the central and local administration – issuance of licences, coordination of the architecture and technical documents, etc.

70. The legalization of the cable market and the need for respect of copyright were used as an occasion for the cable operators to increase the subscription fee, which in 2000 reached EUR 7.50 per month.

b. The Following Events

71. In 2002, the US Trade and Development Agency subsidized both Cable Bulgaria and Eurocom Cable with two grants of EUR 159,826. The agreements for the provision of the aid were signed by the US Ambassador at that time and the Executive Directors of the two companies.

72. Nevertheless, for a period of about a year, no investments were made and, in 2003, the company Bulgaria Broadband S.a.r.l. registered in Luxembourg announced its intention to acquire Cable Bulgaria and even obtained a permit from the Commission on Protection of Competition (CPC). Because of the fact that it owned the other big operator Eurocom Cable, which was acquired in April 2002, the contemplated acquisition would, according to the competitive operators, result in the establishment of a dominant position on the market. Although the particular structure of the ownership of Bulgaria Broadband was not clear, according to sources of information close to the company the main share therein belonged to South-east Europe Equity Fund, which was sponsored and managed by the George Soros fund – Soros Private Funds Management. The procedure before the CPC was initiated on the request for concentration of economic activity. The CPC decided that the contemplated concentration would not lead to the establishment or strengthening of dominant position and even then, it was considered beneficial for the future development of cable services and for the customers. The market share as a result of the acquisition was estimated by the CPC to exceed 20% (Cable Bulgaria had a 17.7% market share and Eurocom Cable had 4.5%). The threshold for the establishment of dominant position had been determined at more than 35% pursuant to the then-effective Law on the Protection of Competition. At the time of the proceeding before the CPC (December 2002), the number of subscribers declared by Cable Bulgaria was 139,000 and the number of Eurocom Cable subscribers was 60,000, mainly located in Sofia. Although the amount of the investment was announced to be USD 12 million and despite the permit received by the CPC, the acquisition ultimately failed.

73. Later, the control in Cable Bulgaria was changed indeed. The company Globaltech Bulgaria acquired the shares of Narizma Holdings Limited, which owned the majority of them – 68.501%. The other shareholders at that time were Clearway Investment Limited (18%), Foresthill Holdings and Investments Limited (10%) and Olds Mobil Investments Limited (3.499%). Two months before finalizing the deal for Cable Bulgaria, Globaltech Bulgaria was granted a telecommunication licence for provision of voice services, which became possible after the removal of the monopolist position of BTC. The acquisition of Cable Bulgaria was part of the plans for the development of Globaltech Bulgaria as a competitor of the BTC in the telecommunication market. Globaltech Bulgaria was owned by Global Communication Technologies Inc. and managed and represented in Bulgaria by Ronald Finley. He confirmed the plans of the new owners to extend the cable network and to negotiate for the acquisition of other operators, among which the company Eurocom Bulgaria, based in the city of Plovdiv. Shortly after the acquisition, the company officially opened and demonstrated an optic cable connection between Sofia and Plovdiv, which happened in November 2003. The company announced its intention to create a national network before the end of 2005 and to invest the amount of EUR 40 million. The next concrete step was the establishment of a similar connection between Sofia and Varna. Cable Bulgaria changed its company name to CableTel and carried out a relaunch at the beginning of 2004. The company offered the so-called triple play package: transfer of data, VoIP and video via a high-speed Internet connection.

74. In October 2004, cable operators again announced a price increase from EUR 7.50 to EUR 9–10 by the end of that year. The justification for the increase stated by some operators were the costs of subtitling, the price increase of resources such as gas, energy and human resources (increased wages), the need for the construction of new technical devices and the maintenance of cable networks. One of the main reasons for the increase, however, was the requirement to place optic cable, which would significantly improve signal quality. The deadline for all cable operators to finish this process was 2007. Some of the operators had started earlier, and this brought them a competitive advantage, as it incentivized subscribers to change operators. The need for investments in order to remain on the market threatened small-sized cable operators, some of which were forced to offer their businesses for sale to the bigger market players. Another reason for the increase which should be outlined is the increase of the fees requested by some of the foreign TV operators who offered their programmes on the Bulgarian market by one to three cents per subscriber. Cable operators were obliged by virtue of the law to notify the Committee on Regulation of Communications in two months in case of such an increase. They were further obliged to provide special fees for persons belonging to the first group of disability,[28] retired persons, kinder gardens and schools. According to the Executive Director of the Association of Bulgarian Cable Operators (ABCO), a Bulgarian customer at that time had the privilege of receiving the best quantity and quality at the lowest prices in Eastern Europe. At the end of 2006, a new price update was discussed. Increased prices for the use of cable television and a reduction of the price of the triple-play service were being contemplated. The reason for such an increase was stated to be the legal requirement for rerouting terrestrial cables through underground ducts in towns that have a population of over 10,000. At that time according to information from ABCO, apart from Sofia and some of the other major Bulgarian cities the percentage of underground cable was insignificant. In practice, the amount of the fees reached the levels EUR 9–EUR 10 in 2007, i.e., the amount which was discussed at the end of 2004.

28. This refers to disabled persons who cannot fully take care of themselves or need constant care.

2. The Saga with the Broadcasting Rights

75. In 2000, a problem with the broadcasting rights granted under the global agreement of 1999 came up. It turned out that some European football championships, of which broadcasting rights had been purchased by the TV operators Ring S.V. and Diema Vision (running the TV channels Ring+ and Diema+, respectively), were broadcasted via the Bulgarian cable networks because of their presence in programmes of some of the foreign channels covered by the 1999 agreement. The two companies notified the Copyright Directorate at the Ministry of Culture about the broadcasting rights infringement because, allegedly, Musicauthor had been obliged to prohibit such illegal broadcasting by ordering cable operators retransmitting such programmes to show a blank screen. As mentioned above, Musicauthor as one of the collective societies was a party to the agreement for simultaneous retransmission via cable of the programmes of thirty-seven public and private televisions from Germany, France, Italy, Spain, Greece (among which RTL, PRO 7, SAT 1, VOX, RAI and ARTE) concluded between the cable operators and the holders of the rights (AGICOA, EBU, the Association of the German Private TV Channels (VRPT) and the collective societies).

76. The legal counsel of Musicauthor, which was one of the parties to the agreement and also authorized to manage the agreement and collect the fees dues thereunder, tried to explain that the agreement granted to Bulgarian cable operators the right to broadcast the programme of the channels designated therein, as a whole and, specifically, all rights with respect to music, films and stage performances, i.e., 80% of all rights. According to him, this was made known to the cable operators at the time of execution of the agreement. The Executive Director of Musicauthor complained that the problem was used by all cable operators in order to refuse payments otherwise due under the 1999 agreement.

77. According to the Executive Director of Ring S.V., Musicauthor was a collective organization with respect to rights concerning only music, and it led cable operators to confusion with respect to the other content of the represented foreign channels. Ring S.V. threatened to initiate Court proceedings because of Musicauthor's offering and sale of rights not held by it. The ABCO decided to wait for the outcome of litigation and instructed its members to refuse future payments under the 1999 agreement, which was done by around twenty cable operators. As a result of the so refused payments as of 2003, the amount due to the right holders reached around EUR 750,000.

78. Representatives of ABCO met with the holders of the rights insisting on price reductions due to, *inter alia*, the unclear situation with the particular volume of the rights. An agreement was not reached, and cable operators excluded all thirty-seven programmes from the offered packages. At the end of 2003, however, one of the ABCO members Centrum Group decided to execute a contract with Musicauthor independently for the broadcasting rights of the channels – SAT1, Pro7, RTL, the Italian RAI and some Spanish, French and other European programmes. As a result, Centrum Group was expelled from ABCO. Centrum Group justified its decision with the enquiries of embassies and ministries regarding the absence of the channels and protests of subscribers. Upon termination of Centrum Group membership with ABCO, some of the other members prohibited the broadcasting of their own channels via the Centrum Group network and refused to broadcast the Centrum Group channel through their networks as a sign of solidarity with the association.

79. ABCO was established in 2000 in order to defend the interests of its members, who agreed that negotiations for the inclusion of new channels would be held by the association so that the best conditions for all members would be achieved. This approach, in practice, guaranteed that the menus of the cable operators would be almost identical in terms of the channels offered. This fact in combination with the virtually identical prices and the similar number of channels offered (between sixty and seventy) further guaranteed that no significant flow of subscribers from one operator to another would be possible. This way, the potential increase in subscribers could be a result only of acquisitions of existing cable operators and not due to a special selection of the channels and employment of good advertising strategies. Furthermore, the very nature of the transmission technology used, namely via cable, did not allow the operators to offer diverse packages at different prices. Change of operators in some cases was impossible due to the different coverage of the various cable operators whereas the preferred operator might not have been present in the particular district of the client. However, even if technically possible the procedure for change required too much effort in order for clients to do it for the sake of watching one or two more specific channels. The absence of real competition in that market was further due to the lack of funds to be invested in research on the preferences of the cable audience. This was the reason why the conduct of Centrum Group was perceived as a threat to the existing status quo on the market.

80. Medium and small-size cable operators set up another organization for the protection of their interests – TV Club 2000.

81. In 2010, the Bulgarian cable industry united by establishing the Bulgarian Association of Cable Communication Operators, the successor of the above-mentioned branch organizations. Among the founders of this organization were the main actors on the market such as blizoo, M-Sat Cable, Telecable, Cable Sat Zapad, Sprint, Videosat and Virginia RN.

82. In 2004, a Court decision in favour of Musicauthor was rendered against the cable operator Eurotour Sat TV, ordering the latter to pay the amount due for the broadcasting of part of the thirty-seven-channel global agreement package, without providing compensation, for a period starting from July 2000. The losing party appealed and maintained that the volume of the rights had not been clarified and that Musicauthor was obliged to register the programmes offered by the Ministry of Culture, which it failed to do. At that time Musicauthor was suing another cable operator Sofia Cable, on identical grounds.

83. In 2005, a new dispute arose between the collective societies and cable operators. Filmauthor tried to convince cable operators that they are obliged to pay fees to the authors of the films they were broadcasting via their networks regardless of the presence of contracts with the TV operators representing the respective channels. The point of Filmauthor was that the retransmission of the programmes via cable is another use of the works contained therein and protected by copyright and with respect to such use, as the law said, a fee would be due. Further, a Filmauthor representative maintained that the broadcasting rights obtained by the cable operators did not cover the copyright fees of the individual elements of the programme. Cable operators opposed this by arguing that they could not be forced to pay double for one and the same thing. The dispute was settled by legal intervention resulting in the introduction of a new provision in the Law on the Copyright and the Neighbouring Rights in December 2005, which entered into force on 1 January 2006. Pursuant to the new Article 21, paragraph 5, where a radio or television organization authorizes the simultaneous, entire and unmodified broadcasting of its programme through the cable network of another organization, the authorization granted by the radio or television organization shall explicitly include also the rights of broadcasting and transmission of the works included in the programme if these rights have been duly granted to it. Prior to the adoption of this provision, there had been no exception from the provision of Article 21, paragraph 1 saying that permission for wireless broadcasting of a work shall include permission to transmit the work by cable by the same organization without paying additional compensation, provided that the transmission is conducted simultaneously with the broadcast, unabridged and unaltered and does not extend beyond the territory of which the right to broadcast has been granted. Therefore, only the television organization, which broadcast the programme was entitled to transmit the works included in its programme by cable indeed, and a separate permission for rebroadcast of a work by cable from the respective collective society, in each case where the cable retransmissions were conducted by an organization other than the television organization itself, such as cable operators, had been required.

84. In 2001, the NCRT declared its intention to solve the existing problems with the real number of subscribers of the cable network, which had been for a long time hidden by cable operators. This fact caused tension between TV organizations and cable operators. In 2003, the organization holding the rights over the TV channel Eurosport TV Plus insisted on receiving a better price for granting cable operators the broadcasting right with respect to that particular channel. According to the National Centre for Public Opinion Research in 2002, 52.3% of Bulgarian households had access to cable network, which corresponded to 1,412,000 households. Cable operators, however, paid on the basis of no more than 300,000 households. The ABCO, which united some of the biggest operators such as Eurocom Cable, Centrum Group, Eurotour Sat TV, Sofia Cable, Eurocom Plovdiv, Cable Bulgaria and MSAT covering at that time about 30% of the market players, paid with respect to only 200,000 subscribers.

85. In 2001, some amendments in the LRT and the Law on Telecommunications were adopted, which entered into force on 5 February 2002. They replaced the licensing regime applicable to cable and satellite operators with a procedure for registration. Although the existence of two separate licences, programme licences issued by the CEM and telecommunication licences issued by the Communication Regulatory Commission (CRC), was retained, the two licences were made interdependent, and the programme licence received more weight because of the obligation conferred on the CRC to issue such licence in all cases of programme approved by the CEM.

86. After the adoption of the Tariff for the Fees for Radio and TV Activity issued by the Council of Ministers, some TV operators applied for deregistration before the CEM, which succeeded the NCRT. In principle, registrations were for unlimited duration and could have been terminated only upon request by the operator. The latter were subject to penalties under the law for breach of their programme concept, profile or scheme. However, the absence of broadcasting of TV programmes was not a ground for imposition of penalties as long as the operator duly pays the fee due under the tariff.

87. In Bulgaria, cable operators are in practice, also TV operators, which is the reason for the variety of programme formats. This is a peculiarity of the Bulgarian market which shows a difference from the European practice according to which cable operators can be only telecommunication operators without having the right to create programmes.

3. Disputes Between TV Organizations and Cable Operators

88. Cable operators and TV organizations have often had disagreements resulting in the temporary absence of some TV channels from the list offered to clients. In 2005, this happened with the channels of Diema Vision Diema+, Diema 2 and Alexandra TV. The CEM took the occasion and organized meetings to solve the problem showing concern about the spectators' interests. The situation happened again in 2007 when the majority shareholder of Diema Vision changed the conditions of the licensing agreement. According to practice, at the beginning of each year, TV organizations would renegotiate the licensing agreements signed with cable operators. At the beginning of 2007, Apace Media requested a price increase of 20%, which left the agreement unsigned. The argument for the increase was said to be the increase of the broadcasting rights for sporting events, constituting the major and most interesting part of the programmes of the channels Diema+ and Diema 2. The company invested more than USD 12 million in such rights, and this fact made the request for a price increase in the eyes of Apace Media quite reasonable and justified. In 2006, Diema Vision acquired the broadcasting rights for the European Championship at the price of EUR 2 million and became the first private media to broadcast such a sporting event on the territory of Bulgaria. Diema Vision negotiated separately with cable operators and, initially, only Centrum Group and Sofia Cable Company accepted the new conditions. At that time according to the data kept with the CEM, the number of the registered TV channels exceeded 200. This fact was considered, however, to be beneficial for customers because of the strong competition for the spectators' attention. However, this was often misused by cable operators who could decide to remove any of the channels from the list without providing any warning or explanation to subscribers. In such cases, cable operators were also relying on the practical difficulties for each customer to shift to another operator, which were already mentioned in this chapter. A compromise was ultimately reached, and Eurocom Cable was the last operator which resumed broadcasting the Diema Vision channels.

89. In 2008, another dispute between a TV organization and cable operators arose. Balkan News Corporation, operating the biggest national television bTV broadcast on air, requested cable operators to pay a fee per subscriber for the transmission of the bTV programme via cable, which had never been an issue before. The amount of the fee was significant: EUR 1.16 per subscriber. This forced eleven cable operators from South Western Bulgaria to stop broadcasting the bTV programme via their cable networks. The Law on Copyright and Neighbouring Rights allowed TV organizations who broadcasted their own programme to authorize its retransmission via cable against payment. Balkan News Corporation took advantage of the expiry of the previous agreement for the transmission of the bTV programme via cable and proposed new conditions for its renewal. According to the TV organization, cable operators charged their subscribers for the inclusion of the bTV programme in the packages they offered without paying anything to the content provider, which was perceived to be an unfair situation, especially with the view of the fact that the three programmes in Bulgaria broadcast on air on the whole territory accounted for around 50% of all programmes watched by Bulgarian spectators.

90. According to the Law on Electronic Communications (LEC), cable operators must carry only the programmes of BNT. Therefore, bTV has not been subject to the must-carry rule.

4. Review of the Recent Changes in the Market

91. In 2006, Centrum Group Sofia encountered a spin-off and, as a result, several cable companies took its place on the market. One of the leading companies in that market, Eurocom Cable Management Bulgaria (ECMB), gradually took over the biggest two – Centrum Group-BG and Centrum Group Cable, after having previously fully acquired the biggest cable company in Plovdiv Eurocom Plovdiv. Centrum Group was among the first companies to offer cable television in Sofia and, for a long period of time, kept its position in the top four of the cable operators in Bulgaria's capital. The acquisition of Centrum Group Cable in 2007 ensured the accession of four more cable operators to ECMB in various parts of the country.

92. In 2007, CableTel announced the acquisition of Evrotur. Evrotur was also a leading player in the Bulgarian cable industry, being the first operator to launch a digital TV service in 2002. Evrotur at the time of the takeover operated under the brand name EstNet in Sofia and had a presence in several other parts of the country.

The Evrotur takeover was commented on as having a cementing effect on CableTel's position as the number one operator in Bulgaria. Less than a year later the single company to compete CableTel and ECMB in Sofia remained Sofia Cable Company.

93. The above-mentioned transactions clearly outline the tendency for consolidation of the market. As an example of the desired development of the market, the Romanian market was indicated where only two companies participated and competed with each other.

94. CableTel encountered two more changes in the ownership up to the moment of writing this country monograph. In 2007, the CPC approved the takeover of CableTel and VICOM Bulgaria by the UK-registered Ramford Alliance Limited. The plans of the new owners included further investment and the introduction of such additional services as HDTV, PVR and VOD within the next two years. Due to the takeover, Ramford ensured the exploitation of the national optic network having an international connection. Conventional and digital television as well as voice services and data could be transferred through the optic ring built. The UK company intended to also invest in a hardware platform for the services provided by VICOM – digital television and interactive technologies in other Bulgarian cities, in addition to Sofia. Ramford further intended to maintain its position in the cable TV market through the acquisition of other regional cable operators which were located in the scope of the fibre-optic network of CableTel.

95. In 2008, the two biggest cable operators in Bulgaria CableTel and ECMB declared their intention to merge. The Dutch company FN Cable Cooperatif was poised to acquire CableTel. This company was part of FN Cable Holdings, a Dutch company controlled by the US investment fund Warburg Pincus Private Equity. FN Cable Holdings B.V. owned the whole registered capital of ECMB. ECMB was the main company of the Eurocom Cable Group offering paid TV, Internet access and fixed phone lines under the trademark Eurocom Cable.

96. The CPC gave permission for the concentration. It took into account the anticipated positive effects because of the investment philosophy of Warburg Pincus and the companies from its group and its intention to support financially the ongoing development of the subject of the contemplated takeover as a modern supplier of paid TV and uplink services in Bulgaria. It further outlined the long experience in the media sector of more than twenty years and knowledge about electronic communications of the potential purchaser.

97. The national association of small and medium cable operators TV Club 2000 opposed the future transaction by noting that the acquiring of direct or indirect control of FN Cable Cooperatif with respect to CableTel and VICOM while retaining ownership over ECMB would mean, in practice, merger between the two biggest cable operators on the cable TV market, which would make them, to a large extent, a monopolist on that particular market or, at least, an undertaking enjoying the dominant position and holding more than 80% of the market.

98. According to market tests published in the press, CableTel and ECMB are the two leading companies in the fields of cable television and cable Internet. The two companies offer identical services and were the single HDTV cable operators as of the moment of issuance of the CPC decision. CableTel used analogue as well as digital technology (73 TV channels via the analogue service and over 140 via digital service). Channels offered by CableTel were almost identical to the ones offered by the ECMB. The CPC emphasized that the hypothetical possibility for abuse of market power could not serve, per se, as a ground for prohibition of the contemplated transaction. As far as such abuse is committed, Article 18 of the Law on Protection of Competition (LPC) provides another remedy through a procedure for the establishment of infringement.

99. The CPC also commented on the planned consolidation from the point of view of the mutual interests of the two sides of the market – TV content providers and cable operators. Well-organized content providers had already been strong players on the part of supply, and, in this context, the appearance of similar strength participants on the side of demand should have a balancing and disciplining effect because suppliers would be prevented from imposing prices and conditions which would be in detriment of the end customer as far as cable operators are very much interested in luring a larger number of subscribers. The CPC concluded that in case future concrete amendment or termination of an agreement would be made as a result of abuse of a dominant position, this might be subject of dispute to be resolved by the CPC; however, it could not constitute an obstacle for the approval of the concentration, although such concentration in the context of the LPC would inevitably occur in the case at hand provided that FN Cable would have the possibility to significantly affect the market conduct of the acquired undertakings. Notwithstanding the CPC finding confirming the future existence of a dominant position in the market as a result of the concentration, the CPC held that the contemplated concentration would trigger modernization of the provision of electronic communication services, and attraction of significant investments from the funds of Warburg Pincus and would better respect the customers' interests, which outweighed the negative impact on the competition of the related markets and, therefore, the concentration would be approved.

100. The analysis of the CPC was based on the presumption that provision of TV content via the Internet (IPTV) and digital television had not still been perceived as real and equal alternatives. This was subject to change in the very near future.

101. Despite the positive decision of the CPC, the takeover was not performed. Instead, in 2009 both companies CableTel and ECMB were targeted by EQT V Limited on behalf of the fund EQT V. The EQT V is a fund mainly investing in Northern Europe. The fund is not a legal entity and operates on the basis of agreement among the investors in the fund and the unlimited liable partner EQT V Limited which has exclusive responsibility for the fund management.

102. First, the intention of EQT V Limited to acquire direct or indirect control over CableTel and the undertakings within its group was submitted for approval to the CPC. As far as the companies participating in the concentration did not act on interrelated markets, the approval was unconditionally granted by virtue of Decision No. 443 of 7 May 2009 of the CPC. Said decision contained an analysis of the situation on the relevant market and the facts and statistics it used are worth being presented for this country monograph. The decision stated that the number of population in Bulgaria is 7,679,290 inhabitants. Considering an average of 2.49 persons per household the total number of households in the country was calculated to be approximately 3,084,052. Paid cable TV covers between 60% and 65% of the households which is equal to 1,850,000 up to 2,000,000 subscribers in the country.

103. More and more new technologies were introduced to the Bulgarian market. Direct-to-home – DTH television is offered for the whole country by the companies Bulsatcom and ITV Partner. Recently, IPTV was presented and is expected to become a major competitor of the existing methods for provision of cable TV. This technology gives the possibility to broadcast and watch TV channels and other TV content via the Internet in the IP[29] environment. The number of operators capable of offering this service is potentially unlimited. The most recently emerged participants in that sector are Vestitel BG, Unix Solutions, Netera and others. In the near future, the paid TV market in Bulgaria anticipates the introduction of other technologies as well such as xDSL, UMTS and others. At the moment, the two main UMTS operators in Bulgaria (MobilTel and Globul) offer access to TV channels and video content through the technology UMTS (3G). Upon the introduction in Bulgaria of digital terrestrial television (DTT), competition in the paid TV market is expected to boost. Under the most recent amendments in the LRT and the LEC, the first stage of digitalization, initially scheduled for 2009, was completed on 1 September 2013. The market promises to encounter interesting developments in view of the fact that electronic media, telecommunication and the computer industry are working in a more and more converging environment where one and the same platforms are used for the provision of fixed-line services, cable TV and the Internet. At the same time, the administrative barriers to entrance to the paid TV market are practically removed following the amendment of the LEC. The provision of this service requires solely notification to the CRC, and the operators who were previously licensed to carry out telecommunication activities through cable networks are deemed to have already notified the CRC. Moreover, the provision of the IPTV service through the Internet does not require any licensing or notification.

104. In relation to Decision No. 443, by virtue of which the acquisition of CableTel was approved by the CPC, and the ensuing notification to the CPC with respect to the potential acquisition of ECMB by EQT, the CPC has been also requested to make an overall assessment of the two transactions which would establish independent control of EQT over both ECMB and CableTel as a result thereof. The CPC had to decide whether the acquired control over ECMB constitutes a separate concentration or if the potential acquisition of both companies by one and the same

29. Internet Protocol.

owner should be regarded as one concentration. As of the date of closing the deal, VICOM Bulgaria was planned to be a fully acquired subsidiary of CableTel. Recently, prior to the procedure before the CPC, eight of the CableTel subsidiaries had been already merged with the mother company and, according to the information disclosed by CableTel in the notification, the procedure for merger of all other CableTel subsidiaries was underway.

105. Other participants in the paid TV market such as M-Sat, SKAT TV and Centrum Group Sofia opposed the contemplated acquisition. The reasoning for the opposition of all companies was identical – namely the establishment of a monopoly position, the possibilities for abuse of that position and unfair competition.

106. The CPC found that the establishment of independent control by EQT V over CableTel and ECMB would trigger transformation, as a result of which the acquiring undertaking would acquire also the possibility to determine the commercial conduct of not only the targeted companies but also the companies included in their groups. The fact that CableTel and ECMB had been undertakings independent from each other and this would change after the transaction led to the conclusion that concentration of economic activity would occur. Pursuant to Article 26, paragraph 1 of the Law on the Protection of Competition, the CPC should permit concentration if this would not trigger the establishment or strengthening of a dominant position, which would significantly prevent effective competition in the respective market. However, the mere presence or strengthening of a dominant position would not suffice if, in the result of a research conducted by CPC, the latter finds no threat to the effective competition.

107. Further grounds for permission of economic concentration despite the presence or strengthening of a dominant position could be the modernization of production or the economy, as a whole, improvement of market structure, luring of foreign investments, etc.

108. Then the CPC referred to the situation of the particular market on the paid TV, which transformation was of concern. The CPC noted that the two companies which had the biggest market shares were much bigger than the shares of all other market participants. The CPC continued the analysis by noting that the majority of cable operators had limited technical and financial resources to compete. Especially the small regional cable operators could not meet the challenges of that market and were acquired by more powerful market participants. This way, the process of consolidation of the market became significantly intensive. The CPC observed that the competition in the paid TV market was shifting from the cable network to a digital platform and, therefore, the providers of digital television like Bulsatcom and ITV Partner should be regarded as competitors to CableTel and ECMB with respect to that market. The development of digital television was found to be beneficial for the competition in the paid TV market.

109. The two groups of CableTel and ECMB disposed of their own infrastructure, which facilitated the connection with their clients throughout the country. Both actively developed and implemented, at the national level, new high technological solutions and converged platforms for receipt of TV programmes and other electronic communications. The ECMB uses both analogue and digital technology to provide paid TV to the subscribers. As of the moment of issuance of the CPC's decision the company offered 65 TV channels through analogue signal and more than 112 via digital signal as well as 3 channels with high definition (HDTV) as a premium service. CableTel offered 73 TV channels via analogue and over 140 via digital signal, respectively. The CPC observed that the two groups owned already built and functioning infrastructure (cable network) which intermediated the connection with their clients in the whole country. The two companies actively developed and implemented, at a national level, high technological solutions and converged platforms for the receipt of TV programmes as well as for provision of electronic communications. This way, the offered services are improved and, furthermore, the development of high-tech information services, as a whole, is encouraged.

110. The CPC concluded, on the basis of the representation of the two groups at the national level, that after the concentration their relations with TV content providers and clients (local suppliers and end customers – subscribers) would continue. For the assessment of the market position of the participants in the contemplated concentration, the CPC took into account also their facilitated access to the end customers because both already had a distinctive brand and a well-developed network, provided services of good quality and were presented in the largest Bulgarian cities.

111. Considering the above background, the entrance of EQT V Limited as a strategic financial investor was perceived as beneficial for the faster digitalization of the cable networks of the two undertakings. This would entail as a result better services to clients and, furthermore, would make it possible for the united group to differentiate the service offered in terms of content and price segments by meeting the needs of the customers more efficiently. The planned investment would further contribute to the development of HDTV services.

112. On the basis of the so presented analysis, the CPC concluded that the united group would not dispose of a dominant position in the paid TV market in the country and, therefore, it would continue being subject to effective competition, which would not grant any possibility for independence from competitors, suppliers and clients. Moreover, the CPC found that the concentration would cause a disciplinary effect on the TV content providers' market and balance the interests of content providers and end clients.

113. The CPC noted the negative character of the opinions gathered for the proceedings by ECMB and CableTel competitors; however, it found them to have been provoked by the natural fear experienced by competitors, whose size, financial and technical abilities were far less than the undertakings subject to the contemplated concentration. At the same time, the market analysis showed that all markets, on which the two groups operated, including the one on paid TV, could develop successfully, driven by strong and financially sound participants.

114. In the context of the common European market of electronic communication services, on which Bulgaria was seriously retarded as concluded by the CPC, it would be absolutely unjustified if the protection of weak operators would prevail and this way, pull back the development of the whole market. Moreover, the stronger the abilities and achievements of a market participant, the stronger the incentive for development that would occur in the rest of the participants. However, the legitimate interests of the competitors are protected by the provisions in the Law on the Protection of Competitions dealing with abuse of a dominant position, unfair competition or entering into prohibited agreements, decisions or coordinated practices and the respective consequences in case of such infringements of the competition legislation.

115. The decision of the CPC also contained an analysis of customers of paid TV services, which at the time of the issuance of the decision did not constitute a uniform mass in view of their various interests. Some of the customers were interested in increasing the quality of service, the implementation of new technologies and the offering of a wider range of options. For such clients, price was not a decisive factor in the choice of provider. As regards the other group of customers, characterized by a low level of income, price had proved to be a leading factor and as such clients would easily make a compromise with the quality or the variety of services offered. The interests of those two groups, according to the CPC, would not be negatively affected by the concentration as far as a large number of small cable operators would continue to exist and there would be a possible supply of paid TV at a different quality and a lower price.

116. The formation of one very large, in terms of market share and financial stability, participant in the paid TV market entailed expectations for offering modern services at prices which, most likely, would keep the existing level or encounter a slight increase. Those customers who could not afford the expected increase would be easily able to shift to alternative providers.

117. The CPC anticipated that the competition in that market would continue at the platform level. The commission finally concluded that the contemplated concentration would lead to modernization in the supply of electronic communication services, attraction of significant investments and better meeting of end customers' interests, which, taken in its totality, would outweigh any potential negative impact on the competition on the relevant market. Consequently, the CPC permitted the concentration and allowed EQT V Limited to acquire direct or indirect independent control over ECMB.

118. In October 2009, the new owners of CableTel and ECMB announced their merger and started offering services under the brand CableTel-Eurocom. At the beginning of 2010, the merged company adopted a new marketing strategy under which the brand name was changed to blizoo. Blizoo was then acquired by Mtel on 29 July 2015. The two operators merged their offer on 1 June 2016 before fully merging on 12 April 2017.

E. *Print Media*

119. The liberalization and deregulation of the whole mass media system also led to the decentralization and emergence of a pluralistic print media. In contrast with electronic media, which are regulated by law and controlled by a specialized regulatory body, the print media in Bulgaria are free from any specific regulations.

120. The statistics indicate a strong presence of print media products in the media market – in 2009 were published 436 journals, 67 of which were daily newspapers. In the same year, 603 magazines and 142 bulletins were published, 96 of which were published in a foreign language.[30] Today some of these media are also available on the Internet.[31]

1. The Market of Periodicals

121. Prior to 1989, there were only seven national dailies in Bulgaria. The liberalization of the market and the absence of specific legal regulation of press activity provided suitable conditions for the appearance of a large number of periodicals.

122. In the first years after the changes, due to the political tensions of very high amplitude and the marginalization of the biggest part of the society divided into either socialists or democrats, the market was dominated by the political press. The key positions belonged to *Duma* and *Demokratsiya* – the official newspapers of the two main parties, namely, the Bulgarian Socialist Party, which was the successor of the communist party, and the Union of the Democratic Forces, respectively. Gradually, this type of press started losing its position and in 2002 *Demokratsiya*, eventually, ceased to exist. However, after some period of absence from the market *Duma* was successfully relaunched in 2001 due to the fact that the Bulgarian Socialist Party was able to assign the issuance of the media to a new publishing house owned by a politically left-orientated businessman and, at the time of writing this monograph, is still available on the market, although far away from its dominant positions at the first years of the liberalized market. The other clearly party-related newspaper is *Ataka*.[32]

123. At the beginning of the 1990s, newspapers marked as hybrid tabloids took the leading positions on the press market. The most popular representatives of this press were the daily '*24 Chasa*' and the weekly '*168 Chasa*' issued by '168 Chasa' EOOD as well as the periodicals sold under the brand '*Trud*' issued by 'Media Holding' AD. The latter was the single brand of a newspaper which existed prior to

30. Fifty-three of them were in English – National Statistical Institute, http://www.nsi.bg/publikacia.php?n=239&r=|3|&P=65&SP=113&PSP=3 (accessed 5 May 2011).
31. Raycheva, *Mass Media Developments*, *supra* n. 23, 161.
32. Expressing the point of view of a Bulgarian nationalist party.

the changes and survived on the market thereafter. They were called hybrid because of the mixture of the high-and low-quality content they offered for covering as large an auditorium as possible.

124. One typical strategy used by such periodicals was the luring of famous persons who enjoyed a high reputation in the country as authors, in order to benefit from their prestige thus creating the impression of belonging to the serious and qualitative press.

125. However, the described cooperation proved to be of mutual interest because such authors received access to a wider audience. This way, some readers were buying hybrid tabloids because of the possibility of reading the opinions of famous authors while keeping their overall disapproval of the style of the particular newspaper. This turned out to be the formula of success for the hybrid periodicals. Publishers who refused to make a compromise with the quality risked remaining with only marginal positions on the market. The absence of a serious press ultimately triggered a similar absence of taste since the public got used to the way of presentation of information and its analysis as provided by the hybrid tabloids.

126. In recent years, some publishers announced their intentions to regain the market positions of the serious press. Nevertheless, the trend showed just the opposite: the most famous hybrid tabloids have even lowered the quality of the content to the level of the boulevard press. This was a result of the influx of boulevard press items on the market and its increasing popularity, which at a certain moment was considered to be a threat to the hybrid tabloids. The already established style of a mixture of serious and popular information strongly influenced other Bulgarian periodicals and allowed for the diversification of the print media.[33] Consequently, the Bulgarian print media consisted of politically dependent or sensationalized print media products, with which arose the question of the credibility of the information and the interpretation of the facts.[34]

127. In 1997, foreign investors entered the Bulgarian market of periodicals. The German Group Westdeutsche Allgemeine Zeitung (WAZ) was very active in Eastern Europe and, similarly to Croatia, Romania, Serbia and Montenegro, and Macedonia, invested in Bulgaria. The established Bulgarian subsidiary WAZ Media Group Bulgaria Holding fully acquired the registered capital of 168 Chasa EOOD and purchased 70% of the shares from the registered capital of Media Holding AD issuing the two most popular and best-selling hybrid tabloids *24 Chasa* and *Trud*. As a result of the two transactions, WAZ obtained full control with respect to the two publishing houses having the most significant presence on the market of

33. In 2010, the mentioned below German media group WAZ that was the creator of the hybrid-press style sold the dailies *Trud* and *24 Chasa* and quit the Bulgarian market.
34. Raycheva, *Mass Media Developments*, *supra* n. 23, 170.

national dailies and the advertising activity performed through them. The two companies controlled by WAZ assigned the selection, printing preparation and distribution of advertising orders to a third company Newspapers Group Bulgaria, which was also controlled by WAZ.

128. In 1998, the two companies had to notify the CPC in view of receiving permission for that practice. The CPC found that the practice had been concerted in the context of Article 9 of the then-effective LPC and prohibited it. The decision of the CPC was subsequently remanded by the SAC with mandatory instructions for the CPC to analyse the possibility of exemption of the practice from the general prohibition on the ground of Article 13, paragraph 1, section 1 of the then LPC providing for such exemption with respect to concerted practice which contributed to the increase and improvement of the production of goods or the provision of services or to technical and economic development by ensuring a fair share of the received benefits to the customers and which did not impose to the respective undertakings limitations that were not necessary for the achievement of the indicated goals.

129. In 1999, at the renewed proceedings before the CPC, the CPC took into account the changed circumstances regarding the participation of WAZ in Media Holding, which at that time was reduced to 30%, as well as the introduction of a new tariff allowing publications of commercials in one of the two newspapers in a certain day of the week and the possibility for access of all interested persons to the services of the Newspapers Group Bulgaria OOD. On the basis of the new findings, the CPC gave permission for individual exemption of the prohibition provided that three conditions would be met: (i) provision of access with respect to all interested undertakings to the services, rendered on equal basis; (ii) the possibility for independent publication of commercials in the two newspapers dependent on the number of orders and not less than one day per week by introducing separate advertising tariffs; and (iii) the possibility for the publishers to decide at their discretion on the location of the big advertising spots in case of absence of specific stipulations about that with the advertisers.

130. In 2001, the CPC checked the performance of the decision and confirmed that the imposed conditions were duly respected.

131. In 2005, several publishers led by Monitor OOD, who together issued a daily by the same title (Monitor), initiated proceedings before the CPC requesting the revocation of the decision for the exemption on the grounds of changed factual background, breach of the conditions for its issuance, provision of untruthful data, on which the decision had been based and abuse of the so granted exemption. The CPC did not grant the request and neither did the SAC at the appeal.

132. As a result of the unsuccessful challenges, WAZ retained its dominant position by receiving more than 50% of the revenue from the market of advertisement via controlled companies.

133. Research conducted on the basis of the financial statements of the companies involved in the media sector for 2001 showed that the business with newspapers had accumulated the largest revenues. The companies controlled by WAZ were ranked first and third in terms of revenues from sales gained by all media companies. The ranking was identical also as regards the generated profit. Other newspaper publishers such as Standard News, Monitor and Sega also qualified in the first ten media companies. However, in 2003, the circulation of newspapers encountered a 16% reduction according to information from the press. Official figures could not be cited at that time due to the absence of official data provided by the Audit Bureau of Circulations. Although the latter was set up in 2001, it had not started functioning in the first years of its existence. As of the time of writing this monograph, still only a few publishers have become members of the Audit Bureau. Neither of the WAZ companies has joined the bureau yet. One of the main activities of the Audit Bureau is the issuance of bulletins regarding the average net sold circulations of the member publishers. The existence of such a bureau is justified because it allows one to discover the real influence of the audited print media in society, and, on that basis, advertising companies could better forecast the effect of the undertaken advertising campaigns. On the contrary, the absence of a body capable of providing reliable data concerning circulations would likely redirect advertising funds from print media to electronic media where the real access to the targeted audience could be adequately measured.

134. At the start of the new millennium, the print media attempted to outweigh the trend of falling circulations by organizing 'games of happiness'. Most of the games were scrutinized by the CPC for compliance with the rules of fair competition and, more particularly, with Article 34, paragraph 6 of the then-effective LPC prohibiting sales in the cases when something is offered or promised in addition to the sales, and its receipt is made dependent on solving assignments, rebuses, questions, riddles; a collection of a series of tokens and the like; and playing games with monetary or objective prizes which value significantly exceeds the price of the product or the service sold. The CPC in its interpretive decision set as a threshold for the amount of the offered prizes ten times the value of the main product if they do not exceed five minimal working salaries. That means that the prize could not amount to more than approximately EUR 2.50 considering the average price of EUR 0.25 for a daily newspaper at that time. However, the daily Monitor offered as such prize an automobile Renault Clio. The CPC imposed monetary sanctions on Monitor and Standard News for infringements of the then LPC. However, the games organized by the WAZ dailies passed the test for compliance with the law. Nevertheless, some newspapers continued to offer games in breach of the law by considering the potential sanctions in the costs for the organization of the game in question whereas the overall effect was deemed to be positive because of the ultimately achieved result of increased sales.

135. The effect of the games on the circulations was analysed by the CPC with respect to *24 Chasa*. In accordance with the figures provided by the printing house Sofia during the game, the average circulation of the newspaper was 181,293 copies per day while for the same period one month before that, it was 131,758 and, therefore, the game turned out to have increased the circulation with approximately 37%. As regards the circulations of Standard and Monitor pursuant to information in the press they exceeded 100,000 copies due to the games. For the sake of comparison in July 2002, they were printed in 55,000 and 75,000 copies, respectively. However, the interest in the games of happiness organized by the dailies gradually weakened, and this strategy for increasing sales was not used in the following years.

136. Newspapers Group Bulgaria, owned by WAZ, had two printing houses in Sofia and Iztok Varnain where the periodicals of 168 Chasa and Media Holding were printed. Most of the other periodicals were printed by Publishing and Printing House Rodina, which was owned by the state. In 2003, the Supervisory Board of the Agency on Privatization approved the transfer of shares in the state printing house from the state to the consortium United Bulgarian Newspapers including the publishers of *Monitor*, *Duma*, *Novinar* and other newspapers. As a result of the transfer, the consortium obtained control of 67% of the registered capital of the privatized publishing and printing house.

137. In 2005, the CPC permitted the concentration on the market of dailies contemplated as a result of the purchase of another 30% of the shares of Media Holding AD by WAZ Media Group Bulgaria Holding.[35] The concentration entailed the WAZ control with respect to 64% of the market of dailies and 60.5% of the market on advertisement, which led to the establishment of a dominant position in the said two markets.

138. It should be noted that in order to ensure compliance with the competition laws of the mirror advertising practice in 1999 WAZ Media Group Bulgaria Holding had been forced to sell exactly 30% of the shares in Media Holding AD to the Austrian Raiffeisen Ost Invest Unternehmensbeteiligungsges m.b.h, which were transferred back in 2005. It was considered that WAZ Media Group Bulgaria Holding had the most serious instruments for pressure on the media market because of the significant number of newspapers and other periodicals issued and in the view of the printing house and the distribution company owned. Considering that background, the so-called mirror advertising practice of publishing identical advertisements in its dailies *Trud* and *twenty-four hours* was viewed as an act of unfair competition. The desire for the withdrawal of the Austrian company was indicated in the decision driven by the ongoing decline in the circulation of the daily press. According to CPC, the contemplated concentration would prevent the seizure of *Trud Weekly* and *Trud at Night*, which at that time experienced temporary difficulties because of the particular situation on the market. Saving two newspapers was assessed by the CPC as beneficial for the competition in the market. The commissioners pointed out that the establishment or strengthening of a dominant position may be allowed if the positive results which it will bring would ultimately outweigh the negative impact on the competition. Among the pros were indicated the

35. Decision of the CPC No. 205 of 20 Jul. 2005.

contemplated significant investments for access of journalists to all world information sources and maintenance of corresponding bureaus of the issued periodicals abroad.

139. Due to those and other arguments, the CPC permitted the concentration. However, it obliged the WAZ Media Group Bulgaria Holding to sell Press Group Utro, which issued the regional newspaper *Utro* in the city of Rousse and its surroundings and had a dominant position on the regional market reaching 73%, to an independent third party. The CPC also imposed further conditions.

140. The obligation for simultaneous publication of advertising spots in the newspapers *Trud* and *24 Chasa* was not found to constitute a barrier to the entrance of other dailies on the market. The newspapers *Dnevnik* and *Telegraph*, which appeared at that time, were provided as examples. Nevertheless, the CPC ordered WAZ Media Group Bulgaria Holding to allow the advertisers to publish commercials separately in *24 Chasa* and *Trud* on two days per week and not just one as under the CPC decision of 1999. According to the CPC, the concentration would not negatively influence the other business sectors in which WAZ Media Group was active such as printing services, distributions, issuance of journals, weeklies and books. However, the German group was directed to provide free access and equal conditions for all interested undertakings willing to take advantage of the services offered by all Bulgarian subsidiaries thereof. The decision was challenged by WAZ Media Group competitors before the SAC which rejected it by two panels thereof.[36]

141. In 2007, New Bulgarian Media Group Holding AD[37] was set up with the main objective of creating and distributing press issues at national and regional levels and more qualitatively satisfying the interests of Bulgarian citizens in receiving information and analyses of pending and general events happening in the Republic of Bulgaria and abroad. For a short period of time after its formation, New Media Group Holding AD formed the basis of its media activity by acquiring 100% of the shares in the companies issuing the national daily Monitor, the national daily *Telegraph*, the weeklies *Politika* and *Weekend*, the local dailies Borba (Veliko Tarnovo) and Maritsa (Plovdiv), the popular sporting daily *Meridian Match*, the journal *Match Magazine* and the journal *Football Bulgaria.*

142. In 2009, the group obtained independent control over the publisher of the national daily *Express*. As a result of the acquisitions, New Bulgarian Media Group Holding took a very significant place in the market of periodicals. The daily *Telegraph*, for instance, held 15% of the total circulation of the central dailies, as of the

36. Decision No. 11285 of 15 Dec. 2005 by the SAC under administrative case No. 7636 of 2005 – three-member panel and, following an appeal, Decision No. 7959 of 13 Jul. 2006 of the SAC under administrative case No. 1494 of 2006 – five-member panel, affirming the first decision.
37. It is considered to be related to the Movement for Rights and Freedoms (the party established after the changes of 1989 as a party of the Turkish ethnic minority), *see* R. Smilova, D. Smilov & G. Ganev, *Media Policies and Regulatory Practices in a Selected Set of European Countries, the EU and the Council of Europe: The Case of Bulgaria* 44–77 (Background Info. Rpt., European Commission 2010).

time of the acquisition, and was printed in 80,000 copies on Friday and 60,000 copies on the other days of the working week. This result placed it on almost equal third position with the newspaper *Standard* on the market immediately after the two market breakers issued by WAZ Media Group.

143. The daily Standard is owned by an offshore company named MCG Holding, registered in Cyprus. In 2007, prior to the financial crisis, this newspaper reported the highest growth of 58%. The current circulation of *Standard* is 35,000 and between 70,000 and 100,000 on Friday and Saturday.

144. Other participants in the market of national dailies which deserve to be noted are Sega AD issuing the newspaper *Sega* and Novinar Media AD issuing the newspaper *Novinar*, respectively. At the beginning of 2012, the shares of the registered capital of Novinar Media AD were sold. A check-up in the commercial register gives interesting information about the other participant in that deal – Agencia Vitosha EOOD. The sole owner of the capital of this company is another actor in the media market – the already mentioned Vitosha FM EOOD bought by A.E. Best Success Services Bulgaria EOOD. There are several speculations that the latter is connected to the monopolist on the market of periodicals – New Bulgarian Media Group Holding AD. It is nevertheless true that this business transaction sustained the process of unification in the Bulgarian media market, proving the fact that different media products fall under the influence of one and the same media actors.[38]

145. The newspaper *Sega* has a circulation of 9,000. The company Sega AD is owned by Overgas AD, which is involved in the process of gasification of Bulgaria.

146. The newspaper *Novinar* had the highest growth in terms of revenues in 2006, i.e., 39.8%, however, in 2007 it noted a reduction of 24.3%. In 2011, according to information published in the press, it was printed in about 12,000 copies and on Saturday and Monday the circulation may reach 14,000–18,000 copies.

a. Market of Business Periodicals

147. Despite the leading role of the hybrid press in the market of periodicals (dailies and weeklies), one segment thereof was reserved for business-orientated periodicals. They rely on qualitative information and analyses and may be defined as a serious press in comparison with the hybrid press. Market leader proved to be the company Economedia AD issuing the daily *Dnevnik* and the weekly *Capital.*

148. Dnevnik was printed in around 10,000 copies. It gained the reputation as the most trustworthy source of information for expats and foreign missions in Bulgaria. *Capital* appeared at the beginning of the 1990s and still maintains its excellent reputation. Together with *Dnevnik*, *Capital* is considered to be the most reliable source of information, and this was one of the main reasons to be largely consulted by the authors of this country monograph during their work thereon.

38. Moreover the group acquired the television channel TV7 in 2008.

149. In the early 2010s, Economedia changed its portfolio as it intensely developed the online format. The business periodical *Pari*, part of the Swedish publishing group Bonnier, was gained by the company and along with *Dnevnik* became part of the periodical named *Capital Daily*. The daily carries on the traditions set by those two leading business periodicals.

150. The other competitor in the market that was meant as an alternative to *Dnevnik* was the newspaper *Klassa*. Its publishing stopped because of poor financial circumstances. Nowadays it can be accessed online on the website klassa.bg.

2. Market of Journals

151. From 2003 onwards, the market of journals experienced a boom because of the entrance of licensed foreign marks. The market became attractive for foreign investments due to the economic growth and the increase in the purchase ability of the population. According to information in the press, a foreign trademark is licensed against a fixed annual amount. The precise amounts constitute trade secrets. Another option for licensing is that, instead of receiving a fixed annual amount, the licensor is entitled to share the revenues generated by the sales and the publication of advertising spots with the licensee. Additional amounts are due with respect to the use of original texts and pictures from the foreign issues of the licensed journal. The local publishers are obliged to meet the requirements of the licensor regarding the paper and design quality of the licensed journal.

152. There are several publishing groups in the market of journals, namely:

- Sanoma Bliasak Bulgaria AD issuing the journals *Bliasak*, *Cosmopolitan*, *Elle*, *National Geographic*, *Maximum*, *Story* and others.
- Attica Media Bulgaria AD issuing the journals *Grazia*, *Maxim*, *Playboy*, *OK* and *Joy*.
- Newspapers Group Bulgaria OOD – *About the Woman*, *Ideal House*, *Media World*, *High Club*, *GEO* and others.
- QM – *Bravacasa*, *Max*, *Amica*, *L'Europeo*.
- Balkan Media Group – *Woman Today*, *Po-zdravi*, *Nash Dom*.
- VIP Group – *Anna*, *Beauty*.

153. In 2007, monthly journals turned out to be the main engine for market growth and for the generation of revenues from advertising activity. The market of journals became the most competitive as compared to other print media. In 2008, the leading position of the dailies for the attraction of investments from advertisers was threatened because monthly journals became almost equal to the dailies in terms of such investments. According to the data provided by TNS/TV Plan regarding the revenues of the print issues generated from advertising activity in the first six months of 2008, the market share of the dailies was 38% while one of the journals was 37%, respectively.

154. It should be noted that WAZ Media Group Bulgaria is active in the market of monthly journals via Newspapers Group Bulgaria OOD. The Group had its own printing house, especially for journals through the fully owned Exprint EOOD. However, the printing machines as assets of Exprint EOOD were sold in 2003 to a third company.

a. Journals for Women

155. One of the most famous journals during the communist regime in Bulgaria was *Woman Today*. It continued to be printed and distributed after the changes. The competition among the journals orientated to women is especially noteworthy. This specific segment of the market has been penetrated by a large number of world-famous brands. In 2004, the publishing company Sanoma Bliasak Bulgaria AD introduced the US magazine *Cosmopolitan* on the market with an initial circulation of 50,000. The company constituted a joint venture between the Bulgarian publishing house Bliasak Media OOD and the Dutch company Sanoma Magazines International B.V. (SMI), each of them holding 50% of the shares. At the end of 2005, a Bulgarian version of the famous French *Elle* having a circulation of 40,000 also appeared on the market issued by the same company. At the end of 2008, Sanoma Bliasak offered the US journal for fashion *Harper's Bazaar* to Bulgarian customers in Bulgarian language.

156. The other biggest publishing house on the market of journals is Atica Media Bulgaria OOD, which is a subsidiary of the Greek company Atica Media. The prices announced for advertising in the two magazines were the highest in comparison with those of the competitors, among which *Woman Today*, *Eva*, *Moda*, and the Bulgarian version of the Italian magazine *Grazia*, owned by the biggest Italian publishing house Mondadori and issued in Bulgaria also by Atica Media Bulgaria may be highlighted.

157. Nevertheless, the market leader remained the Bulgarian brand *Eva*, which journal was issued by the company Agency Eva OOD (according to data provided by TNS/TV Plan). The leading position of that magazine was not surprising considering the overall tendency in Europe, according to which the local market leaders retained their positions and the success of the licensed brands needed a longer period for adaptation.

158. The situation in the women's journals market was analysed by the CPC on the occasion of the contemplated concentration as a result of the intention of Antenna Bulgaria EOOD to acquire direct control over the Agency Eva OOD by purchasing 80% of the registered capital of the latter company.[39]

159. The CPC emphasized in its decision the process of constant expansion of the possibilities for delivery and receipt of information and advertising messages to the customers. The channels for access to information are print media (newspapers

39. Decision of the CPC No. 253 of 3 Apr. 2008.

and journals), electronic media (air and cable televisions, radio stations, information agencies as well as Internet-based informational websites). In this respect, the growth of the women's journals market was found to be a part of the overall trend for the development of the media and advertising market.

160. The CPC noted that no economic (structural and strategic) as well as administrative and legal barriers for penetration on the women's journals market and the advertisement therein existed. From an economic perspective, launching the issuance of magazines containing information about women does not require significant amounts of investments, special technologies or access to limited resources. Yet, some barriers have been indicated such as: (i) necessity for initial capital investments for the purchase of computer and editorial techniques as well as hiring qualified personnel (journalists, experts in pre-printing design and technical assistants); (ii) attachment of the customers to journals already existing on the market (product differentiation); and (iii) financial resources necessary for purchasing licences of world-famous brands. The stated barriers with the exception of the means for the creation of material basis are not obligatory and their absence would not prevent the possibility for the performance of such economic activity according to the CPC. The latter statement is proved by the presence of a large number of participants in that market and its constant growing. Also, the necessary initial capital investments cannot be said to be hard to overcome structural barriers as long as there is a qualified workforce and access to the necessary equipment.

161. The most difficult for overcoming structural barrier is likely to be customers' inertia and the loyalty of the readers to the already existing brands. In this context, the new market participants need to make significant expenses for advertisement and promotion of the new product and other activities, which determines the lowered possibilities for achieving positive economic results in comparison with the already present market players.

162. The CPC further took into account the beneficial factors of the respective market, namely, the presence of unused capacity of printing houses, the well-developed distribution network and retain and increase interest of the readers in journals. Therefore, the CPC concluded, that despite the existence of certain barriers for entry of women's journals in the market, they are not significant and would be overcome within a reasonable period of time.

163. In its decision, the CPC outlined also the tendencies at the national and world levels for market development towards consolidation. The CPC permitted the concentration and, this way, another player Antenna Bulgaria OOD entered that market.

b. Journals for Men

164. The first journal targeted the men's auditorium appeared immediately after the changes in 1990. This was the journal *Club M*, which from the very beginning of its existence until the time of writing this country monograph awards the title the

Man of the Year. However, this segment of the market was quite underdeveloped for a long period of time. The world-famous brands of such journals started to enter the Bulgarian market in 2002 when *Playboy* was offered to men in Bulgaria by Attica Media Bulgaria. It was followed by *Maxim*, which was licensed to the same company. In 2006, a newly formed company Independent Publishing Group obtained the right to distribute another world-famous brand from this category *FHM*. Shortly after that, the company QM started issuing the journal *Max*, which original version is Italian.

c. Other Segments of the Market of Journals

165. Other segments of the market of journals that may be identified are lifestyle, analytical (having political, cultural and other analyses) and celebrity.

166. The first Bulgarian lifestyle journal *Egoist* was quite successful in the 1990s but started gradually losing positions and ceased to exist at the beginning of 2007.

167. In 2006, the first licensed brand in the segment of the analytical weeklies, i.e., the Bulgarian version of *Business Week*, was launched on that market by Kesh OOD.

168. Another specific niche is the segment of the monthly journals directed to business. It is taken by the local brand *Manager*. In 2009, Attica Media Bulgaria announced its intention to launch a Bulgarian edition of *Forbes*.

169. In the segment of celebrity journals the launch of the UK journal *OK!* in 2007 should be noted. Among the most famous local brands are *Bliasak* and *High Club*, for instance.

3. Market of Free Newspapers

170. Recently, free informational periodicals formed a newly emerged segment of the market of periodicals. The first such periodical was the weekly cultural guide *The Program*, which appeared in 2002 having a circulation of 25,000 copies per week. It was followed by *One Week* in Sofia (sixty-four pages, 20,000 copies per week), *Sofia City Guide* (in the English language), *Weekly Mail* (400,000 copies per week) and others. However, for a long period of time, the Bulgarian market lacked free informational dailies and, in this respect, it deviated from the world trend. According to the data provided by the World Association of Newspapers (WAN), in 2006, there were more than 100 free informational dailies issued in thirty-seven countries.

171. In 2006, the publishing group Economedia AD announced its intention to issue free informational daily and stated its readiness to launch it in the fall of that year. This perspective for the development of the market of dailies was severely opposed by the leaders thereon *Trud* and *24 Chasa* issued by WAZ Media Group Bulgaria. Several publications followed announcing 'the death of the free press' and analysing the differences between 'the newspaper and the free newspaper'.

172. The owners of the two leading newspapers promised to react to the challenge by launching their own free daily only with the intention to hinder the development of the free newspaper to be issued by Economedia AD and force it to leave the market. Upon that moment WAZ would also close down their free newspaper.[40]

173. The other main concerns justifying the WAZ position as stated on the pages of one of its dailies were related to the poor quality of the product, the threat to the existence of serious print media and freedom of speech because of undermining the economic basis of the serious journalism.

174. The contemplated counteractions against the Economedia free daily were presented as a defence of the real journalistic activity. Similar reactions against the existence of free informational periodicals were followed also by the publishers of the newspapers *Standard*, *Zemya* and *Duma*, who called free informational periodicals 'killers of the truth'.

175. As a result of the pressure, the publishing group Economedia abandoned its work on the project by stating that obviously Bulgarian media market had not developed to the extent, in which business goals could be achieved only through market instruments and in a fair competition environment.

176. Nevertheless, in September 2008 the first free informational daily *19 Minutes* was issued by Ball Media AD in 100,000 copies (A4 format, twenty-four pages). It was distributed in the most crowded places in Sofia – the metro, the biggest shopping centres, the Sofia airport, the central train and bus station and the like.

177. Two months later, the publisher declared that the circulation reached 200,000 copies and only 1% remained undistributed. In terms of content, *19 Minutes* almost lacked its own journalistic materials and the information published was provided mostly from information agencies and other media, which were quoted. Advertising spots and announcements took one-third of the area, however, in some issues, advertisements have not been placed. Soon after its launch in Sofia, *19 Minutes* appeared in the other major Bulgarian cities such as Varna, Plovdiv and Bourgas. An online version www.19min.bg also started functioning. Svetla Tsankova in her study Free Periodicals – A Threat or Incentive for the Newspapers' Market in Bulgaria? – observed that in 2009 the distribution of *19 Minutes* was not that effective and the special stands of the first free daily in Bulgaria as well as its distributors disappeared from many institutions, public transport stops and other crowded places where they used to be at the beginning of its issuance.

40. Newspaper *Trud*, issue 17 Aug. 2006.

178. Two months after its start, *19 Minutes* happened to be in the centre of a scandal. In several articles, the daily published unchecked information about the credibility and financial stability of some of the famous Bulgarian banks. Article 152 of the Law on Credit Institutions made punishable the disclosure of untruthful information or circumstances concerning a bank, by which the good name and credibility of that bank are undermined. The publisher defended himself by saying that the information was presented in the form of a rhetoric question, which, according to him, was allowed and did not breach the prohibition laid down in Article 152.

179. Almost in parallel with the start of *19 Minutes,* a free periodical appeared on the market of weeklies; however, it targeted a very specific group – the inhabitants of the Sofia district Lyulin. It was issued by Metropolis OOD and sponsored by the biggest Internet provider in that district Lyilin Net. The relatively poor quality in terms of format and content forced the publisher to turn it into a monthly periodical.

180. On 10 November 2008, Economedia AD dared to launch the first issue of its free *Gradski Vestnik*, which became the second free daily after *19 Minutes*. It started with 100,000 copies, sixteen pages, standard newspaper format, coloured. The idea of the newspaper was that it becomes a forum for civil journalism by urging its readers to publish their opinions concerning the most topical issues. *Gradski Vestnik*, as its name suggests (it means City Newspaper) was mainly devoted to the news and events from Sofia. Also, it had an online version at www.gradski.bg.

181. Although at the beginning of 2009, *Gradski Vestnik* took second place in the free periodicals market due to reaching 23% market share, Economedia AD discontinued its issuance because of financial problems arising out of the pending financial crisis.

182. However, the first free weekly entered that specific niche of the market of periodicals exactly in the heat of the financial crisis. On 16 March 2009, the free newspaper *Anons* with a circulation of 100,000 copies, twenty-four pages and an online version at www.anons.bg. was launched in the market. The project was accomplished by the second largest media group in Belgium Rossel & Cie. Its Bulgarian subsidiary Rossel Media Bulgaria EAD became the publishing company of that newspaper. A distinctive feature of Rossel's business strategy was the establishment of its own distribution network, which was announced to be the main advantage and a guarantee for the realization of 100% of the copies and provision of conditions for effective advertisement. About 40% of the pages were reserved for advertising spots.

183. The financial crisis did not constitute a barrier to the entrance of a new participant on the segment of the free dailies either. On 13 April 2009, *Novinite Dnes* issued by AS Media AD started simultaneously in the biggest four Bulgarian cities with a circulation of 100,000 copies in Sofia, 20,000 copies in Varna, 15,000 copies in Plovdiv and 15,000 copies in Burgas, respectively. The optimism of the publisher was justified by the expectations that in a situation of crisis, advertisers were keen on attempting different advertisement carriers, which may prove to be more effective than the conventional ones. However, the initial plans failed and since November 2009 *Novinite Dnes* has been offered at the price of EUR 0.10 per copy.

184. Svetla Tsankova analysed the 'phenomenon' of free periodicals in her study quoted above. She noted that it appeared in Bulgaria in a period when the market of periodicals was forced to change due to the decreasing interest of the readers. The trend of decreasing circulation has characterized the market in the past five years. Free periodicals indeed threatened the revenues of a part of the paid newspapers but mainly those of information periodicals. The serious periodicals relying on analytical materials and creative approach towards their readers may reasonably expect that their circulations would remain unaffected. Svetla Tsankova concluded that free information periodicals should not be perceived as a threat to the newspaper market in Bulgaria but rather as an incentive for finding new ideas, approaches and concepts as well as for offering more qualitative information on the part of the paid press.

4. Other Print Media Products

a. The Segment of Business to Business Journals and Periodicals

185. Business-to-business (b2b) periodicals are newspapers or journals which are issued for the purpose of supporting professional activity in specific business fields. Examples of b2b periodicals in Bulgaria could be the following: *HoReMag* (tourism), *Regal* (specialized periodical for the business with fast circulating products), *MD* (medicine), *Legal World* (law: targeting lawyers and other professionals engaged in the field of law), *Bulgarian Accountant* (accountancy), *Details* (architecture), the weekly *Construction the City* (construction, architecture and investments) and *Luxurious Properties* (real estate). In comparison with other European countries, this specific segment of the market may still be specified as underdeveloped. One of the big advantages of the b2b periodicals is the loyalty of their readers and the fact that they are purchased mostly under the conditions of subscription. Also, their audience is bigger than the number of copies issued because usually a whole office is subscribed for one issue and, therefore, one copy is read by all professionals working in that office. Furthermore, the readers of b2b periodicals often consult previous issues in their everyday work.

b. The Market of Periodicals for Expats

186. This is a specific segment of the market of periodicals because of having a specific target group – expats living and/or working in Bulgaria. The first periodical aiming to address this target group was the weekly *Sofia Echo*, issued in the English language for the first time in 1997 by Sofia Echo Media EOOD. Upon the accession of Bulgaria to the European Union (EU) on 1 January 2007, this niche of the market became particularly attractive in view of the expected growing number of expats to move to or visit Bulgaria for various purposes – permanent residence, buying properties or just tourism. As a result, Economedia AD decided to cover that segment by acquiring 60% of the shares in the Sofia Echo Media EOOD. In addition to its presence on the stands in the major Bulgarian cities, *Sofia Echo* is distributed in the biggest resorts and is offered free of charge in the biggest hotels and popular restaurants in Sofia.

187. The portfolio of Sofia Echo Media included also the journal *Property Wise*, which is issued once per two months and directed to potential investors in real estate properties in the country.

188. The boom in the market of English language periodicals for expats led to the appearance of a lot of new issues such as small travel guides containing useful information and distributed free of charge. In 2006, the monthly journal *Vagabond* issued in the English language was launched on that market. In 2005, the distribution of the free bilingual *Highlights* started at the Sofia airport.

c. The Market of Periodicals for Retired Persons

189. In fact, the most read periodical in Bulgaria is *Treta Vazrast* directed entirely to people in pre- or post-retirement age. This newspaper is printed each week in an amazing 310,000 copies. The price is EUR 0.10.

d. The Boulevard Press Market

190. This type of press is currently enjoying its boom in Bulgaria. The market leader is the weekly *Weekend* with 180,000 copies. The success of the boulevard press is the main reason for the current tendency of turning the hybrid press into a press very near to the boulevard one in terms of style and way of presentation of information.

F. Online Media

191. The online media include radio and television as well as newspapers and magazines which can be consulted on the Internet.

1. Development of the Internet in Bulgaria

192. The development of the Internet market in Bulgaria started in the 1990s, and the development of online communications was very fast. The number of Internet service providers (ISP) was constantly growing. At the time Bulgaria became one of the pre-accession countries for the EU in 2005, there were over 170 ISP, which ranked Bulgaria second behind Poland among the eight countries of Central and Eastern Europe, which just became Members of the EU in 2004.[41]

193. The paradox is that at the same time, the Internet access in Bulgaria was limited. In the beginning, the most popular way of accessing the Internet was the Internet cafes. The situation changed in 2000 when Internet access from home was generalized.[42] In 2010, 89% of the people using the Internet were connected from home. Still, according to the E-Communications Household Survey carried out in November and December 2009 by Eurobarometer, just 37% of all households in Bulgaria had access to a computer, which ranked Bulgaria at one of the last places in the EU.[43]

194. In 2010, the Internet penetration rate in Bulgaria was of the order of 45% (45 users per 100 inhabitants). Despite this growth, according to a Bulgarian social research agency, 43% of the households declared using the Internet in 2011,[44] which is still behind most of the EU Member States. Nevertheless, according to the Economist Intelligence Unit, the total number of Internet users per 100 inhabitants is expected to rise to 75 in 2015.[45]

195. Finally, it should be stressed that at the beginning Internet access in Bulgaria was made through dial-up connections, replaced later by cable and LAN access, as well as by ADSL. Today Internet access through/via optical fibre is also available, and its part is expected to grow. With the improvement of the quality of connections, more people became Internet users from home. However, Internet access remains a problem in the small villages due to the low demand. Indeed, Internet users are mainly from the 18 to 40 age group, and most of them live in the cities.

2. Development of the Online Media

196. With the development of the Internet, many broadcasting media (television and radio) and print media created their own websites, thus allowing for online access to their programmes.[46] Access to their sites is possible either through a paid

41. R. Middlehurst & S. Woodfield, *The Role of Transnational, Private, and For-Profit Provision in Meeting Global Demand for Tertiary Education: Mapping, Regulation and Impact*, summary report on a case study, 7.
42. About 87% of the people having Internet access declare to connect from home according to Alpha research agency for marketing and social research.
43. E-Communications Household Survey carried out in November–December 2009, published in 2010, https://data.europa.eu/data/datasets/s791_72_5_ebs335?locale=en (accessed 5 May 2011); Lozanov & Spassov, *Media and Politics*, *supra* n. 17, 136.
44. According to Alpha research agency.
45. *See* http://www.eiu.com/index.asp?layout=ib3Article&article_id=1207918905&pubtypeid=1162462501&country_id=1870000187&category_id=775133077&rf=0.
46. http://www.listenlive.eu/bulgaria.html (accessed 5 May 2011).

subscription or can even be free. In 2008, bTV was the first television channel to propose on its web page a video archive and real-time video streaming. It was the most visited website in 2010.

197. In addition, several web-based media exist: mediapool.bg, novinite.com, news.bg, dir.bg, etc.[47]

G. The Current Media Situation in Bulgaria

198. David Ben-Gurion once defined the freedom of criticism as the test of democracy.[48] It is now widely acknowledged that a healthy democracy relies on a pluralistic media market. Indeed, media pluralism allows for the expression of diverse points of view. This can only be reached by ensuring media independence.

199. This section will discuss the media situation in Bulgaria particularly the problem with the independence of the media.

1. On the Media Control and Independence

200. How can one judge the media independence in a country? The answer to this question is considered to be threefold.

201. First, to be independent, the media should not be controlled, influenced or interfered by the state. This is true even if sometimes a state intervention is possible without the media losing its independence. This is the case, e.g., when the state takes measures to stop powerful political or economic groups from taking control over the media, thus preventing them from manipulating the information and ensuring better media pluralism. This is also the case when the state intervenes in the defence of laws such as, e.g., laws for the protection of minors.[49] Not only the media are a source of information but also they are a powerful tool to influence public opinion by providing comments and criticisms on various events, groups of people or institutions.

202. Furthermore, media can also be made dependent through its ownership[50] or financial subsidies.

47. Daskalova, *The Bulgarian Media System after 1989: Restructuring in Three Directions*, *supra* n. 15, 9.
48. http://www.quotegarden.com/censorship.html (accessed 5 May 2011).
49. E. Psychogiopoulou & R. Craufurd Smith, *Policy Implications of MEDIADEM, an EU-funded Research Project on Media Policies in 14 European Countries for Media Freedom and Independence*, 3 (Mediadem – European Research Project June 2011).
50. Media Ownership, *Impact on Media Independence and Pluralism in Slovenia and Other Post-socialist European Countries*, Sandra B. Hrvatin, lenart J. Kuèiæ & Brankica Petkoviæ, Peace Institute, Mediawatch.

203. Finally, its constant need for information can also, under some circumstances, put the media in a situation of dependence. In 2009, the Bulgarian-British writer and journalist Julian Popov noted that 'the media are … moving in another direction … they are increasingly becoming media of headlines, not of content. That is why those who control the headlines also control the media.'

204. What certainly has changed in Bulgaria since the 1990s is the way the media are controlled. Under the communist regime, the media served the state to manipulate society: the control on media was strong and direct. Today, twenty years after the changes which led to democracy in Bulgaria, such direct control is no longer possible. Much however has still to be done to improve and ensure the media independence.

2. Overview of the Situation for the Different Media

a. Public Broadcasting Media

205. As public media the BNT and BNR are considered to be the less reformed, mainly due to weaknesses in their management and financing.[51]

206. In Bulgaria, the period 1989–1990 is characterized by the construction of democratic institutions, including BNT and BNR. State monopolies with a lack of pluralism, had to be democratized and modernized.[52] At the time, the Managing Directors were appointed through a secret vote by a regulatory commission, whose members were appointed partly by the president and partly by the National Assembly. Thus, most of the Managing Directors were loyal to the governing majority. Between 1989 and 1990, three Managing Directors succeeded each other at the head of the BNT. The same situation occurred between 1992 and 1995. In addition, many programme modifications were decided in such a way that journalists or emissions criticizing the majority were silenced.[53]

207. In addition, BNT and BNR receive state subsidy for programmes that serve the public interest. As pointed out by Danail Danov, a media expert in Sofia: The media funded from the state budget are obviously in a state of dependence on the parliamentary majority.[54]

b. Private Broadcasting Media

208. The independence of the private media is also problematic in Bulgaria, albeit for a somewhat different reason. Private media are indeed controlled by powerful economic entities, which may exercise pressure and/or manipulate the information.

51. Lozanov & Spassov, *Media and Politics*, *supra* n. 17, 16.
52. V. Chichovska, *The Political Censorship in Bulgaria* 230 (University Ed. Chernorizec Hrabar, 2003).
53. *Ibid.*, 230–231.
54. *Ibid.*

According to Reporters Without Borders (RWB), a mafia-influenced economy is gradually taking control over the Bulgarian media. In its 2009 report, RWB notes that organized crime groups that have understood the advantages that can be derived from controlling news and information have extended their ascendency over the media. The grey economy's hold over the press is now threatening news diversity and the survival of investigative journalism.[55]

209. Not only private broadcasting media can be influenced by powerful economic groups but also politicians can interfere in their editorial line. While they cannot give money through subsidies like for the BNT and BNR, political entities can provide indirect financial support, e.g., through the distribution of budgets for advertising government initiatives. In order to make the operations less obvious, the money goes first to public relations agencies, which then redistribute it to the media.[56] Svetla Petrova, a popular journalist who was working until recently in Bulgaria's largest private television channel (bTV) reveals that in popular emissions where politicians are interviewed *everything is arranged, even the critical question.*[57]

c. Print Media

210. Since Bulgaria's access to democracy, the main characteristic of the country's press market is its continuous monopolization. It started in the 1990s when the German group WAZ acquired the newspapers *Trud* and *24 Chasa*. This tendency was confirmed when business-related or politically oriented groups started to build up a monopoly on the private press.

211. In 2011, RWB noted that a large number of titles were acquired by the New Bulgarian Media Group. Jean-François Julliard, the General Secretary of the non-governmental organization, comments that because of the lack of transparency in media ownership, it is very difficult to identify the real identity of those who provide financial support.[58] An illustration of the influence of ownership on the editorial line of a journal is the acquisition of the dailies *Monitor* and *Telegraph* by the New Bulgarian Media Group, connected to the Turkish minority party DPS. While the journal was always expressing strong criticism towards DPS, its attitude changed immediately after the transfer of ownership.[59]

212. As was already mentioned, the use of the Internet is growing in Bulgaria. It is a source of unlimited and diverse information. Due to the initial limited audience, the

55. *See* http://en.rsf.org/bulgaria-resignation-or-resistance-bulgaria-05-02-2009,30207.html (accessed 9 Sep. 2011).
56. S. Krasteva, *KAS Democracy Report 2008, Media and Democracy*: *Bulgaria*, Vol. 2, 58 (Konrad Adenauer Stiftung 2008).
57. *See* http://www.bivol.bg/index.php?option=com_flexicontent&view=items&id=819:wikileaks-bulgarian-media&Itemid=195 (accessed 9 Sep. 2011).
58. *See* http://www.novinite.com/view_news.php?id=123931.
59. Krasteva, *KAS Democracy Report, supra* n. 56, 44.

authorities were not initially very interested in the online media. At the time, the main users of Internet media were indeed young people, mainly from cities, or Bulgarians living abroad.[60] More recently, however, the Internet has become more and more used in Bulgaria as a source of information. The authorities then began to change their attitude towards the online media, social networks, blogs and forums.

213. Some foreign observers have already expressed their concerns about the rising control over the Internet space and electronic communication.[61] In the last few years, there has been a significant development in blogging as an independent way of communication. More and more blogs are focused on social and political issues:[62] people do not always accept the official media version; they want to evaluate and discuss the facts by themselves and look for opposite opinions. More and more people are going on blogs or are using social networks such as Facebook, Twitter and My space.[63] According to a ranking on bloggers, the most popular ones are those talking about the hot topics of the moment, including privacy and communication rights, and freedom of speech.[64]

214. Hence, the authorities have started to take an increasing interest in online activities. Despite this, journalists and bloggers continue to reveal corruption cases, post online comments about the new law regulations, censorship or any other official attempts to restrict independent news coverage, etc.[65] Still, of all the Bulgarian media, the Internet is considered to be the most independent. That is the reason why it has become an important source of information for more and more significant parts of the Bulgarian population.

60. *Ibid.*, 45.
61. *See* https://www.giswatch.org/ca/node/20 and references therein.
62. Krasteva, *KAS Democracy Report*, *supra* n. 56, 45.
63. The social media provides new opportunities for information and communication and encourages a more interactive Internet usage. For example, the social network Facebook is used also to spread important information and news, as a space for different civic causes. For example, groups are often formed in order to support various causes, such as to save the Rila Mountains (protest against the construction of a ski lift and hence massive felling of trees or foothill area which becomes construction sites). The information is posted on the 'walls' of the different members and is quickly spread among their friends. The organizers reported that by mid-February 2008 they had to gather 70,000 signatures – which is the absolute minimum to allow a priority consideration of a petition by the European Commission, and which can have pressure on the government to stop illegal construction on time. The Facebook users are able to make comments on each cause or information posted in Facebook. An example of a very successful initiative is *Spasi gorata* (Save the Forest) which has been initiated by BlueLink, a network for civil action, and supported by leading environmental NGOs in Bulgaria and the Executive Forestry Agency of the Bulgarian government combining traditional and innovative interactive tools. More precisely, *Spasi gorata* is an online platform for posting citizens' alerts about suspected illegal logging activities. Similar initiatives have been started elsewhere in the environmental sector, *see* https://www.giswatch.org/ca/node/20.
64. V. Staevska & A. Kashumov, *Bulgaria blueLink and Access to Information Programme*, 3, available at topbloglog.com.
65. The blogs are less suspected of serving commercial or political interests.

II. Broadcasting Infrastructure

215. In 2010, in the television sector, 102 providers of audiovisual media services distributed their 136 programmes via cable electronic communications networks and/or satellite. Cable electronic is the most popular way to receive television in Bulgaria. Less than 30% of the population watches programmes via terrestrial television broadcasting and a very small share, about 3%, via satellite networks.

216. Twenty-four providers have licences for the broadcasting of thirty-three television programmes distributed via terrestrial analogue or digital broadcasting. Of those thirty-three programmes, four have national coverage and are distributed via analogue terrestrial networks broadcasting: Kanal 1, bTV, Nova Television and the online BG Pro.

217. BNT is transmitted mainly by powerful transmitters, built at strategic and high points in order to cover the greatest possible areas. A large number of low-power repeaters allow for the coverage of large areas. The analogue network consists of a total of 677 transmitters and re-transmitters, allowing coverage of 98.3% of the population of the country. The broadcasting of bTV television is done in a similar way: its analogue network consists of 676 transmitters and re-transmitters, allowing coverage of 97% of the population of the country. The broadcasting of the third television with national coverage – Nova Television – is smaller, about 70% of the population, with 143 transmitters and re-transmitters.[66]

218. Over 70% of the households in Bulgaria receive TV programmes through cable networks. Broadcasting via cable is characterized by its regional principle. Most of the local cable operators broadcast their own programmes, but the quality of the programmes as a whole is unsatisfactory. They do not have the resources or desire to invest in training their staff. The cable networks cover all the cities and only 28% of the villages.[67]

219. Concerning the radio sector, in 2010 seventy-six providers had licences to air 285 radio programmes distributed via terrestrial analogue broadcasting. Three radio programmes have national coverage: Horizont and Hristo Botev (BNR) and the private Darik Radio Bulgaria. Thirty radio service providers, which have registered the airing of thirty-two radio programmes, provide their programmes via cable electronic communications networks and/or satellite.[68]

66. Plan Introducing Digital Terrestrial Television Broadcasting (DVB-T) in Bulgaria, 10.
67. *Ibid.*, 8.
68. *Ibid.*

III. Technological and Economic Developments in the Media Markets

A. *The Digital Switch-Over*

1. Introductory Remarks

220. Terrestrial television in Bulgaria is undergoing a switch-over from analogue to digital broadcasting. The digitalization process is expected to be completed by the end of 2015 and has been decided by the EU. Indeed, digitalization may allow for a stronger plurality and diversity in the broadcasting field (the corresponding broadcasting spectrum allows more users/programmes than with the analogue system). In order to encourage this plurality, the digitalization process should, however, be controlled so that risks like monopolization are reduced. To do so, a legal basis containing safeguards for public interest, freedom of expression and access to information is necessary.[69]

2. The Digital Switch-Over and the EU

221. Each European Member State's digital switch-over will be monitored by the EU. Bulgaria opened its market as a result of the EU ascension in 2007 and transposed the EU's communications regulatory framework into its national law. The first action taken by the EU in the field was the Television Without Frontiers Directive (TWF) (89/552/EEC)[70] which established a single market in television broadcasting services. In 1997, the Directive 97/36/EC[71] of the European Parliament and the Council amended Directive 89/552/EEC of the Council concerning the coordination of certain provisions of laws, regulations and administrative acts of the EU Member States related to the pursuit of television broadcasting activities. In its Resolution B5-0488/2002 of 16 September 2002, the European Parliament 'requests the European Council to adopt … an EU action plan for the successful introduction of digital television in Europe'. And at the same time, it 'calls on the Commission and the Member States to make the development of digital television and the availability of digital television to the public at large a top priority on the political agenda … '.[72]

69. K. Nyman-Metcalf, *Organization for Security and Co-operation in Europe*. The Representative on Freedom of the Media.
70. Council Directive 89/552/EEC of 3 Oct. 1989 on the coordination of certain provisions laid down by law, regulation or administrative action in Member States concerning the pursuit of television broadcasting activities (OJ L 298 of 17 Oct. 1989).
71. Directive 97/36/EC of 30 Jun. 1997 amending the Council Directive 89/552/EEC (OJ C202/60 of 30 Jul. 1997).
72. *See* http://www.europarl.europa.eu/sides/getDoc.do?type=MOTION&reference=B5-2002-0488&language=HU (accessed 27 May 2011).

222. On 19 December 2007, the Directive 2007/65/EC[73] entered into force to account for the changes in the audiovisual media services field. The new EU Directive covers all audiovisual media services – traditional television (linear service) and video on demand (non-linear services) – and had to be implemented by 19 December 2009 at the latest. On 5 May 2010 entered into force Directive 2010/13/EU[74] which is the codified version of the Audiovisual Media Services Directive and superseded the other three directives.

223. The Digital Agenda for Europe is one of the seven flagship initiatives of the Europe 2020 Strategy launched in March 2010 by the European Commission. Bulgaria is already late compared to the other EU Member States and its switch from analogue to digital broadcasting by the end of 2012 is most likely impossible. For that reason, the government announced January 2015 as a new date. Finally, the switch from analogue to digital broadcasting happened earlier and the analogue signal was stopped in September 2013.

224. Since 2014, the European Commission has been tracking the digital progress of the EU Member States through the Digital Economy and Society Index (DESI). In 2021, Bulgaria was 26th among EU countries in the European Commission's Index for the penetration of DESI.[75] In its Decision No. 493 (21 July 2020), the Council of Ministers of Bulgaria adopted a National Strategic Document 'Digital Transformation of Bulgaria for the period 2020–2030'.[76] The document sets out the principles of digital transformation. One of the main priorities of the strategy is to improve the existing infrastructure by ensuring the wide deployment and use of very high-capacity networks. The document contains seventeen impact areas where measures need to be taken, including the stimulation of the demand for Internet-based services by citizens and businesses, but also the fight against misinformation and the need to increase Bulgarian citizens' digital skills.

B. The Launch of Digital Television in Bulgaria

1. The Digitalization Process

225. In Bulgaria, the first step towards the digital switch-over was taken in October 2000 when BNT got a contract for acquiring digital video equipment and a

73. Directive 2007/65/EC of the European Parliament and of the Council of 11 Dec. 2007 amending Council Directive 89/552/EEC on the coordination of certain provisions laid down by law, regulation or administrative action in Member States concerning the pursuit of television broadcasting activities (OJ L 332, 18.12.2007, p. 27).
74. Directive 2010/13/EU of the European Parliament and of the Council of 10 Mar. 2010 on the coordination of certain provisions laid down by law, regulation or administrative action in Member States concerning the provision of audiovisual media services (Audiovisual Media Services Directive) (OJ L 95, 15.4.2010, p. 1).
75. https://digital-strategy.ec.europa.eu/en/policies/countries-digitisation-performance.
76. https://egov.government.bg/wps/portal/ministry-meu/strategies-policies/digital.transformation/itis-national-strategic-documents/national.strategic.document.digital.transformation.

facility for non-linear broadcasting in Sofia. The next year, in June 2001, the State Telecommunications Commission granted a twelve-year licence to the BTC to establish a network for experimental digital terrestrial broadcasting.[77] In 2004, in Sofia, the experimental broadcasting in digital format by the NURTS Company/BTC started.[78] Bulgaria adopted the standard DVB-T/MPEG-4.

226. According to the Geneva plan of 2006 frequencies III, IV and V were to be used for the needs of digital terrestrial broadcasting. Bulgaria has a radio resource permitting it to build ten networks for DTT signals with national coverage, thirty-four networks with regional coverage and twenty-three networks with regional coverage for the territory of Sofia and Varna.[79]

227. The same year, in March 2006, an expert group at the Ministry of Culture was created in order to elaborate a national strategy for the development of the audiovisual sector in Bulgaria, especially in the context of the switch-over to digital broadcasting. The expert group included members of CEM. However, this group failed to initiate a public debate on the transition to digitalization, which remained limited to the institutional level.[80]

228. In August 2006, the State Agency for Information Technology and Communications (SAITC)[81] appointed a working group to draft a plan to introduce DTT (DVB-T) in Bulgaria[82] which was adopted in 2008 by the Council of Ministers.

229. According to this Plan, digitalization must begin in 2008 and end in 2012. It specifies that digital terrestrial broadcasting will be done through digital broadcast stations situated in densely populated cities and areas (so-called *island* principle). The country will be divided into twelve regions: Sofia, Plovdiv, Varna, Burgas, Stara Zagora, Vidin, Ruse, Blagoevgrad, Smolyan, Kardjali, Pleven and Shoumen. They will operate on the same radio frequency (SFN), covering their relevant areas *(allotment zones*).[83] Furthermore, it also specifies the obligations of the state and the changes that need to be made in the regulatory framework. It also mentions the release of radio frequencies currently used by the Ministry of Defence for civilian needs through a gradual replacement with frequencies operating in the European harmonized frequency bands table. The strategy defines two stages in the development of the broadcasting sector.

---

77. E. Ibroscheva & M. Raicheva-Stover, 'Development of Digital TV in Bulgaria: Opportunities and Problems', 3 *Intl. J. Commun.*, 87–107 (2009).
78. The package included the programmes BNT 1, bTV, Nova Television, TV7, BBT and the Voice.
79. Plan Introducing Digital Terrestrial Television Broadcasting (DVB-T) in Bulgaria, 22.
80. O. Spassov, *Public Service Television in Bulgaria at the End of the Analog Age* – in *Public Service Television in the Digital Age* 8 (S. Miklos & A. Isanovic (eds), Mediacenter 2008).
81. Created in 2005 as an institution under the Council of Ministers.
82. The plan was adopted by the Protocol No. 5.24 Council of Ministers of 31 Jan. 2008, amended by the Protocol No. 11.35 on 19 Mar. 2009 and Protocol No. 51.13 on 30 Dec. 2009.
83. Programme to realize the transition from terrestrial analogue to DTT broadcasting, 2010.

230. The late adoption of the Plan resulted in the timetable of the digital switch-over being delayed. December 2012 is the date for the switch-off of analogue broadcasting, and by 2015, the digital broadcasted television programmes are expected to reach full coverage of the territory and the population. The introduction of digital technologies will actually allow the population living in remote and sparse areas to have access to the Information society.[84]

231. According to the plan adopted in 2008, the transition from analogue to DTT broadcasting is composed of two phases.

232. Under this plan, the available free channels in the first phase will be distributed between three national networks for terrestrial digital TV broadcasting, two for commercial television operators, one for national public network operators and twelve regional networks for commercial operators in Sofia, Plovdiv, Varna and Burgas. The second phase provides for the inclusion of another three national networks and fifteen regional. Two companies have licences to build the networks of the first and second phases – the Czech Towercom[85] and the Latvian Hannu Pro.[86] Since 2010, Towercom has effectuated test broadcasting in the big cities. Hannu Pro will operate the national network for digital terrestrial broadcasting for the public operators BNT and BNR, as well as the three national networks of the second phase.[87]

233. The digital broadcasting in the country will be done by six national networks (multiplexes). Each of these multiplexes[88] will contain four to eight programmes. One of them will broadcast only the programmes of the public service broadcasters BNT and BNR, while the other five will contain the programmes of the private operators. The total number of programmes that will be broadcasted after the transition to digital broadcast television will reach the number of channels in the cable networks.

2. Major Challenges

234. The transition from analogue to DTT will be difficult as it puts major challenges on the media policy, the regulation of radio frequency resources, as well as the financing of the transition.

84. Strategy of the Commission for Communication Regulation for the period 2008–2012. In this connection, in 2008, the Bulgarian government adopted a new programme aimed at accelerating the development of Information Society in the country for the period 2008–2010, *see* https://joinup.ec.europa.eu/sites/default/files/document/2014-12/Bulgaria%2520Country%2520Report.pdf.
85. The Towercom Czech Republic is 100% owned by Towercom Slovakia. It comes from Slovak Telecom established in 1999. In 2000 Slovak Telecom was privatized and 51% of its shares are acquired by Deutsche Telekom.
86. The company was founded in 1993 as a studio for computer graphics under the name of Silicon Graphics. Later the company started to work as a systems integrator in two-third of the big projects for TV broadcast in Latvia, Lithuania and Estonia.
87. *See* http://www.predavatel.com/bg/digital/plan (accessed 26 May 2011).
88. The multiplexes are digital platforms which serve as intermediaries between the television and the transmitters.

235. It is obvious that at the beginning, digital terrestrial broadcasting will need financial support. However, the government plan of 2008 says nothing about the cost of the digital switch-over.

236. Another major problem is the fact that a substantial part of the spectrum is used by the state for other purposes. In reality, a very limited frequency resource is available at this moment because some of the spectrum is currently occupied by the Ministry of Defence, and because the frequency resource is common to the analogue and digital broadcasting television programming, the licensing of analogue channels thus reduces the spectrum for digital ones. That's why the transition from terrestrial analogue to terrestrial digital broadcasting is not as smooth as digital broadcasting through cable or satellite networks.

237. Until 2008, it was still possible for an operator to apply for a licence for terrestrial analogue broadcasting and, of course, now this is a problem due to the insufficient free frequency resource. The main advantage of digital terrestrial TV is the variety of programmes – on one television frequency could be broadcast up to eight television programmes with digital quality. Thus, digital terrestrial broadcasting will allow better use of the available frequencies, as well as better quality. The unprecedented amount of spectrum that will be freed up in the switch-over from analogue to digital terrestrial TV is known as the Digital Dividend. The Digital Dividend spectrum is located between 200 MHz and 1 GHz. This spectrum is very valuable also because of its excellent propagation characteristics.

238. Unfortunately, the digitalization process was not spared from politicization. While six companies applied for a licence,[89] the CRC granted a licence to only two winners of the first stage – Towercom for the two commercial networks with national coverage and Hannu Pro for the national public network operators BNT and BNR.

239. For the second phase, six candidates submitted applications for participation in the competition – Interactive Media Services Limited, Bulsatcom Corp., Hannu Pro Bulgaria, Towercom Bulgaria, Adepto Limited and Tesla Bulgaria Limited.[90] To participate in the final procedure, two of them were allowed, respectively, Hannu Pro Bulgaria and the second-ranked Adept Limited. In the end, the CRC issued an authorization to Hannu Pro to operate the three national commercial multiplexes of the second phase. The other three companies (Interactive Media Services Limited, Bulsatcom Corp. and Tesla Bulgaria Limited) were not admitted to the competition because their documents did not fulfil the conditions of the competition. Towercom Bulgaria, which took the licence for the first two multiplexes, was dropped from the competition.

89. BTA, Interactive Media Services Ltd, ORS (Osterayhishe rundfunkzender GmbH), Techno Entertainment Ltd, Towercom Bulgaria and Hannu Pro Bulgaria, https://crc.bg/en/news/640/six-candidates-have-submitted-documents-for-participation-in-the-contest-for-development-of-digital-television-networks-in-bulgaria (accessed 1 Jun. 2011).

90. *See* http://money.bg/news/id_1952431647 (accessed 1 Jun. 2011).

240. With its Decision Nos 358 and 360 of 8 April 2009, the CRC has also announced two competitions for remote participation in the competition, respectively, for the first and second stages of the plan for digitalization. To participate in the first competition, documents have also been submitted by six candidates[91] and four[92] for the second one.

3. Monopoly on the Digital Television in Bulgaria

241. In 2010, NURTS Bulgaria AD, which has inherited a monopolist position by acquiring a system of relay facilities covering the country's entire territory, acquired Towercom Bulgaria, one of the two multiplex[93] operators licensed by the CRC. According to some sources, a merger between Hannu Pro and Towercom has been undertaken. As a consequence, related companies will manage all multiplexes in the country, and they will have a common owner. A single entity will control the entire – private and public – broadcasting in the country.

242. Moreover, one can regret the lack of transparency in considering the choice of media entities. For example, according to its offer, Hannu Pro will provide only ninety transmitters to cover the territory. According to specialists in this field, this is not sufficient to ensure a good-quality signal. For comparison, in another offer, the provided transmitters were close to 700. However, neither the fact that the offer is technically incorrect nor the concentration apparently worried CRC. Another problem with the proposal of Hannu Pro is that it directly contradicts LRT. The law provides that the public multiplex must broadcast up to four TV and four radio programmes of BNT and BNR. The offer of Hannu Pro, however, indicated that their multiplex will broadcast ten programmes: four programmes will have a standard definition, and six other programmes a high definition. At the same time, the broadcasting will be of 19 megabits, for a standard of 6 megabits for TV with high definition. In these conditions, the consumers are unlikely to receive a good quality of broadcasting.

a. The Broadcasting Legislation and the Digitalization

243. According to Article 47a of the LEC, radio and television operators cannot be authorized by CRC to use individually assigned scarce resource – radio frequency spectrum for the broadcasting of electronic communications by electronic communications networks for terrestrial digital broadcasting. This restriction also applies to persons related to the operator under the Commerce Law.

244. Under Article 48 of the law, a company or its affiliates under the Commerce Law, which was granted permission for use of individually assigned resource

91. BTA, M-Tel, Towercom Bulgaria, Hannu Pro Bulgaria, DVBT and NURTS Bulgaria.
92. DVBT, BTA, M-Tel and Hannu Pro.
93. These are companies that manage the transmission of digital signals from television studios to the transmitters throughout the country.

– radio spectrum for the provision of electronic communications by electronic communications networks for terrestrial digital broadcasting is banned from being radio or television operator, as well as to create radio or television programmes. Simultaneously, these persons according to paragraph 5 of Article 48 LEC are not allowed to build an electronic communications network for radio and television programmes broadcasting.

245. According to paragraph 5a of the final and transitional provisions of LEC within the procedure under Article 48, paragraph 1, the CRC defines one operator, which is authorized to use an individually prescribed limited resource – radio spectrum for the provision of electronic communications by electronic communications networks for terrestrial digital broadcasting with national coverage as provided for the first stage of the Plan for implementation of DTT broadcasting (DVV-T) in the Republic of Bulgaria, adopted by the Council of Ministers.

246. The above-mentioned amendments of the LEC of 2009 permitted Towercom to be the only winner for the two networks with national coverage of the first stage and in the second phase of digitization. There was a reaction to the changes. On 3 April 2009, a case was opened at the request of fifty-one MPs (members of Parliament) of the 40th National Assembly, connected for joint processing and resolving constitutional case No. 2 of 2009, which started on 2 April 2009 at the request of forty-eight MPs from the same National Assembly. The complainants were asking for the establishment of the unconstitutionality of, between other articles, Articles 47a and 48, paragraphs 3, 4 and 5 of the LEC, as well as paragraph 5a of the final and transitional provisions of the LEC.

247. The complainants consider that Article 47a of the LEC is in contradiction with Article 19, paragraphs 1, 2 and 3 of the Constitution. This article guarantees to all citizens and legal persons equal legal conditions for economic activity, preventing abuse of monopoly and unfair competition, protects the consumer and provides that the investments and economic activities by Bulgarian and foreign citizens and legal persons are protected by law.

248. The Constitutional Court considered that the provisions of Article 47a do not contravene the provisions of Article 19, paragraphs 1, 2 and 3 of the Constitution of the Republic of Bulgaria. This article is aimed at preventing vertical and horizontal mergers and monopoly situations. The purpose of this provision is clearly to differentiate the entity that will provide electronic communications (here the multiplex operator) from the entity which will create the media content (the radio and television broadcasters).

249. Concerning Article 48, paragraph 5, the Constitutional Court considers that such a provision is contrary to Article 19, paragraphs 1, 2 and 3 of the Constitution because Article 48, paragraph 5 of the LEC limits free economic activity and does not guarantee the legal persons equal legal conditions for business. The ban on the construction of electronic communications networks for radio and television programmes broadcasting to enterprises, which is authorized to use individually assigned resource – radio spectrum for the provision of electronic communications networks for terrestrial digital broadcasting, does not guarantee the constitutionally enshrined rights of citizens to pluralism of opinions, neither prevents the possibility to influence on the operators, creating radio and television programmes. Moreover, the entity that will build the digital broadcasting networks will be forced to hire a transportation network. The legislator unduly restrains the business initiative of the operators of multiplexes to develop and use their own transmission networks. The Constitutional Court declared it unconstitutional.

250. Indeed, some argued that the multiplex operators with their own transmission network may restrict its access, which would create conditions for abuse. However, it should be noted that the practical application of the above-mentioned provision requires the identification with a legislative act of the enterprises that will provide pivotal networks for the future multiplex operators, without the possibility for the latter to build their own networks. This is a prerequisite for monopoly abuse.

251. Similarly, according to the Constitutional Court, paragraph 5a of the final and transitional provisions of the LEC also creates conditions for monopoly abuse. It provides that one legal person within a competition will become the owner of two multiplexes in the first phase of digitalization. This provision does not stimulate competition in digital broadcasting and thus negatively affects the interests of consumers of the media market. On those grounds, the Constitutional Court concluded that paragraph 5a of the final and transitional provisions of the LEC is in conflict with Article 19, paragraphs 1, 2 and 3 of the Constitution and declared it unconstitutional.[94]

b. The EU Supervision of the Process of Digitalization

252. At the time of issuance of the licence of Towercom, a decision of the Constitutional Court already declared unconstitutional to give two or three frequency groups in one competition, as this is not in the interest of the market. CRC, however, hurried to issue these licences and did not wait for the decision, which publication was delayed for several weeks and finally published in the State Gazette twelve days after the decision of CRC for the first stage. For the second stage, at its meeting on 14 July 2010, CRC granted Hannu Pro Bulgaria the last licence for digital television broadcasting in Bulgaria for the so-called public multiplex. The commission claims that the decision of the Constitutional Court was only for Towercom because in accordance with the last amendments of the law, the first two frequencies are given in one contest to one enterprise and the last three are given in another contest, but nowhere is written to one or more enterprises. Therefore, according to CRC, it could only be attacked what the law says – the words ‘a’ and ‘one’ in the first paragraph of paragraph 5a of the final and transitional provisions of LEC.

94. Decision of 4 Jun. 2009 of the Constitutional Court under constitutional case No. 3 of 2009, promulgated in the State Gazette, issue 45 of 16 Jun. 2009.

253. In 2011, the European Commission (EC) decided to examine the compatibility of the Bulgarian legislation with the European one, as well as the practice of issuing licences for digitalization. The EC observed at that time that Bulgaria failed to meet its obligations under three EU Directives[95] by limiting the number of participants that can be assigned to establish electronic communication services for the broadcasting of television and radio programmes, to two. The EC sent a letter to the Bulgarian Ministry of Transport, Information Technology and Communications (MTITC) in which it criticized the selection procedure of multiplex operators in Bulgaria. Furthermore, according to experts of the EC, the CRC knew that the tender procedure was based on the rule of law which was declared unconstitutional.[96]

254. The EC recommended what measures Bulgaria had to take to remedy the violations. Considering that the infringement was still taking place, on 24 January 2013, the EC referred Bulgaria to the EU Court of Justice[97] considering that the procedure followed by Bulgaria was based on disproportionately restrictive award conditions, leading to the exclusion of potential candidates which hampers competition and is in breach of the applicable EU Directives on electronic communications.[98]

255. In its decision of 23 April 2015, C-376/13 – *Commission v. Bulgaria,*[99] the EU Court of Justice held that Bulgaria had indeed infringed EU law. This decision is not a sanctioning one and Bulgaria has not had to pay any fine for now. Yet, Bulgaria has to bear the costs of the case before the Court, and it possibly will have to compensate the winners of the previous tender procedure that will see their licences revoked.

256. It is clear, however, that if the country does not take action quickly to remove the effects of the vicious licensing, sanction proceedings will be launched that will impose fines on all Bulgarian taxpayers. In order to avoid penalties that may reach thousands of euros per day, Bulgaria must withdraw the current licences and conduct new digital broadcasting tenders.

257. The Act to Amend and Supplement the LEC[100] suppresses the restrictions hindering the competition in the digital market. The LEC amendment permits all interested parties to participate in the new tender procedure.

258. By Decision No. 33 of 19 January 2017, the CRC started public consultations on the conditions for the authorization and use of individually assigned frequency spectrum for the broadcasting of television and radio programmes with national coverage. By Decision No. 91 of 16 February 2017, the CRC announced

95. Namely the Authorization Directive 2002/20/EC, Framework Directive 2002/21/EC and Directive 2002/77/EC on competition in the markets for electronic communication networks and services.
96. Decision No. 3 of the Constitutional Court from 4 Jun. 2009.
97. In support of the criticisms of the EC is the suit action taken by M-Tel and DVB-T, which participated in the second contest for multiplex operators, announced by CRC.
98. *See* http://europa.eu/rapid/press-release_IP-13-46_en.htm.
99. *See* http://curia.europa.eu/juris/liste.jsf?language=en&jur=C,T,F&num=c-376/13&td=ALL.
100. Promulgated State Gazette No. 103 of 27 Dec. 2016.

its intention to start the tender procedure. Interested parties have to submit their application within thirty days of the publication of the announcement in a national daily newspaper and on the website of the CRC.

259. Since late 2017, the CRC opened public consultation procedures for the authorization and use of different MHz spectrums for digital television broadcasting (the distributed licences will be valid until 2030). This time, the CRC announced that operators who have already obtained an authorization for the use of individually assigned frequency spectrum in Bulgaria could not submit an application in this procedure. The reason for the above conditions is simply to promote competition in the sector and introduce new market participants.

260. Finally, one should note that, in general, it is considered that the digital switch-over is a bigger challenge for the smaller countries in the EU because they have less developed and not enough regulated media markets. Many media specialists consider that the Bulgarian regulatory framework is not developed enough concerning both its elaboration and its implementation.

§3. Sources of Media Law

I. Introduction

261. Since 1989, important legislative efforts have been made in order to regulate the now-free media in Bulgaria. The process of liberation started immediately after the fall of communism in November 1989. On 17 November 1989, the Plenum of the Central Committee of the Communist Party dismissed Todor Zhivkov from his position of Secretary General and the National Assembly released him from his duty as President of the State Council. The same day, Article 271 of the Penal Code which prohibited any criticism against the regime was cancelled. The communist Constitution was also repealed. Provisions guaranteeing a free press were included in the new Constitution adopted in 1991.

262. Today media freedom in Bulgaria is protected by the Constitution and several laws. Currently, radio and television activity is subject to the most serious legal regulation in Bulgaria.

263. It should be noted that the regulatory framework of media law applies only to electronic, i.e., television and radio, media. There is not a proper law on the press in the country. It is a matter of self-regulatory journalistic ethics codes. These codes define the qualities that a newspaper should have, such as accuracy, impartiality, diversity of opinion, fairness, independence and respect for the law. There are no state subsidies and no reductions in value-added tax for the press media. Their only limitations are contained in Article 39, paragraph 2, and Article 40 of the Constitution, which apply to all types of media.

264. As previously mentioned, the main problems with the print media are the lack of transparency in their ownership and their concentration in the hands of a few. For that reason, in September 2009, the Union of Publishers in Bulgaria (UPB) urged the government to take active steps towards the regulation of the ownership of print media, the origins of the investments there, as well as media concentration. An inclusive working group was formed to prepare the necessary regulations and thus in 2010 amendments were made to the Law on Obligatory Depositing of Print and Other Products. These amendments require that all print media must publish in their annual first issue information about their actual owner. Any changes in the ownership need to be also reported in due time. The Ministry of Culture has to publish information on print media ownership on its official website. The responsibility of complying with the new rules belongs to both publishers and distributors, while the control over compliance with the regulation belongs to the municipal authorities.[101] The violators will face fines, which will go to the municipal budgets.

265. Similarly, there are no special regulations or restrictions concerning the Internet in Bulgaria.[102] In 1999, there were discussions for the licensing of Internet operators in the country. But 'Internet Society – Bulgaria'[103] filed a lawsuit against an order[104] of the President of the Committee on Telecommunications (CPT) in its part on the licensing of the operators. This all finished with a decision of the SAC of 18 November 1999 to end a charge after the CPT, after the CPT introduced a new order that the Internet operators go to free mode.

266. In 2010, during the last amendments of LRT, the possibility that the CEM would also monitor the audiovisual content on the Internet was discussed. So far the regulator controlled only the content of the programmes broadcasted on radio and television. The experts in the media considered that the Internet should fall in the scope of the new regulation because some programmes with audiovisual content were available on the Internet. But it was more a question of regulating the radio and television programmes that are distributed through the Internet rather than regulating this form of communication.

---

101. R. Smilova, D. Smilov & G. Ganev, *Media Policies and Regulatory Practices* 25 (Mediadem – European Research Project 2011).
102. Bulgaria has special legislation concerning the cybercrime, mentioned in the Bulgarian penal code. Bulgaria also participates in a cooperation against child pornography on the Internet. With regard to safer Internet exists a hotline operation managed by the Applied Research and Communications Fund in partnership with the State Agency for Child Protection, the Bulgarian Ministry of Interior, the Ministry of Education and Science, the MTITC and under the general supervision of the Public Council on Safer Internet Use in Bulgaria, The European Network and Information Security Agency.
103. On 4 Dec. 1995 was created the Internet Society Bulgaria (ISOC). The principal aims of ISOC are the reliability of the information and the development of Internet in the country. The main areas concerned by the interest of ISOC are: promotion of more rapid development of Internet in Bulgaria; promotion of the Information Society; free and open-source software – development, education, application, services; promotion of e-Government initiatives and protection of human rights on the Internet.
104. No. 723/99, items 4, 9 and 11 of RD 09-235/98.

267. In 2010, attempts were made to introduce changes in LEC. It was foreseen that mobile operators and Internet providers have to keep for a certain period of time information about their customers' conversations, email correspondence and any other communication. However, after active protests from some Bulgarian non-governmental organizations, the changes were not voted.[105]

268. Currently, the Internet is still a telecommunication activity which is not regulated and is not subject to licensing. It does not fall within the scope of the LRT as a means of providing media services. Bulgarian legislation does not treat blogs, social networking sites, etc., as media. Such content is not regulated because they are considered a form of personal communication.

II. Constitutional Provisions

269. The Constitution stipulates the basic rights of Bulgarians, such as freedom of expression, association and religious beliefs, as well as the rights to privacy, property, inheritance and economic initiative.

270. Article 39, paragraph 1 of the Constitution enshrines the right of everyone *to express opinions or to publicize them through words – written or oral, sound or image, or in any other way*. At the same time, paragraph 2 of Article 39 precises that these rights are not absolute. They *shall not be used to the detriment of the rights and reputation of others, or for the incitement of a forcible change of the constitutionally established order, the perpetration of a crime, or the incitement of enmity or violence against anyone.*

271. The freedom of the media faces constraints because there are other important values, such as state security, social peace or personal rights.[106] Such limitations of the media's freedom of expression are possible in a democracy, but they must be set in law or mentioned in the Constitution.

272. Article 40 of the Constitution regulates the media freedom and the prohibition of censorship, as well as the suspension and confiscation of printed matter or another medium of information:

> (1) The press and the other mass information media shall be free and shall not be subjected to censorship. (2) An injunction on or a confiscation of printed matter or another information medium shall be allowed only through an act of the judicial authorities in the case of an encroachment on public decency or incitement of a forcible change of the constitutionally established order, the

105. M. Pesheva, et al., *The Words of the Media Transition* 55 (Faber Ed., 2010).
106. According to Art. 17, para. 1 of the *International Covenant on Civil and Political Rights* to which Bulgaria is a side, *no one shall be subjected to arbitrary or unlawful interference with his privacy, family, home or correspondence or to unlawful attacks on his honor and reputation.*

perpetration of a crime, or the incitement of violence against anyone. An injunction suspension shall lose force if not followed by a confiscation within 24 hours.

273. As for Article 41 of the Constitution, it declares the right of everyone to seek, receive and disseminate information:

1. Everyone shall be entitled to seek, obtain and disseminate information. This right shall not be exercised to the detriment of the rights and reputation of others, or to the detriment of national security, public order, public health and morality.
2. Everyone shall be entitled to obtain information from state bodies and agencies on any matter of legitimate interest to them which is not a state or official secret and does not affect the rights of others.

274. In its interpretive Decision No. 7 of 1996,[107] the Constitutional Court confirmed that the rights under Article 39, Article 40 and Article 41 of the Constitution are fundamental rights and defined them as essential to individual and societal development. Along with the fundamental right to freely express and disseminate opinions is the principle that the press and other media are free. Censorship is explicitly banned. The Constitutional Court notes that the three provisions are found in a systematic and functional relationship. It declares that the restriction of these rights is acceptable only to ensure the protection of other constitutional rights and interests and can be done only on grounds provided in the Constitution. The limitation by law of those rights for reasons different from those specified in the Constitution is strictly forbidden.

275. At the same time, the constitutional provision of paragraph 6 of the transitional and concluding provisions provides a legislative framework only for the electronic media, and even more precisely only for BNT and BNR. The Constitutional Court ruled in Decision No. 7 of 1996 on the reasons for the introduction of regulation for the radio and television broadcasters and its rejection of the other types of media. The Court argued that the reasons for the establishment of special regulations on radio and television activities are legal, financial, technical or technological.

276. According to Article 18, paragraph 3 of the Constitution, the state shall exercise sovereign rights over the spectrum which is the means for the broadcasting of radio and television programmes. Therefore, state intervention is inevitable in the allocation of spectrum which in view of the actual technical level is still a 'scarce resource'. The limited technical frequency resource justifies state intervention in the field of terrestrial broadcasting.

107. Promulgated in State Gazette No. 55 of 1996.

277. As regards the distribution of programmes by other technical means, there are practically no restrictions. In fact, the broadcasting of radio and television programmes via cable, satellite or other technical means is not connected with the use of limited radio frequency resources. The principle of free economic activity enables the state to interfere in this case.

278. This distinction between terrestrial broadcasting and broadcasting via cable, satellite or other technical led to the creation by the legislator of two different modes for broadcasting, providing for two different regimes. For that reason, fifty deputies from the XXXIX National Assembly considered unconstitutional individual texts[108] of the Law amending the LRT. They contended that the law imposes a licensing and registration framework, resulting in two distinct legal regimes differing in content and severity for the same broadcasting activity. For that reason they considered the law amending LRT contrary to Article 19, paragraph 2 of the Constitution.

279. The registration system is a simplified system compared to the licensing one. This regime facilitates the operators who wish to broadcast radio and television programmes through a range which has no connection with limited resources. This helps to extend the reach of the individuals to seek, receive and impart information (Article 41 of the Constitution). The Constitutional Court considered that the regime is consistent with those reflected in the Constitution the right of free economic initiative. For the Court, it is reasonable to accept therefore that the objective prerequisites for the licensing of terrestrial radio and television broadcasting shall not have the effect of introducing similar arrangements for other operators, broadcasting programmes through other technical means. The difference in the two regimes is not a prerequisite for their participation, but a consequence of their choice. However, once the operator has made his choice, he is subject to differences in the framework of the particular regime.

280. For the claimants, the inequality of radio and television broadcasters is also active in case of withdrawal or termination of their telecommunications licences. In Bulgaria, each broadcaster needs two individual licences – one in accordance with LRT for the programmes and one for the broadcasting in accordance with the Telecommunications Law (TL). In case of termination or revocation of the programme licence, the telecommunications licence for the broadcast on certain frequencies to which the state has sovereign rights is also revoked. This is necessary due to the functional dependence of both licences. However, for the operators broadcasting through technical means other than radio resource, only the registration is delayed because there is no functional dependence between the mentioned programme and

108. Decision No. 1 of 26 Mar. 2002 under constitutional case No. 17, 2001. Some of the texts are, for example, Art. 105, para. 1 that reads as follows: Radio and television broadcasting through existing and/or construction, maintenance and utilization of new telecommunications networks for terrestrial broadcasting is based on a licence issued by the CEM in the terms and conditions of this law; Art. 125a, para. 1 according to which persons who wish to create radio or television programmes for broadcasting through technical means other than terrestrial broadcasting should be registered.

the frequency network. The termination will result in the prohibition of broadcasting only the programme through its own or foreign cable network, satellite or any other technical means. Therefore, Article 126a,[109] paragraphs 3 and 4 of the LRT are not unconstitutional.

III. The Law on Radio and Television

281. Presently, the radio and television in Bulgaria operate on the basis of the LRT from 1998. In fact, the first LRT dates back to 1996 but was met with sharp criticism and political stand-offs.

282. The initial LRT in its redaction of 1996 established a regulatory body named NCRT. A majority of this council's members (five out of nine) were to be elected by the government and the ruling majority in the Parliament. In addition, Article 89 of the initial LRT provided NCRT with powers for imposing compulsory administrative measures. These measures imposed *following a warning and in case there was no result*[110] are listed exhaustively in the first paragraph of Article 89. They consist of (i) giving binding recommendations to the directors of radio and television organizations; (ii) temporarily suspending the broadcasting of particular programmes; or (iii) temporarily suspending the broadcasting of radio or television organizations.

283. The Constitutional Court considered in its decision that Article 40, paragraph 2 of the Constitution governs the grounds for suspension and confiscation which are possible only by a judiciary act. It is obvious that the provisions of Article 89 do not meet the constitutional requirements. This is the reason why two years later, in 1998, a new LRT was adopted.

284. The new law guarantees the independence of the electronic media from political and economic pressure (Article 8, actual Article 5, paragraph 1), protects their freedom from censorship (Article 9, actual Article 5, paragraph 2), stipulates that every opinion can be freely expressed in radio and television broadcasting (Article 11) and grants the media the right to receive information from the state institutions (Article 13). The LRT of 1998 established a regulatory body named CEM. This body is concerned with the content of the programmes and the respect of the law by the electronic media. According to the law, four members of the CEM are appointed by the President and five from the parliamentary majority. The LRT

109. The article reads as follows: (1) In violation of conditions of licences, which does not constitute a breach of Art. 126, a penalty sanction of EUR 250 to EUR 2,500 is applied. (2) In case of a second violation of the conditions of licences, which does not constitute a breach of Art. 126, the penalty sanction is doubled. (3) For the breach of the programme project, programme design, programme profile or schedule by the operator, a penalty sanction of EUR 1,000 to EUR 2,500 is applied. (4) In case of systematic violation of the law by the registered operator, the registration is deleted.

110. Decision No. 21 of 1996 published in State Gazette No. 102 of 1996.

regulates public and private broadcasters, controls their programming content and outlines the licensing procedures for new broadcasters, as well as advertising and sponsorship in broadcast media.[111] Since 1998, the LRT has been amended many times.[112]

285. The general principles of LRT are defined in its Article 10, paragraph 1:

- the right of free expression and the right of information should be guaranteed;
- the confidentiality of the source of information should be respected;
- the privacy of the citizens should be protected;
- the broadcasting of programs impressing hate and intolerance among citizens should be prevented, so should be the broadcasting of programs, which are contrary to the good moral, especially if they contain pornography, laud or exculpate atrocity or violence or incite to hatred based on race, sex, religion or nationality;
- the right of reply in the programs should be ensured, as well as the copyright and related rights in the broadcasts and programs;
- the purity of the Bulgarian language should be preserved.

286. These principles are developed in the articles of LRT. For example, the above-mentioned Article 11, paragraph 1 declares that any opinion can be expressed freely. Article 16 declares that the media service providers cannot create and provide for broadcasting programmes containing information related to the privacy of citizens without their consent and are responsible for the content of the programmes (Article 17, paragraph 1). The media service providers are also obliged to respect the rights of children covered by the Law on Child Protection and other regulations and are forbidden to make children participate in programmes that could threaten or harm their physical, psychological, moral and/or social development (Article 17a). According to Article 18, individuals or state and municipal authorities offended in a linear media service where they did not participate personally or through a representative have the right to respond.

287. Finally, it should be noted that according to Article 17, paragraph 4 media service providers are not responsible for the disclosed information and its content when obtained: (i) through a formal way; (ii) from quotations of official documents; and (iii) as an accurate reproduction of public statements.

---

111. Ibroscheva & Raicheva-Stover, *Development of Digital TV in Bulgaria: Opportunities and Problems*, *supra* n. 77, 12.
112. The LRT has been amended twenty-eight times since it was first published in November 1998, and this led to the fact that LRT began to resemble more a patchwork of clauses rather than a coherent unit of legislation.

IV. Law on Electronic Communications

288. The regulation of electronic media is done in accordance with the provisions of two major laws – the LRT and the LEC.[113]

289. In 1998, the TL which regulates the transmission of electronic messages through electronic communications networks used for terrestrial analogue broadcasting of television signals was adopted. This law established a second regulatory body – the Commission on Telecommunications. On 7 October 2003, the State Gazette published the new TL which entered into force the same day and cancelled the one of 1998. According to the new TL, the Commission was succeeded by the CRC which is responsible for overseeing the telecommunication licences. In accordance with the provisions of the new law, telecommunication activities can be carried out in three possible modes: on an individual licence, the registration under a general licence and a free mode. The new TL explicitly states that Internet access is a free-provided service if the provider of Internet access is using the network of other operators and does not build or maintain his own telecommunications network. Compared to the repealed law, several activities have changed regime and moved from individual licensing regime to licence registration under a general licence – these are the construction and operation of cable network operators and networks for data.

290. The TL was replaced by the LEC adopted in May 2007. The provisions of the LEC and the powers of CRC will be examined below respectively in the part concerning the licensing requirements and the part concerning the regulatory bodies.

V. Transposition of the European Legislation

291. As already said in §2, III, A, 2 'The Digital Switch-over and the European Union', the TWF was the main instrument for the audiovisual sector in Europe. The directive was punctually amended in 1997 and more substantively in 2007 harmonizing key areas that were likely to hinder the free movement of television broadcasts across borders, the promotion of European works and works by independent producers, advertising, sponsorship and teleshopping, the protection of minors and public order, the right to reply, the events of major importance to society.

113. The European Commission considers that Bulgaria has incorrectly transposed the provisions related to the imposition of financial sanctions on providers of electronic communications networks and services contained in Directive 2002/21/EC of the European Parliament and of the Council of 7 Mar. 2002 on a common regulatory framework for electronic communications networks and services (Framework Directive) and Directive 2002/20/EC of the European Parliament and of the Council of 7 Mar. 2002 on the authorization of electronic communications networks and services (Authorization Directive), as amended by Directive 2009/140/EC. In that regard, the LEC is under amendment in order to have national effective system of appropriate, proportionate and dissuasive sanctions and measures designed to ensure compliance in cases of violations of regulatory decisions.

292. In 2010, the revised TWF Directive was subsequently codified by Directive 2010/13/EU of the European Parliament and of the Council in order to take into account the rapid development of the audiovisual market. Since then, this latest revision was amended by Directive EU 2018/1808 of the European Parliament and of the Council of 14 November 2018[114] in order to take into account the latest technical developments and user experiences. The media consumption patterns have significantly evolved, in particular for the younger audiences. Established platforms now include video-sharing sites, social media, and various forms of user-generated content. These changes necessitated a legal framework overhaul to mirror market evolutions and balance the accessibility of online content services, consumer safeguards, and market competitiveness.

293. As a Member of the EU, Bulgaria adopted the policy and legislation of audiovisual standards of the EU. The 1998 LRT transposed only partly the provisions of the TWF Directive. Amendments to the LRT made in 2000 and 2001 completed the transposition of the revised TWF Directive.

294. Just after that, the LEC was adopted. It introduced the European regulations governing electronic communications. This law actually provides the legal framework for digital radio and television broadcasting.

295. Bulgaria also ratified the European Convention on Transfrontier Television adopted in 1989, as well as the Amending Protocol[115] whose main objective is to encourage the free circulation of television programmes and thus to promote the free exchange of information and ideas. In fact, the convention served as a basis for the preparation of the TWF. In December 2020, Bulgaria introduced the latest revision (Directive 2018/1808) of the European media legislation with amendments to the LRT. In terms of technology, the LRT already contains the new European requirements for digital media and platform services.[116]

296. The liberalization of the media market leads to more choices of services for consumers and better realization of the right to information. The EU legislation guarantees the promotion of competition, protection of the interests of the citizens and the development of the EU internal market. LRT contains these principles; for example, freedom to provide audiovisual services, development of public television

---

114. Directive (EU) 2018/1808 of the European Parliament and of the Council of 14 Nov. 2018 amending Directive 2010/13/EU on the coordination of certain provisions laid down by law, regulation or administrative action in Member States concerning the provision of audiovisual media services (Audiovisual Media Services Directive) in view of changing market realities (OJ L 303 28.11.2018, p. 69).
115. The Convention was amended on 9 Sep. 1998 in order to take into account the technological developments and important changes in the broadcasting sector, as well as to maintain coherence with the TWF revised in 1997. The protocol amending the Transfrontier Television Convention entered into force on 1 Mar. 2002.
116. For example, Art. 2(6) and (7) LRT promulgated in the State Gazette, issue No. 109 of 2020, in force as of 22 Dec. 2020.

which guarantees pluralism and protection of the public interest and uniform regulation of public and commercial operators.

297. Bulgaria also ratified some other EU legislation and conventions which also concern the electronic media environment, such as the Framework Convention on Protection of National Minorities,[117] the Convention on the Protection of Human Rights and Fundamental Freedoms,[118] as well as the Directive 2000/31/EC on electronic commerce, concerning certain legal aspects of the information society services.

117. Ratified by the National Assembly of Bulgaria in State Gazette, issue No. 78 of 3 Sep. 1999.
118. Ratified by the National Assembly of Bulgaria in the State Gazette, issue No. 80 of 10 Feb. 1992.

Part I. Freedom of Speech

Chapter 1. Constitutional Framework

298. The right to freedom of expression and freedom of the press is settled, as was mentioned above, on a constitutional level in the provisions of Articles 39, 40 and 41 of the Constitution of the Republic of Bulgaria. The systematic interpretation of the texts of Article 5, paragraphs 1 and 2 leads to the conclusion that these norms are directly applicable and no other norms shall contradict them. Furthermore, the provision of Article 57, paragraph 1 of the Constitution indicates that the fundamental rights of citizens shall be inalienable. The Constitutional Court has had a lot of chances to declare the unconstitutionality of different provisions because of their contradiction with the mentioned norms.[119]

299. The significance of the rights set in these three provisions evolves mainly from their belonging to universally recognized values. These rights are individual subjective rights guaranteed to all persons in the legal system. Nevertheless, the freedom of the press is interpreted mostly as institutional freedom.

300. In the opinion of the Constitutional Court expressed in Decision No. 7 of 4 April 1996 under constitutional case No. 1 of 1996, the leading constitutional text is based on Article 39 which determines the right to freedom of expression. This article emphasizes the right of the legal persons to express and spread freely their opinions in different ways, including through the press, radio, and television. According to the Court, the freedom of expression is sui generis legal boundary before the regulative powers of the state in different spheres of public life. This right is the legal basis of political pluralism and the reason for the absolute prohibition of monopole in the political, ideological and intellectual sphere as a whole.

301. The Court uses the non-legal term ‘communication rights’ to generalize the rights expressed in the three constitutional provisions. The subjective right of free expression of opinion has its origin in the freedom of thought. According to the Court, as it is the richest in content, this right incorporates in a specific way the other rights. Nevertheless, the three constitutional provisions include, along with this main right, a catalogue of additional, specific rights, such as the right of freedom of

119. For example, Decision No. 4 of 11 Feb. 1997 under constitutional case No. 29/1996; Decision No. 10 of 25 Jun. 1999 under constitutional case No. 36/1998; and Decision No. 17 of 6 Nov. 1997 under constitutional case No. 10/1997.

the press and the other mass information media and the right to search, receive and disclose information. These rights are constitutionally guaranteed by the absolute prohibition of censorship (Article 40, paragraph 1 in fine) and the obligation of the state bodies to give the requested information (Article 41, paragraph 2).

Chapter 2. Legal Grounds for Limitation of the Rights

302. Logically, the legal grounds for limitation of the mentioned subjective rights are settled in the Constitution. The existence of such possible limitations proves the fact that these rights are not absolute. In the above-mentioned decision, the Constitutional Court divides the legal grounds for limitation, conditionally classifying them by the kind of interests which have to be protected:

(a) protection of the constitutionally established order (Article 39, paragraph 2 and Article 40, paragraph 2);
(b) protection of the national security (Article 41, paragraph 1);
(c) keeping the public peace and prevention of criminality (Article 39, paragraph 2; Article 40, paragraph 2 and Article 41, paragraph 1);
(d) protection of public health and morality (Article 40, paragraph 2 and Article 41, paragraph 1);
(e) protection of the reputation and the rights of the other citizens (Article 39, paragraph 2; Article 40, paragraph 2 and Article 41, paragraphs 1 and 2); and
(f) keeping a secret (Article 41, paragraph 2).

303. The Court notices an interesting question related to these limitations, namely if the latter are subject to hierarchization, i.e., are they equally significant or some of them are more important than others? The constitutional judges refuse to take a strong position on that question but, however, underline the fact that the concrete constitutional texts and the spirit of the Constitution, as a whole, give preference to the rights of the individual. Thus the intensity of limitation of the right to freedom of expression is the strongest when the latter is exercised against the rights and the reputation of someone else.

304. According to the Supreme Court of Cassations, the question of balance in exercising constitutionally guaranteed rights can be settled after a concrete estimation of the facts in each case. However, the freedom of the press and the other mass information media does not include the possibility of spreading false information that infringes individual rights.[120]

120. Decision No. 404 of 13 Jul. 2010 of the Supreme Court of Cassations under civil case No. 907 of 2009.

Part II. Regulation of Print Media

Chapter 1. The Journalists' Profession

305. The activity of journalists working for print media is not specifically regulated as far as there is no special law on the press effective in Bulgaria. Therefore, such activity is governed by the provisions in the Constitution regarding the freedom of expression (Article 39), the freedom of the press (Article 40) and the freedom to search, receive and disclose information (Article 41). It is, consequently, subject to the limitations described in the said articles.

306. Regarding the activity of journalists working for radio and TV operators, there have been public debates on the issue of the internal freedom of journalists; however, they have been conducted only with respect to the state radio and television and did not touch on the private media. According to Radomir Tcholakov, the battle of the political class for the ruling of the state media included the appointment of journalists close to the persons holding the political power. However, the already appointed journalists pleaded for lack of interference in their jobs whenever there was a change in the governing political forces. Political parties often used the internal freedom of journalists as an instrument for removing those who happened to be unsuitable and not as a matter of principle.[121]

307. In 1992, the Bulgarian Parliament amended the Labour Code by inserting the provision of Article 328b, which granted the right to employers to terminate the labour agreements of their employees unilaterally by giving two-month notice if the latter are managers in cultural institutions, BNT, BNR and Bulgarian Cinematography. Such termination could have been done without any need to provide a special reason revealing some culpable behaviour on the part of the employee. The amendment was used by the government formed by the Union of the Democratic Forces to trigger collective dismissals of journalists in the state radio and television as the number of the dismissed only in the BNT exceeded 700 within several months. The same legal basis was again used by the socialists who dominated the next Parliament. In 1995, seven correspondents of the BNR were dismissed because, in the opinion of the then management of the state radio, they had written their materials in a hostile manner towards the government. This case triggered very serious tensions, and, ultimately, the article of the Labour Code was revoked by the

121. R. Tcholakov, et al., *Media Law: Dictionary of the Main Concepts* 197 (Publishing House Trud 2005), Медийно право: речник на основните понятия (in Bulgarian).

socialist parliamentary majority. However, this precedent of politically driven dismissals of journalists along with the often cases of threatening journalists induced the legislators to include provisions in the LRT of 1998 in order to safeguard and guarantee the internal freedom of the journalists working for radio and TV operators.

308. As a result, Article 11 of the LRT was adopted, which, in its currently effective version, provides that every opinion can be expressed freely in media services. The next paragraphs of Article 11 confers a special protection of the journalists working for media services providers for the sake of free expression of their opinions.

309. Journalists and creative workers who have concluded contracts with media service providers shall not receive instructions and directives for their activity from persons and/or groups other than the bodies of management of the media services providers. The type of contracts that may be entered into is not specified, meaning that they may also be other than employment agreements, i.e., civil law-based contracts. Therefore, the single requirement for someone to work as a journalist with a media service provider is to have concluded a contract with that provider.

310. This provision not only refers to journalists but also covers creative workers. According to Radomir Tcholakov,[122] creative workers are meant as persons who hold copyright with respect to audiovisual work, i.e., director, scriptwriter and operator pursuant to Article 62 of the Law on Copyright and the Neighbouring Rights. Further, managers of media services providers may avail of this provision and oppose any attempts to interfere with the freedom of journalists and creative workers made by third parties. In this respect, the protection of journalists and creative workers under this article is further extended to the managers of such media services providers.

311. Public criticism regarding media services providers on the part of their employees shall not be considered disloyal to the employer. However, this provision is hardly applicable with respect to private media services providers. Its applicability would be possible mainly with respect to public media services providers.

312. Journalists who have concluded contracts with media services providers shall have the right to refuse the fulfilment of assigned tasks if they are not related to the fulfilment of the provisions of this law or of the respective contracts and contradict their personal convictions; technical and editorial processing of programme material and news cannot be refused. It should be noted that this provision concerns only journalists and not creative workers. Therefore, such contracts must provide for the performance of journalistic activity with a particular media services provider.

313. The LRT provides for the possibility of the conclusion of editorial statutes. These statutes can be established through agreements between the owners and/or

122. *Ibid.*, 200.

management of media service providers and the journalists who have contracts with them. These statutes outline the guidelines for working in the field of publicity. The editorial status must contain concrete definitions and measures for:

(i) protection of freedom and personal responsibility of journalistic work in fulfilment of the assigned task;
(ii) protection of journalists in the context of (i);
(iii) professional and ethical norms for journalistic activity of the respective media services providers;
(iv) ways of taking decisions which refer to journalistic activity; and
(v) establishment of an internal body for settlement of occurred disputes related to journalistic work.

314. In 1999, such editorial statute was concluded in the BNT with respect to the journalists and editors working there. It should be noted, however, that the conclusion of editorial statutes is not legally mandatory and is left entirely at the discretion of the contracting parties.

315. Some of the prohibitions stated in the Law on Personal Data Protection (LPDP) with respect to the processing of personal data are explicitly made inapplicable to journalistic activity. Pursuant to Article 4, paragraph 2 thereof, personal data processing is admissible in the cases when it is done for journalistic activity, literature or artistic expression as long as such processing does not infringe the right of personal life of the person, to whom the data refer. In such cases, the provisions of the LPDP setting the obligations of personal data administrators shall not apply. Likewise and subject to the same conditions, journalistic activity is exempted from the prohibition under Article 5 of the LPDP for the processing of personal data, which reveal race or ethnic origin, political, religious or philosophical beliefs, membership in political parties or organizations, associations having religious, philosophical, political or syndical objectives or related to health, sexual life or the human genome. Transfer of personal data to a Member State of the EU and European Economic Area (EEA) is exercised freely in compliance with the requirements of the LPDP. With respect to non-member countries, such transfer would be admissible in all cases, in which it is done solely for journalistic activity, literature or artistic expression as long as such processing does not infringe the right of the personal life of the person, to whom the data refer (Article 36a of the LPDP).

316. Bulgarian case law has not commented so far on the issue of the legal position of bloggers and whether they might be equated to journalists in order to avail themselves of the special legal protection conferred by virtue of the LRT. The principle followed regarding publications on the Internet is that everything which is forbidden outside the Internet is forbidden also on the Internet.[123] The specification of the precise legal position of bloggers is difficult because of the absence of clear-cut definitions of the terms 'journalist' and 'media'.

---

123. N. Ognyanova, *Audio-Visual Policy and Legislation of the European Union* 185 (University Press Saint Kliment Ohridski 2005).

Chapter 2. Journalists' Rights

§1. Role of Journalists as Watchdogs of Society

317. It is often said that the media is the fourth state power. Such a statement makes sense especially when we have in mind the function and the aims of this power. The latter serves as a corrective of the official state powers (legislative, executive and judiciary) by monitoring their work. The media asks uncomfortable questions, the answers of which are of public interest. Its main role as a democracy keeper predetermines the great influence that the media has on people's lives.

318. However, to be watchdogs of democracy, journalists have to be independent not only from the government but also from any economic interests. This independence makes them impartial, and this impartiality strengthens their position as a real power.

319. In the authors' opinion, this is not the only question of personal sense of responsibility. The society also has to participate in that process by insisting on the freedom of media. Although this freedom is explicitly recognized in the Constitution, it has to be gained again and again not only by words but also by actions.

§2. Journalists' Independence

320. In 1996, the President requested the Constitutional Court to clarify the meaning of Articles 39, 40 and 41 of the Constitution.[124] With regard to Article 40, paragraph 1, the following understanding has been expressed, namely that the freedom of the means for mass information has two dimensions: (i) freedom from the state interference through its bodies in the reflection of facts and events; and (ii) freedom of journalists in a given means for information to express their opinions in accordance with the nature, objectives and policy of the respective media. The request in this part has been further elaborated by the Parliament through the opinion of the Chair of the Permanent Commission on Human Rights and Religions. The opinion suggested that no state body could interfere in the work of a private media. In case of state media such as BNT, BNR and Bulgarian Telegraph Agency, their management bodies are the single ones which have been authorized to determine their policy, and they shall be liable before the body, which has elected them, i.e., the Parliament.

321. The opinion of the Chair of the Permanent Parliamentary Commission on Human and Religion Rights submitted for the case further reads that the right of journalists to express freely their opinions should correspond to the nature, objectives and policy of the respective media, and if it is private and the opinion of a journalist does not coincide with the point of view of the owner of the media, the former

124. *See* the above-mentioned Decision No. 7 of 4 Jun. 1996 under constitutional case No. 1 of 1996.

has the freedom to express his opinion in another media and leave the media, in which he is working. The same conclusion should be valid also with respect to journalists from the state media, whose opinions deviate from the objectives and policy designated by the management of the respective media. In such cases, they would have the option to leave in order to keep the whole freedom of expression of their own opinion. The management would have the equal option to dismiss them from work if such journalists exercise their own policy, which does not correspond to the policy of the media.

322. The Constitutional Court disagrees with the aforementioned understanding of the freedom of journalists to express freely their opinions in accordance with the nature, objectives and policy of the respective media because such understanding actually contained limitations of the freedom by making it dependent on the nature, objectives and policy of the respective media. However, the Constitutional Court did not go more into that issue by concluding that the potential conflict should be left to the future development of the jurisprudence.

323. A sociological survey conducted in Bulgaria in 2000 by the agency Alpha Research among 286 Bulgarian journalists from the print and electronic media at the national and regional levels showed that only 7% of the journalists considered the media in Bulgaria to be free and independent. According to the journalists who participated in the survey, the most frequent interventions in their materials have been done by the management of the respective media (25%), followed by the interventions of politicians (22%) and auto censure.

324. In the report Attacks on the Press 2001 issued by the Committee to Protect Journalists, it was stated that media outlets that criticized ruling authorities faced harassment, while journalists investigating politically sensitive issues, such as official corruption and organized crime, continued to suffer threats and intimidation for their work. Independent media outlets continued to face indirect government harassment, especially when politicians used their influence to divert advertising revenue to loyal media outlets and away from more independent and critical outlets according to the report.

325. In 2001, the BNT announced that the reporters and editors working for the BNT would not be allowed to participate in the promotions of products, or trademarks as well as in commercial events. They would be further not entitled to own or be shareholders, managers, members of supervisory bodies and independent consultants in sociological, advertising and PR agencies. The said requirements were included in the Regulations of the BNT on the Activity of the News Department. Furthermore, the employees leading the information emissions of the BNT were not allowed to express publicly their opinions regarding topics and issues from the news. The prohibition was included in the job description for the positions 'editor' and 'reporter'.

326. The first private national television bTV also restricted the persons leading the news from participating in advertisements and having shares in PR companies or agencies. They are also not allowed to make commentaries, which differ from the position of the media. All these requirements have been written in the employment contracts of the journalists. According to the Managing Director of bTV at that time the said rules followed 'the world model'.

327. The restrictions imposed on the journalists leading the news emissions of the BNT were criticized in view of the fact that they do not correspond to the LRT. The latter prohibited the use of voices and images of journalists leading news emissions in commercial messages but allowed such persons to participate in the popularization of a cause or idea. The absence of explicit prohibition in the law for participation of such journalists in activity related to advertising or PR was construed as their right to do so, which could not be limited through the internal acts of the respective media.

328. In the report of the organization, RWB devoted to the status of the media sector in 173 states all over the world for the period 2007–2008. Bulgaria has been ranked 59 in terms of freedom of media freedom. In 2013, Bulgaria was ranked 87 out of 179 countries and has the lowest ranking of all the EU Member States.[125]

§3. Protection of Journalistic Sources

329. Pursuant to Article 15, paragraph 2 of the LRT, journalists are not obliged to reveal their sources of information not only to the audience but also before the management of a media service provider except in the cases of pending Court proceedings or other proceedings initiated by an affected person. Moreover, journalists are obliged to keep secret the source of information provided that this was explicitly requested by the person who provided the information (Article 15, paragraph 4). Likewise, media service providers are not obliged to reveal their sources of information to the CEM subject to the same exceptions (Article 15, paragraph 1). The keeping in secret of the source of information is also included among the principles, by which media service providers shall be governed while carrying out their activity (Article 10, paragraph 3). Media service providers are entitled to include in their broadcasts information of unknown sources after having expressly indicated this fact (Article 15, paragraph 3).

330. Although protection of journalistic sources is granted by virtue of the LRT, it applies also to journalists working for print media. In a verdict of the Sofia Regional Court of 19 February 2004, it is said that the protection of journalistic sources is one of the main conditions for freedom of the press. This right of journalists (not to disclose their sources) is explicitly settled in the effective LRT, and, further, it is protected according to the practice in the application of the European Convention on Human Rights (ECHR).

125. *See* Reporters Without Borders, *Bulgaria: Police Attack Journalists Covering Protest Outside Parliament*, 26 Jul. 2013, available at: https://www.refworld.org/docid/57b5b28ac.html (accessed 17 Aug. 2024).

Chapter 3. Journalists' Liability

§1. Liability System in Bulgaria

331. In Bulgaria, there is no liability system applicable only to journalists. In general, like all citizens, journalists are liable for unlawful actions with culpable intent. Such actions trigger civil, criminal or administrative liability.

I. Civil Liability

332. Article 45 of the Law on Obligations and Contracts (LOC)[126] states the general liability of every person to redress the damage he has faultly caused to another person. Tort, as described in Article 45 of the LOC, represents a complex legal fact consisting of the following elements: act (action or omission); damage; unlawfulness of the act; cause–consequence connection between the act and the damage incurred; and guilt of the wrongdoer. All these facts are united by the legal rule and must be cumulatively present. Further to the tort liability under Article 45 in the cases where damage has been caused during the performance of a work assigned by another person, the latter will be vicariously liable. This liability serves as a guarantee that the actual damage will be ultimately efficiently remedied. That is why vicarious liability does not require the presence of guilt on the part of the assignor of the work.

333. The burden of proof with respect to the unlawful action, the damage and the cause–consequence connection between the act and the damage lies on the claimant in the procedure initiated pursuant to the Code of Civil Procedure by the person, who suffered the damage. The presence of fault is presumed, and the responsibility for the rebuttal of this presumption is left to the respondent.

II. Criminal Liability

334. A significant part of the crimes, which could be committed through media outlets, such as insult, defamation and disclosure of the secret of adoption, are prosecuted on the basis of complaints by the injured. This is called in Bulgarian legal doctrine private prosecution. When criminal proceedings are initiated upon the complaint of the injured the latter takes the procedural role of private prosecutor. Notwithstanding the actual filing of a complaint even if it is not barred by the statute of limitations, criminal prosecution will not be initiated if six months have passed following the day when the injured has become aware that the crime has been committed (Article 84 of the Criminal Code).

126. Law on Obligations and Contracts, promulgated in the State Gazette, issue No. 275 of 22 Nov. 1950, in force as of 1 Jan. 1951.

335. The right of complaint arises at the moment of commitment of the crime or at the moment the injured has become aware of the commitment. However, if the injured has filed his complaint within the six-month period from the moment he has become aware of the commitment of the crime, the Court will refuse to initiate criminal proceedings in case the period provided for in the statute of limitations has expired because the said period has started running from the commitment of the crime. The injured will be considered to have known about the commitment of the crime when he has not only become aware of the fact of commitment but also knows the perpetrator of the crime. This is particularly important for the crimes of insult and defamation, which, according to the Court practice, shall be prosecuted within six months from the moment the injured has become aware of the author of the anonymous material and not of the mere fact of the commitment of the crime.[127]

III. Administrative Liability

336. In some specific cases, journalists or their employers may bear administrative liability. For instance, the Law on Credit Institutions provides for the imposition of fines with respect to persons, who disclose false information or circumstances for a bank via means of mass information, by which the good name and the trustworthiness of the bank are infringed. Such sanction may be imposed only if the act would not qualify as a crime under the Criminal Code. In case of legal entities which have disclosed such information, they will be subject to monetary sanctions.[128] The administrative offences provided for in the Law on the Credit Institutions are certified by official persons authorized by the deputy governor of the Bulgarian Central Bank heading the Bank Supervision Department.[129]

337. The Law on the Protection from Discrimination also provides for administrative liability of persons and legal entities, which have committed discrimination or have failed to meet an obligation arising from that law. Journalists and media may be subject to such sanctions in case of writing, publishing or broadcasting materials that might constitute direct or indirect discrimination in the context of Article 4 of the Law on the Protection from Discrimination. The acts for the establishment of the offences shall be prepared by certain members of the Commission on the Protection from Discrimination designated by its chair.

338. Pursuant to Article 153, paragraph 3 of the Law on the Credit Institutions, the issuance, the appeal and the enforcement of the penal orders shall be done in accordance with the procedure set in the Law on the Administrative Offences and Penalties. The latter is also applicable with respect to matters which are not settled in the Law on the Protection from Discrimination.

127. Decision No. 430 of 16 Jul. 1971 under criminal Case No. 347/71, I criminal department.
128. Article 152, paras 3 and 4 of the Law on the Credit Institutions.
129. Article 153, para. 1 of the Law on the Credit Institutions.

IV. Ethical Liability

339. In the beginning of 2006 in Bulgaria over 200 newspapers, magazines and radio and TV broadcasters signed the Code of Ethics for the Media. Its norms were planned to be enforced through two commissions – one for the press and one for the electronic media. The main rule is that everybody who refers to one of the commissions has to point out which provisions of the code he or she considers to have been infringed. It is not a must for the one who files the complaint to be personally affected because he or she may raise concerns about a violation of the public interest. In case the commission confirms the infringement of the code, the media, which printed or broadcast the respective material or programme, is obliged to publish the decision of the commission as well as to apologize to the persons affected by its misconduct. The two commissions consist of twelve members divided into three quotas having four members. The quotas belong to the journalists, media owners and one independent quota, which includes representatives of the society.

340. In the preamble of the code, the fundamental freedom of expression, access to information, protection of dignity and inviolability of the personal life and the right to safety and security are proclaimed as leading principles. The code also refers to the practice of the European Court of Human Rights to invoke the principle that the public persons shall have a lower level of protection of their personal lives and this would be the justification for disclosure of such information by the media but only in case the protection of public interest imposes such disclosure.

§2. Review of the Case Law

341. As already mentioned above journalists might be held liable for tort under Article 45 of the LOC. In the cases where damage has been caused during the performance of a work assigned to the journalist by the publisher, the latter will be vicariously liable on the grounds of Article 49 of the LOC regardless of the presence of guilt on the part of the publisher.

342. Bulgarian case law contains examples of litigations against journalists and their employers based on Articles 45 and 49 of the LOC. In a case decided recently by the Supreme Court of Cassations,[130] the latter confirmed, as a Court of last instance, the amount of EUR 3,000 to be paid as compensation for the infringement of the right of the good name of a Bulgarian composer, who was also the organizer of a traditional music fest in the city of Burgas. The claim was directed against a woman leading a TV show on one Bulgarian television having national coverage through cable transmission and the legal entity holding the licence for broadcasting the programme of the said television. The Court accepted as proven the facts that the first defendant had disclosed information about the plaintiff, which was false,

130. Decision No. 352 of 23 Apr. 2009 of the Supreme Court of Cassation under civil case No. 6517/ 2007.

and insulting, blaming him for corruption and creating the wrong image of his activity as organizer of the musical festival. The Court held that this conduct of the defendant was unlawful and triggered her liability under Article 45 of the LOC to compensate the damages she had caused culpably. The Court also made the other defendant severally liable for the payment of the compensation on the grounds of its vicarious liability under Article 49 of the LOC.

343. In case of moral damages, the Court shall decide on the amount of the compensation on the basis of the rules on justice, i.e., the judge has the discretion to rule on this issue. In the case discussed above the Supreme Court of Cassation found the amount of EUR 3,000 even insignificant in view of the evidence taken during the proceedings and the rules on natural justice. To reach this conclusion, the Court took into account the publicity of the statements broadcast on the TV and the image and popularity of the person, who suffered the damage. However, due to the absence of a claim from the respective party for the increase in the amount of compensation, the Court left it unchanged.

344. In 2009, a publisher in Bulgaria was held vicariously liable for damages incurred by a reader's letter. The regional weekly *Videlina* has been ordered to pay EUR 14,000 for publishing a reader's letter in October 2007 accusing a local politician of corruption. The fine has been upheld by an appeal Court in the southern city of Plovdiv. In the meanwhile, however, the enforcement proceedings have been completed, and the newspaper has been forced to pay the full amount of the sanction despite the appeal, which cannot suspend the execution of the judgment of the Court of the second instance. The judges who passed the two decisions found that *Videlina* had the capacity of principal with respect to the author, i.e., the reader Kunka Delcheva, who wrote the letter. This reasoning provoked severe debates and reactions. The organization RWB published its opinion under the title 'Weekly's survival threatened by disproportionate fine'.[131] *It is deplorable that a newspaper or magazine can be convicted for publishing a reader's letter*, RWB said:

> Videlina cannot be blamed or held responsible for the views expressed by one of its readers, who anyway said she assumed complete responsibility for what she was writing. The people who were criticized by this reader, Kunka Delsheva, should have used their right of reply in Videlina instead of suing it.

345. RWB added:

> The size of this fine is totally disproportionate, especially in a European Union member country, and threatens the magazine's survival. We urge the judges to at least await the decision of the higher appeal Court before seizing the money from its accounts. And the higher Court should overturn the judgment on the grounds that it violates the basic principles of press freedom.

131. http://en.rsf.org/bulgaria-weekly-s-survival-threatened-by-08-07-2009,33756.html.

346. The position of the Bulgarian Association of the Regional Media was that:

> the creation of such legal precedent hangs down as an axe over the reader's letter, the reader's opinion, the freedom of expression and the right of the society to be informed.[132]

347. The saga continued as the Supreme Court of Cassation reversed the appealed judgment because of breaches of the procedural rules and returned the case for a new examination by another panel of the appellate Court.[133] Later the Court of Appeal reduced the fine to EUR 1,750. The judgment was appealed again before the Supreme Court of Cassations, but the latter did not admit it to cassation appellate review.[134]

348. In June 2002, the Supreme Court of Cassations decided as a Court of last instance another case which focused on the media interest and was considered to establish conditions for serious restrictions on the right of Bulgarian citizens to receive information as well as on the media freedom in general. The publisher of the national daily *24 Chasa* was ordered to pay EUR 3,750 to a person who suffered moral damages as a result of publication in the said periodical. One of the claims of the injured persons was directed against the publisher of *24 Chasa* for publication, in which certain words said at a press conference by another journalist, not associated with *24 Chasa* in any manner, had been merely cited. As a result, many journalists were alarmed that the decision questioned their freedom to use citations because they could be convicted for the words of third parties.

349. At the end of 2004, Bulgarian jurisprudence concerning journalists' rights obtained its landmark case. In November 2004, the Romanian journalist George Buhnic was arrested by Bulgarian authorities after he secretly shot smuggling affairs in the duty-free shops at the border between the two neighbouring countries by using a small camera attached to his glasses. The journalist was accused on the grounds of Article 339a of the Criminal Code providing for imprisonment from one to six years of every person who in the absence of a duly issued permit, required by the law, produces, uses, sells or holds a special technical means designated for secret collection of information and the technical means shall be expropriated by the state. The said provision was inserted in the code in 1997 and was intended to prevent police officers from abusing special investigation techniques at their disposal. However, being directed against the investigating journalists, who objectively would not be able to do their jobs without using such means, Article 339a was seen as a real threat to the freedom of expression.

---

132. *See* http://www.europe.bg/htmls/page.php?category=5&id=22898 (no longer available).
133. Decision No. 581 of 30 Sep. 2009 of the Supreme Court of Cassations under civil case No. 1019 of 2009.
134. Ruling No. 1371 of 28 Oct. 2011 of the Supreme Court of Cassations under civil case No. 587 of 2011.

350. Despite the strong public reaction in December 2004, George Buhnic was found guilty by the Regional Court in Rousse. At the appeal, the Rousse District Court cancelled the first verdict and remanded the file to the prosecutor's office. On 15 September 2005, the Regional Court in Rousse issued an acquittal under the renewed criminal proceedings. The verdict was protested by the prosecutor's office before the Rousse District Court, which affirmed it. The following protest of the prosecutor's office with the Rousse District Court before the Supreme Court of Cassations was withdrawn by the prosecutor's office to the latter Court and this way the proceedings were terminated. As a result, the Romanian journalist was allowed to take his camera back.

351. As of the time of writing this monograph, Article 339a of the Criminal Code is still present without any amendments following the outcome of the Buhnic case. However, it should be expected that future cases of use of hidden cameras for the purpose of journalistic investigation would not result in criminal proceedings but rather the aggrieved person, who has been recorded contrary to his will could avail himself of the legal protection provided by the civil law.

352. At the end of 2008, the publisher of the free daily *19 minutes* was sanctioned by the Bulgarian Central Bank for publishing materials implying financial difficulties of one Bulgarian bank without indicating the author and the sources of information. This act of the publisher was considered to constitute an infringement of the Law on Credit Institutions because such conduct could affect the image and the credibility of the bank.

353. The first decision of the Commission on the Electronic Media in application of the Code of Ethics for the Media was adopted on 3 August 2006 in reply to a petition filed by a popular man, who was leading a TV show in the programme of the BNT, against another television having national coverage bTV. The complaint was provoked by a TV show broadcast on bTV, in which a photo of the claimant was shown to the guest in the studio (a former Ms Bulgaria and owner of an agency for models) and a hidden voice said that he was inspired by her to become a woman, that he wanted to participate in the next Ms Bulgaria competition, and asked for advice how to improve his way of walking. According to the claimant, the broadcasting of his image and this insulting text constituted a moral and ethical duress towards his personality. He opined that the electronic media were obliged to respect human dignity and that journalists should be responsible for truth, morals and the good name of people. The respondent argued that the format and the nature of the particular TV show allowed such caricatures and that the claimant was a public person.

354. The commission emphasized that the freedom of expression is not absolute and is limited in the cases where human dignity is affected. In order to mark up the borderline between freedom and its limitations, the commission cited the following paragraph from the Decision of the Constitutional Court No. 7 of 1996:

> The freedom of speech is one of the fundamental principles, which is the basis for the growth of each democratic society and one of the major conditions for its progress and for the development of each person. It is valid not only for 'information' or 'ideas', which enjoy good acceptance and are not considered to be insulting or are accepted with indifference, but also for those who insult, shock or embarrass the state or whatever else part of the population. These are the requirements of pluralism and tolerance without which a democratic society will not be able to call itself in such a way.

355. The commission reminded in its decision that the Code of Ethics of the Bulgarian Media was based on the Constitution of Bulgaria and the international agreements in the area of human rights, including the ECHR. According to the commission, the Code of Ethics is an act which serves as a legal ground for the limitation of the freedom of expression if its rules are breached. The commission found as undisputable the fact that the personal dignity of the claimant, which is a protectable value, was affected in the case at hand. However, it applied the test under Article 10, paragraph 2 of the ECHR requiring, in addition, that the potential limitation of the freedom of expression is necessary in a democratic society. In this connection, the commission found it important to consider the format and the nature of the TV show, the speech and the expression used therein, whether the claimant qualifies as a public person and, if so, what the implications from this fact would be.

356. The commission noted that humour, caricature and grotesque have been known since ancient times and that they had an enormous impact on the development of art and culture. The inevitable tolerance in a democratic society, according to the commission, falls foul of the imposition of any limitations regarding style and way of expression, which are part of the freedom of expression. In this context, the creation of models in advance (which would be the main consequence if the way of expression is sanctioned) conflicts with the values of a democratic society.

357. The commission agreed that the claimant has been personally affected and has morally suffered as a result of the broadcast of his image in that TV show. However, for the commission, he had the status of a public person, although the claimant did not admit that fact attributing this status only to persons who occupy public positions.

358. The commission referred to the practice of the European Court of Human Rights in order to demonstrate that there is no difference between public and famous persons whatsoever. Public persons may also qualify as actors, businessmen, etc., as the criterion is not the particular position or occupation but the influence of that person on public opinion.

359. The commission relied on the well-known and largely recognized principle that public persons shall bear the freedom of speech and expression to a larger extent in comparison to private persons. They shall accept critique not only towards their statements and opinions but also to their personality, as a whole. Also, they must admit the fact that they will be more often subject to publicity in the media, comments and all forms of judgments. The claimant was leading a weekly TV show on the BNT enjoying a large audience. He participated in discussions on various issues and influenced the formation of public opinion on them. Therefore, there was no doubt for the commission that the claimant was obliged to be more tolerant and adaptable to different forms of his reflections, including the one used by the TV show on the bTV.

360. During the procedures before the commission, the representative of the bTV showed the readiness of the television to apologize to the claimant. The commission noted that any media may apologize or give a right to reply even if they are not obliged to do so under the Code of Ethics, and this is entirely left at their discretion. Ultimately, the commission found no infringements of the Code of Ethics and rejected the claim.

§3. Defamation and Insult

361. Very often journalistic materials might affect the good name of people who are investigated or commented therein. Good name as a value including also the honour and dignity of an individual may be a subject matter of the crimes of insult, i.e., intentionally humiliating the dignity of a given person through mistreatment and defamation, i.e., the conscious disclosure of untruthful and shameful acts for a given person or imputing criminal offence to another person.

362. A constitutional case dated 14 July 1998 was initiated in order to question the compliance with the Constitution of the provisions in the Criminal Code about the penalties provided for insult and slander as criminal offences. More specifically, the penalties provided for these crimes at the time of the proceedings before the Constitutional Court – 'up to six months of imprisonment' for insult and 'up to one year of imprisonment' for defamation – were deemed too high and disproportionate to the nature of the crimes. Further, according to the fifty-five members of the Parliament, who initiated the challenge, Article 148 of the Criminal Code provided for discriminatory procedure for realization of criminal liability. The penalties for the crimes of insult and defamation were more severe in the cases where the perpetrator or the victim was a state official (two years of imprisonment). Also, the crimes committed by or against such officials were prosecuted by the state ex officio, unlike the other cases of insult and defamation which were to be initiated following a claim by the aggrieved party. The effect of limitation on the freedom of expression as a result of the severe penalties for insult and defamation would fall foul of Article 10, paragraph 2 of the ECHR. Furthermore, the provision of even more severe sanctions and different procedures for prosecution regarding the cases involving state officials would contradict the constitutional principle of the lower level of defence of public figures and state officials as well as the one for the equality of citizens.

363. In its analysis, the Constitutional Court specifies that the freedom of expression is not absolute and subject to limitations. Such limitations are set forth in the Constitution and also in Article 10 of the ECHR, which states that the exercise of these freedoms, since it carries with it duties and responsibilities, may be subject to such formalities, conditions, restrictions or penalties as are prescribed by law and are necessary in a democratic society, for the protection of the reputation or rights of others and for the protection of other values specified therein. Therefore, the Court concluded, that civil and criminal liability as means for protection of honour, dignity and good name constitute a legitimate restriction of the freedom of expression, which is permitted both by the Constitution and the ECHR. The Court confirmed the requirement for proportionality of the restrictive measures vis-à-vis the nature of the protected values, which also followed from the previous case law on that issue.[135]

364. However, the Court did not find the penalties in the Criminal Code disproportionate. It stressed that personal dignity is proclaimed as a supreme constitutional principle and many of the personal rights derive from it. The Court observed that the penalties applicable to insult and defamation are among the least severe compared to those for all other crimes against personal rights. It further noticed that other European countries which ratified the ECHR had similarly provided for imprisonment with respect to defamation.

365. Likewise, the Constitutional Court did not find the more severe penalties in the Criminal Court and the difference in the procedures for the prosecution of cases of insult and defamation involving state officials in any conflict with the Constitution and the ECHR. It emphasized the requirement that state officials may be subject to stricter liability for insult and defamation or entitled to higher protection when suffering from such crimes only if, upon the commitment of the crime, they acted in the performance of their official duties. The rationale behind the special treatment of such cases is that the respective provision in the Criminal Code is designed also to protect the prestige of the institution, to which the particular state official belongs.

366. Nevertheless, the possibility of criticizing state officials is not affected according to the Constitutional judges. They quoted previous practice of the Constitutional Court where it was stated that 'statements concerning the activity of state bodies or constituting critique of political figures, public officials or the government deserve a higher level of protection'. Therefore, the extent to which such persons may face critique is larger compared to private individuals. At the same time, such critique cannot exceed the limits of the freedom of expression stated in the Constitution including the protection of good name.

367. The criteria for demarcation of the borderlines are not clear and should be judged on a case-by-case basis. Yet, the Court concluded that the criminal liability

135. Decision of the Constitutional Court No. 7 of 4 Jun. 1996 under constitutional case No. 1 of 1996.

for insult and defamation did not prevent criticizing persons belonging to the political system or the system of state bodies and, ultimately, did not grant the request for declaring the challenged provisions of the Criminal Code incompliant with the Constitution.

368. However, following the amendments of the Criminal Code in 2000, imprisonment as a penalty was substituted by a fine amount ranging between EUR 50,000 and EUR 1,500 for insult and between EUR 1,500 and EUR 3,500 for defamation. In the latter case, the Court is obliged to impose also public reprimand while for insult this is optional. In case of insult and defamation committed by a public official or directed against such person, the penalties are: (i) fine between EUR 1,500 and EUR 5,000 and public reprimand for insult and (ii) fine between EUR 2,500 and EUR 7,500 and public reprimand for defamation.

369. The organization for protection of human rights, the Bulgarian Helsinki Committee, conducted in 2001, a research on the litigations against Bulgarian journalists for insult and defamation. It was observed that more often the protection of a good name from insult and defamation is sought through criminal liability than civil liability. Out of ninety-seven Court proceedings, there were sixty criminal and thirty-seven civil. The cases based on defamation prevailed: thirty-three cases for defamation, fifteen for insult and forty-four for both insult and defamation. The research showed inequality in the number of proceedings initiated in the capital and the other areas of the country. The report noted the long duration of the proceedings, the high amount of compensation requested and the low percentage of successful cases against journalists. At the time of the research in 2001, twenty-three proceedings had been completed and only one journalist was ordered to pay a fine and subjected to public reprimand.

§4. Privacy

370. Pursuant to Article 32 of the Constitution of the Republic of Bulgaria:

> privacy of citizens shall be inviolable. Everyone shall be entitled to protection against any illegal interference in his private or family affairs and against encroachments on his honour, dignity and good name. No one shall be followed, photographed, filmed, recorded or subjected to any other similar activity without his knowledge or despite his express disapproval, except when such actions are permitted by law.

The right to privacy is not absolute, and its breach may be justified in certain cases when other legitimate interests impose that. However, such cases must be explicitly provided for in the law as Article 32 of the Constitution requires.

371. One of the effective laws in Bulgaria allowing intervention in the personal lives of citizens is the Law on Special Investigation Techniques. Special investigation techniques are defined in Article 2 of the said law as the technical means and the operational methods for their application, which are used for the preparation of exhibits such as cinema recordings, video recordings, audio recordings, photos and marked objects. Technical means are electronic and mechanical facilities as well as substances, which serve to document the activity of the controlled persons and objects. Operational methods are observation, tapping, retracing, penetrating, marking and checking correspondence and computer information, controlled delivery, confidential transaction and investigation through undercover officers,[136] which are applied in the process of use of technical means.

372. Special investigation techniques shall be used in cases when this is indispensable for preventing and discovering grievous crimes pursuant to the procedure set in the Code of Criminal Procedure on the condition that the necessary data cannot be collected in another way.[137] Special investigation techniques shall be used for the preparation of exhibits as well as in relation to activities connected with the protection of national security.[138] Therefore, the legitimate interest justifying intervention in citizens' personal lives as specified in the Law on Special Investigation Techniques is the prevention and discovery of grievous crimes and national security protection.

373. The Constitutional Court has stated that the possibilities for state intervention with respect to constitutional rights in the cases when such possibilities exist in the effective law shall be construed restrictively and narrowly in order to remain as an exception.[139] That is why every law which contains such a possibility for state intervention with respect to the constitutional rights of citizens must also provide mechanisms for the prevention of potential abuse of the exception. In the Law on the Special Investigation Techniques, the guarantees against potential abuse of such techniques are related to the precise specification of bodies, which may have the right to request use of special investigation techniques, the procedure for issuance of permits for such use, the term for use of such techniques and the obligation for the destruction of the data obtained as a result from the use of special investigation techniques.

374. The right to request the use of special investigation techniques and to use the so collected data and exhibits in accordance with their competence shall have:

---

136. Confidential transaction is used by the undercover officer and constitutes execution of fictitious sale or other transaction having material subject matter in order for the undercover officer to win the trust of the other party to the transaction. It is defined in Art. 10b of the Law on the Special Investigation Techniques. The undercover officer is a public servant of the competent offices established under the Law on the Ministry of Interior, the Law on Defence and Military Forces or of National Investigation Office who has been authorized to establish or maintain contacts with a controlled person in order to receive or discover information for commitment of grievous culpable crime and for the organization of criminal activity.
137. Article 3, para. 1 of the Law on the Special Investigation Techniques.
138. Article 3, para. 2 and Art. 4 of the Law on the Special Investigation Techniques.
139. Decision No. 7 of 1996 of the Constitutional Court.

(i) the Head Department Combat against Organized Crime, (ii) the Head Department Criminal Police; (iii) Head Department Security Police; (iv) the Head Department Border Police; (v) Department Internal Security; (vi) regional departments of the Ministry of Interior; (vii) specialized departments (with the exception of Department Technical Operations): territorial departments and independent territorial units of State Agency National Security; (viii) the offices Military Information and Military Police with the Minister of Defence; and (ix) the observing prosecutor in pre-trial criminal proceedings following a written request to the Court stating reasons. Bodies other than the specifically enumerated in the law may not request and use special investigation techniques.

375. The procedure for issuance of permits for use of special investigation techniques is commenced upon the initiative of the heads of the bodies listed in the previous paragraph or the observing prosecutor, who submit the request to the chairmen of the Sofia City Court and the district Courts or to deputy chairmen authorized by them and with regard to the persons engaged in the army – to the chairmen of the district Military Courts or a deputy chairman authorized by them. They shall issue a permit in writing or reject it by stating reasons.[140] The respective body requested for the issuance of the permit shall rule on the request immediately upon its receipt. The described procedure is designed to guarantee a serious review of the requests and to permit the use of special investigation techniques only if judicial bodies find that there is sufficient information for a grievous crime or other ground for tapping and retracing.[141]

376. The term for use of special investigation techniques shall be up to two months. In case of necessity, it can be prolonged following the procedure described in the previous paragraph; however, the total duration shall not exceed six months.[142]

377. The information received as a result of the use of special investigation techniques, which has not been used for the preparation of exhibits regardless of whether it constitutes classified information, shall be destroyed by the bodies using such techniques within ten days following the termination of the use.[143]

378. Despite the legal guarantees against abuse of special investigation techniques, the practice for the application of the law has shown that only 1%–2% of the issued permits are related to procedures ending with a guilty verdict.[144]

379. The LEC is another piece of legislation, which provides for state intervention in citizens' personal lives. For keeping electronic messages confidential, it introduces the general rule prohibiting tapping, recording, retention or other types

140. Article 15 of the Law on the Special Investigation Techniques.
141. N. Ognyanova, *Bulgarian Media Policy and Law: How Much Europeanization*, 2 Central European Journal of Communication, 27–41 (2009).
142. Article 21, paras 1 and 2 of the Law on the Special Investigation Techniques.
143. Article 31, para. 3 of the Law on the Special Investigation Techniques.
144. Ognyanova, *The Audio-Visual Policy and Legislation of the European Union, supra* n. 143, 276.

of interception or retracing of messages from persons other than the sender and the receiver of the message without their explicit consent save for the cases when this is provided for in the law.

380. The prohibition does not apply to undertakings operating electronic communication networks when: (i) retention is necessary due to technical reasons or it is a significant part of the provision of the service; and (ii) authorized persons by virtue of the LEC are carrying out checks of the technical parameters of the service. In the cases described in (ii), the undertakings are obliged to erase the retained messages immediately after the grounds for the retention have been removed.[145]

381. Further, the general rule is not applicable with regard to the recording of messages and related traffic data if the retention is necessary and provided for in law with the purpose of evidencing the conclusion of commercial transactions and if the sender and the receiver of the messages have been notified in advance about the recording, the objectives and the term of storage as well as about their right to refuse that. The messages and the related traffic data recorded shall be retained for a period not longer than the period, in which they can be used.[146]

382. Other exceptions are stated in Chapter 19 of the LEC titled Creation of Conditions for Interception of Electronic Messages Related to Protection of National Security and Safeguarding of Public Order. It lays down the obligation of the undertakings providing public electronic communications networks to provide the possibility for real-time interception of electronic messages and the possibility for permanent surveillance as well as real-time access to data related to a given call. When those data cannot be provided in real time they shall be delivered to a special department of the Ministry of Interior and the State Agency National Security in the shortest possible term after the end of the conversation. The possibilities for interception, permanent surveillance and data access related to a given call in real time shall be carried out only following the procedure set in the Law on Special Investigation Techniques.[147] The reference to the Law on the Special Investigation Techniques is intended to serve as a guarantee against potential abuses.

383. The undertakings providing public electronic communications networks and/or services shall provide, enter into exploitation and maintain on their behalf the detecting interfaces, from which the detected electronic messages may be delivered to the facilities of the specialized department at the Ministry of the Interior or to the State Agency National Security.[148]

384. The term 'interception' is defined in the LEC as an activity for providing access to and the delivery of the electronic messages of a given subscriber and the

145. Article 246 of the LEC.
146. Article 247 of the LEC.
147. Article 304 of the LEC.
148. Article 305 of the LEC.

data related to his calls to the bodies listed in the Law on the Special Investigation Techniques as competent to request the issuance of permits for use of special investigation techniques.

385. 'Detecting Interface' is defined as a system of monitoring centres and other input-output programmes and technical techniques of an undertaking carrying out electronic messages, where access to the detected electronic messages or the data related to the call is provided.

386. The undertakings providing public electronic communication networks and/or services are obliged to provide the possibility for delivery of the detected electronic services to the facilities of the specialized department of the Ministry of Interior and the State Agency National Security through fixed or commutated lines.[149] In order to provide safeguards against abuse of interception, the LEC states that interception shall be exercised in a way excluding a possibility for unlawful interference and ensure the protection of the information connected with the interception. The intercepted electronic messages shall be received only by the specialized department of the Ministry of Interior and the State Agency National Security following the procedure set in the Law on Special Investigation Techniques.[150]

387. Section III of the LEC deals with the protection of the customers' data. The undertakings providing public electronic communication networks and/or services are entitled to collect, process and use customers' data when such data are necessarily designated for provision of electronic communication services. The customers' data include, *inter alia*, traffic data, i.e., data, necessary for provision of electronic communication services, for billing, forming the customers' accounts as well as for proving their authenticity such as: (i) number of the calling and end customer and number of the card for electronic payment; (ii) beginning and end of the call identified with date and hour, with precision to a second if technical possibility is available and/or in case of data transfer – the size of the data transferred for billing purposes; (iii) type of the service rendered; (iv) points of mutual connection at the time of realization of the call, beginning and end of their use, identified with date and hour, with precision to a second if technical possibility is available; (v) data for the type of connection or zones, time and territorial, necessary for the specification of the value of the service; and (vi) location of a user of service, which is provided from a mobile network including the provision of the service 'roaming'.[151]

388. The undertakings providing public electronic communications services, which collect, process and use traffic data for the purpose of a specific call or the establishment of a connection, must erase the said data or make them anonymous upon termination of the said call or connection unless the said data are directly necessary for the establishment of a new call or connection or in the cases provided for

149. Article 308 of the LEC.
150. Article 309 of the LEC.
151. Article 248, para. 1 of the LEC.

in the LEC. The said undertakings must provide the users with accurate and full information about the type of traffic data which are processed for billing purposes and for interconnection payments, and about the duration of such processing. They shall further store and process traffic data for billing subscribers and interconnection payment until the payment is effected, except in the cases where they are challenged or payment is pursued according to the procedure established by the LEC.

389. Also, they shall provide information about traffic data to the Commission for Regulation of Communications at its request, in connection with the settlement of disputes on access, interconnection and billing. The undertakings may use the data covered for market research, including the extent to which the electronic communications services provided by the said undertakings satisfy the requirements of users, or for the provision of value-added services, requiring further processing of traffic data or location data other than the traffic data necessary for the conveyance of the communication or for the billing of the communication, solely where the said undertakings have obtained the consent of users.

390. The personal data on end users, received in connection with the research, shall be made anonymous. After obtaining the prior consent of users, the undertakings referred to in Article 248, paragraph 1 of the LEC may process the information about the types of traffic data for market research. The said undertakings shall provide users with accurate and full information about the type of traffic data which are processed, as well as about the duration of such processing. After obtaining the consent of users, the undertakings shall have a right to provide traffic data related to the users for the provision of value-added services requiring further processing of traffic data or location data other than the traffic data necessary for the conveyance of the communication or the billing of the communication. They shall include a mechanism in their relations with the users, making it possible for the user to withdraw the consent thereof given for market research at any time.[152]

391. Legal entities providing public electronic communication networks or services shall retain for a period of twelve months data created or processed in the course of their activity relating to the traffic of messages and necessary for: (i) tracing and identifying the source of connection; (ii) identifying the direction of the connection; (iii) identifying the date, hour and duration of the connection; (iv) identifying the type of connection; (v) identifying the end electronic communication device of the user; and (vi) establishing identifier of the cells used.[153]

392. The retention of the data shall be guaranteed for a certain period of time with a view to the use of all or a part thereof for discovering and investigating crimes, regarding which two or more years of imprisonment is provided in the law as a penalty as well as for discovering and investigating computer crimes prosecuted under Chapter 9a of the Criminal Code and for search of missing persons. According to the reasons for the amendments of the LEC, the category of missing

152. Article 250, para. 1 of the LEC.
153. Article 250a of the LEC.

persons embraces in addition to accused and other persons on trial, attempting to avoid criminal prosecution, and sentenced or persons attempting to avoid imposed penalties, also other cases, which might not be related to committed crimes.

393. Such cases might be, for instance, a search for persons, who have disappeared without a trace or persons, although not announced for search as disappeared without a trace, whose precise location must be quickly established for the sake of preserving their lives and health. Examples of the latter are persons who have disappeared in mountains due to avalanches or other reasons. According to the reasons for the amendments, the LEC following the amendments distinguishes between the data referring to the traffic of messages from their content and the regime applicable to them.

394. No other data, including such revealing the content of the messages, may be retained under the procedure set in the LEC as explicitly stated therein.

395. The LEC lays down the obligation of the undertakings providing public electronic communications networks and/or services to destroy the data after the expiry of twelve months with the exception of those, which have been accessed and stored.

396. Access to the stored data shall be provided following the permission of the chairman of the regional Court or of a judge located in the seat of the body, which has requested the access. An order for the provision of access shall be issued.[154] According to the reasons for the amendment of the LEC, the level of chairman of a regional Court is enough to guarantee the respect of the procedure for access to the data. The LEC sets the procedure for provision of such data to a competent body of another country if such obligation follows from an international treaty, which is in force with respect to Bulgaria.[155] Permits and rejections given by the respective Courts shall be entered in a special registry, which is not public.

397. In case of access to the data, exercised by the specialized department of the Ministry of Interior through interface, the head of the body, which has requested the access, is obliged to notify the undertaking of the necessity for retention of the data. The above-mentioned requirements have been introduced in implementation of Article 7b of the Directive 2006/24/EC of the European Parliament and of the Council of 15 March 2006 on the retention of data generated or processed in connection with the provision of publicly available electronic communication services or of public communications networks and amending Directive 2002/58/EC. The said article provides for the obligation of the Member States to ensure that providers of publicly available electronic communications services or of a public communications network respect, as a minimum, the principle, *inter alia*, that the data shall be subject to appropriate technical and organizational measures to protect the data

154. Article 250c of the LEC.
155. Article 251 of the LEC.

against accidental or unlawful destruction, accidental loss or alteration, or unauthorized or unlawful storage, processing, access or disclosure.

398. The directive further provides for the obligation of each Member State to designate one or more public authorities to be responsible for monitoring the application within its territory of the provisions adopted by the Member States pursuant to Article 7 regarding the security of the stored data. Those authorities may be the same authorities as those referred to in Article 28 of Directive 95/46/EC. The authority designated by Bulgaria for monitoring the security of the stored data is the Commission on Personal Data Protection, which is also the authority designated pursuant to Article 28 of Directive 95/46/EC.

399. In order to guarantee the rights of citizens related to the process of traffic data, a new provision has been inserted in the Criminal Code. Article 171a thereof provides for imprisonment up to three years or probation with respect to persons who unlawfully acquire, reveal or disclose traffic data, which are collected, processed, stored or used pursuant to the LEC. Article 327 of the latter provides for administrative liability of any person, who violates the rules regarding the protection of confidentiality of communications and the related traffic data sent over public electronic communications networks. The administrative penalties shall be a fine of EUR 50,000 or exceeding this amount but not exceeding EUR 5,000 in case the act does not constitute a criminal offence. Pursuant to the new Article 332a of the LEC, any official of a state body or undertaking providing public electronic communications networks and/or services, who breaches the duties thereof or abuses the data stored under Article 250a, paragraph 1 of the LEC, shall be liable to a fine of EUR 50,000 or exceeding this amount but not exceeding EUR 5,000, unless the act constitutes a criminal offence.

400. The changes in the LEC allowing the Ministry of Interior through the officials working for the specialized directorate for Operational Technical Operations to have constant access to the traffic data in real time triggered serious debates in the Parliament and on media. The parties in opposition objected to the contemplated changes by raising their concerns regarding the infringement of the constitutional rights of Bulgarian citizens through interception of their communication on the Internet. Representatives of the civil society also criticized the changes. According to Alexander Kashamov from the Foundation Programme for Access to Information, the guarantees against misuse of direct technical access to the traffic data by the specialized directorate of the Ministry of Interior are quite insufficient and inefficient.

401. The fact that a permit given by the Court is required for receipt of the data from the said directorate does not remove the main problem that exactly the officers working there have unlimited technical access without needing a Court permit. According to Kashamov the registries, in which the information requested by other directorates and offices will be entered, would not solve the problem either because nothing prevents the officers of that directorate from doing an unlimited number of searches exercising their right of direct access. The Commission on Personal Data

Protection could not control efficiently the potential abuses because of lacking capacity for that. Kashamov expressed his puzzlement as to why the Ministry of Interior does not oblige the mobile operators and Internet providers to submit the requested data in short terms and, in case of their failure to provide the data, to seize them by applying the Code of Criminal Procedure. The presence of so simple solution makes the persistence of the governing party to introduce the changes in the LEC unclear according to Kashamov. That is why the dubiety about the possible real reasons for the access remains especially in the view of the traditions in Bulgaria for tracking political opponents, investigating journalists and business rivals.

402. The objective of the LPDP is to guarantee the inviolability of persons and private life through provision of protection of individuals in case of unlawful processing of personal data related to them in the course of the free data circulation.[156] The LPDP defines 'personal data' as any information related to a natural person, who is identified or may be identified directly or indirectly by an identification number or through one or more specific indices. Pursuant to the LPDP for personal data processing will qualify any action or set of actions which may be carried out with respect to personal data by automatic or other means such as collecting, recording, organizing, storing, adapting or modifying, restoring, consulting, using, disclosing through delivery, disseminating, submitting, updating and combining, blocking, erasing or destroying.

403. The processing of personal data is allowed in certain cases which are listed exhaustively in the LPDP. Two of them deserve a special note. The processing of personal data will be lawful if the natural person, to whom the data refer, has given his/her explicit consent. Also, in the cases where the processing is performed only for journalistic, literature or artistic expression, as long as the procession does not violate the right of the private life of the person to whom the data refers.

404. The Code of Ethics of Bulgarian Media contains provisions concerning privacy. In point 2.3.1 of the Code of Ethics of Bulgarian Media, the parties thereto declare that they shall respect the inviolability of everyone's personal life. In point 2.3.2, the parties undertake to avoid the publication of images and recordings, made outside public places if the persons affected have not given their consent for such use.

156. The Law on Personal Data Protection, promulgated in the State Gazette, issue No. 1 of 4 Jan. 2002, in force as of 4 Jan. 2002.

Chapter 4. Right to Reply

405. Decision No. 7 of the Constitutional Court of 1996 recommends the introduction of the right to reply in Bulgarian legislation. The particular text therein reads as follows:

> A recommended element of the legal regulation regarding all means for collective information is their obligation to provide a right to reply to persons affected from factual statements or to remedy the implications of an objected statement by providing a possibility for publication or broadcasting of its rebuttal.

406. This recommendation has been taken into account by the drafters of the LRT. Article 18 thereof grants a right to reply to natural persons and legal entities as well as state and municipal bodies affected by linear media services, in which they have not participated, regardless of whether in person or through a representative. Within seven days following the day of the broadcast, such persons or bodies are entitled to request in writing the provision of their reply for dissemination from the respective operator.

407. The practice shows that the right to reply may be exercised personally by the affected individuals or by the legal representatives of the affected body and not by a third party on their behalf. The short period of time provided for reaction by the Bulgarian legislator is justified considering that the negative effect of the broadcast cannot be successfully remedied if not timely addressed. However, the lack of quick reaction on the part of the affected person could be reasonably construed as a lack of affection or at least as proof of the insufficiency of the affection to trigger the right to reply.

408. The request must contain the objected statements as well as the date and the hour of the broadcast. The operator is obliged to ensure the inclusion of the reply in the next edition of the same broadcast or in equivalent time up to twenty-four hours following the receipt of the reply and must not allow the amendment or curtailment of the text. The provision for dissemination of reply shall be free of charge for the persons and bodies affected by the respective broadcast. Article 18 specifies also the duration of the reply which may not exceed the duration of the objected part of the broadcast. Non-compliance with the latter condition is used very often in practice by electronic media to oppose the requested right to reply.

409. A similar provision granting a right to reply with respect to print media is not available in the effective legislation due to the lack of a general law on the press. The right to reply is left at the discretion of the respective print media, i.e., it is a matter of self-regulation. However, part of the press which signed the currently effective Code of Ethics for the Media is bound by its provisions.

410. Notwithstanding the absence of a general law on the press, the effective Election Code lays down the right of publication of reply. The latter is granted not to all legal persons. Pursuant to Article 131, paragraph 1 of the Election Code, any media service provider except the electronic media, which has published an item that infringes the rights and damages the reputation of any candidate or of any person who represents a party, a coalition of parties or the nomination committee, shall be obligated to publish a reply immediately after the receipt of the latter. The reply shall be laid out in the same position and the same typeface as the item where it is reacting and shall appear unaccompanied by any comment. The reply shall be published free of charge.

411. The LRT sets the obligation of media services providers to apologize publicly to the affected persons in case they have breached the prohibition under Article 16 for the creation and provision for dissemination of broadcastings, containing information, related to the personal lives of citizens without the consent of the latter. Public apology does not deprive the affected person of his or her right to seek relief in Court. The above-stated prohibition is not applicable to information in the public interest concerning the private lives of citizens who exercise state powers or citizens whose decisions influence society. Media service providers are allowed to include such information in their broadcasts. Public apology as provided in the LRT reveals some similarity with the right to reply. In both cases, there is a person who has been affected by a media services provider's broadcasts. However, the right to reply is a relief available also for legal entities and state and municipal bodies whereas public apology may be requested only by citizens, i.e., natural persons. Obviously, the latter could choose between the two options, i.e., to request the broadcasting of the reply or to insist on a public apology.

412. It is interesting to observe that Article 16 of the LRT explicitly mentions the independence of the relief sought by the Court from the receiving of public apology whereas Article 18 is silent on this issue. This fact does not mean that persons whose right of reply has been exercised cannot refer to the Court. The affected person is entitled to claim damages from the respective media services provider and/or the particular journalist as well as to initiate criminal law proceedings for slander against the latter. However, the timely publication of the reply could mitigate the negative consequences of the broadcasting and, consequently, the amount of the damages due. Furthermore, it is likely that the affected person would be satisfied by the exercise of his or her right to reply and would not be willing to have recourse to the Court system. Therefore, the provision of the right to reply by a media services provider would lower the amount of the damages and the threat of litigation against the particular media. This conclusion was made by Radomir Tcholakov. He also pointed out that the voluntarily provided right of reply in a correct manner will be considered in some cases by the Courts as a fact mitigating the culpability.[157]

413. The enforcement of the right to reply and public apology are further safeguarded by Article 126, paragraph 1 of the LRT providing for monetary sanctions

157. The same conclusion was made by Radomir Tcholakov, *see* R. Tcholakov, *Media Law: Dictionary of the Main Concepts* 309 (Trud 2005).

in all cases of infringement. The sanctions are imposed by the CEM, and their amounts are ranging between EUR 1,500 and EUR 10,000.

414. Bulgarian legal literature has analysed some problem questions concerning the right to reply. For instance, whether right to reply is due in case a person is affected by satiric shows? Nelly Ognyanova, for instance, in her book *Media Regulation: Principles and Case Law* concluded that the wording of the LRT and the then effective applicable provisions of the European Convention on Transfrontier Television and the Directive Television Without Frontiers do not give any room for interpretation meaning that any kind of show is included. However, as Ognyanova noted, such a broader interpretation would give a right to reply also to persons affected by statements made in a film or documentary as well as in reality programmes. According to her in such cases, the judgment of whether infringement is in place should belong to the media council.

415. Another problem question concerning the right to reply is whether the right to reply must be provided by a media services provider in case a person is affected by a commercial shown by such provider. As far as commercial, as such, does not constitute a broadcast, the answer to that question should be negative, and this is confirmed by Nelly Ognyanova in her study mentioned above.

416. The issue of whether a publication on the Internet would entail a right to reply has been for a long time debatable. The reason for that was that in its previous versions, Article 18 of the LRT used the term radio and TV operators instead of media services providers. After the most recent amendments of that law, which took place in 2010 provoked by the corresponding amendments in the TWF, the term audiovisual media service/radio service was defined as follows:

> a service in the context of Article 56 and 57 of the EU Treaty, which is within the editorial liability of a media services provider and which main objective is the provision of audio-visual broadcasts/radio broadcast for information, entertainment or education of the public through electronic communication networks in the context of the Law on the Electronic Communications.

The latter contains a definition of the term electronic communication network, which explicitly mentions the Internet as a fixed terrestrial network used for radio and TV broadcasting. Therefore, radio and TV broadcasts performed through the Internet qualify for audiovisual media services covered by the LRT and, consequently, they are subject to the obligation for the provision of a right to reply in case the conditions set in Article 18 are present. However, as far as the content published on the Internet does not constitute a broadcast, such as information published in a blog, for instance, this provision would not apply.

417. Radomir Tcholakov suggested that although not settled in the law, the requirement for publication of a reply should apply also to Internet sites.[158] Nelly Ognyanova points out that the Council of Europe adopted rules regarding the right to reply in the new media environment by adopting Draft Recommendation Rec (2004) on the Right to Reply in the New Media Environment. Those rules apply to each communication means by which periodical dissemination to the public of editorial content, offline and online such as newspapers, journals, radio, television and Internet-based information services. The EU has analogous rules adopted with a Recommendation of the Council and the Parliament 2006/952/EC. According to those rules, the Member States are obliged to ensure the right to reply online by legal means or alternatively through self-regulation.

158. *Ibid.*, 303.

Chapter 5. Access to Public Information

418. Accessing public information was not an easy thing in Bulgaria. The former communist regime was widely secretive, and access to official documents and/or records was possible only at a certain level and with special authorizations.

419. Today the right to access public information is enshrined in the Bulgarian Constitution of 1991 and by the Law on Access to Public Information (LAPI).[159] Even before the LAPI entered into force in 2000, the Access to Information Programme Foundation (AIPF) was created, whose purpose was to fight for the improvement of access to information in Bulgaria. More precisely, the goals of the AIPF were to promote and assist the exercise of the constitutional right of access to information, to encourage the citizens to demand information through civic education and to promote transparency in the work of public institutions at the central and local levels.

§1. Public Documents

420. Efficient public participation in democracy requires effective access to public information and documents for the public, especially for citizens and media. A transparent and democratic society should thus provide efficient and free access to public documents.

421. The LAPI has a very large scope as it does not narrow the right to access information by specifying categories of information or applicants to this right. According to Article 2 of the LAPI shall be considered public information any information related to the social life in the Republic of Bulgaria or any information that may allow the citizens to form their own opinion on the activities of the persons having obligations under the LAPI.[160] Furthermore, according to Article 4 of the LAPI every Bulgarian or foreign citizen or any person without citizenship, as well as any Bulgarian or foreign legal entity has the right to request access to information. The LAPI also ensures equal conditions for access to public documents to anybody (Article 6 of the LAPI): no distinction can be made between the different types of applicants, e.g., between private individuals and journalists.

422. In addition, the person requesting access to an official document does not have to provide reasons for his/her request. According to Article 24 of the LAPI, the request for granting access to public information should be made in the form of

159. Bulgaria also ratified the Aarhus Convention on Access to Information, Public Participation in Decision-making and Access to Justice in Environmental Matters, the European Convention on Human Rights and the International Covenant on Civil and Political Rights.

160. It is important to be noted that the right of access to information held by the public authorities is not equivalent to the 'publication of the acts of government' because in the first we have the right of the citizens to have an insight in a *document* containing information of *public* importance and in the second one is the duty of the State to let the public know its decisions: bills, laws, rules, resolutions, etc.

a written application or verbal request. This request can however not be anonymous. The information can be granted to the requester by a verbal explanation, paper copy or copy on technical bearer (Article 26 of the LAPI). The time limit for the authority to issue a decision is fourteen days, and the access must be free of charge (Article 20, paragraph 1). The only costs to be covered are the material costs (Article 20, paragraph 2), which may not exceed the rates set out by the Minister of Finance.

423. Moreover, Article 15 of the LAPI states that it is the public authority's duty to help the requestor identify the requested document. On this point, the tendency is to enhance the openness of the public administration so that it operates in an open and transparent manner. The efforts to improve openness and transparency include a legislative framework to promote public entities and citizen partnerships. More precisely, regarding the process of accessing information, journalists are much better aware of the procedures for obtaining such access. The LAPI greatly helped their journalistic investigations and journalists have used the LAPI to investigate government misconduct, to unveil corruption and to trigger public debate on questionable topics. Some journalists have also used the LAPI to access the historic files of Communist Bulgaria's former security services. Today more and more journalists are using the LAPI procedures and, in general, the journalists prefer verbal questioning to obtain quickly up-to-date information.

424. The LAPI deals with access to information from all the state and local authorities, as well as from all the public legal entities subject to public law and all individuals and legal entities financed by the state budget, subsidies from the EU funds or allocated through EU projects and programmes (Article 3 of the LAPI).[161] In accordance with Article 2, paragraph 2 of the LAPI information shall be deemed public irrespective of the kind of physical bearer they are held on. The term 'document' is not only restricted to paper-based documents. Thus, public sector information applies to any kind of information materialized on paper, electronic or other carrier, including audio or video records as far as they are collected or generated by a public sector organization (paragraph 3). Paragraph 4 nevertheless specifies that the LAPI does not apply to personal data.

425. Concerning mass media, Article 18 of the LAPI specifies which information from this media is regarded as public so that access to it shall be granted. The media shall provide information related to the persons who take part in their management or those who exercise effective control over their management or activities. Information on the business-related parties taking part in the management of other mass media (i.e., which allows them to exercise effective control over their management, their activities or editorial policy) is also considered public. Access should also be granted to announce statements on the mass media public goals, as

161. The amendments to the LAPI in 5 Dec. 2008 included the regional offices of central authorities and bodies financed under the EU programmes and funds.

well as principles and internal rules applied by the mass media to guarantee correctness and objectivity of disseminated information. Finally, information about the financial results of the mass media owners and the dissemination of their production are also to be made public.

426. The aim of Article 18 of the LAPI is to encourage transparency in media activities, which is strengthened by Article 19 which states that 'The access to the information under Article 18 shall be exercised in compliance with and with balance of the principles of transparency and economic freedom, as well as of personal data protection, commercial secrecy and the secret of the sources of the mass media that wished to remain secret.'

427. The right to access official documents is not absolute.[162] Public authorities can place limitations on the disclosure of public information in order to protect particular rights or interests. All refusals should however be an exception and must therefore be duly justified.[163] The LAPI defines in its Article 37 exemptions for the provision of information by governmental bodies. Information can be refused if it is personal or private information, a state or official secret, a trade secret, or pre-decisional material.

428. In fact, Article 37, paragraph 2 of the LAPI stipulates that grounds for refusal to grant access to public information are in place where *the access is of a nature to affect third party's interests and the third party did not give its explicit written consent for the disclosure of the requested public information, unless there is overriding public interest.* The paragraph protects simultaneously two types of interest – the personal information of an individual and the business interest of the legal entities. Considering the provisions of the LPDP, Article 8 of the ECHR and Article 17 of the International Covenant on Civil and Political Rights, an official document, which contains personal or other private information, may be limited in access. The difficulty is that the law does not clearly define the level of harm needed to substantiate the withholding of the required information.

429. In 2002, Bulgaria adopted the Law on the Protection of Classified Information (LPCI), which regulates the rules and process of collecting, processing and storing classified information as well as the public access to it. In accordance with

162. Article 10, para. 2 of the ECHR recognizes that freedom of expression may, in certain prescribed circumstances, be limited. The exercise of these freedoms, since it carries with it duties and responsibilities, may be subject to such formalities, conditions, restrictions or penalties as are prescribed by law and are necessary in a democratic society, in the interests of national security, territorial integrity or public safety, for the prevention of disorder or crime, for the protection of health or morals, for the protection of the reputation or rights of others, for preventing the disclosure of information received in confidence, or for maintaining the authority or impartiality of the judiciary.
163. Cases where Member States have justify restriction on freedom of expression and/or other human rights by arguing on national security considerations have often be considered by the European Court of Human Rights. The Court has emitted clear warnings on the need to clearly lay down precise information on these considerations in order to prevent any abuses. *See Klass v. FRG*, Application No. 5029/71, 6 Sep. 1978, *The Observer and Guardian v. the United Kingdom*, 26 Nov. 1991, Application No. 13585/88.

Article 1 of this law, classified information is applied to national, as well as to foreign classified information when stipulated by international agreements[164] signed by Bulgaria.

430. The state can decide to restrict access to public information because it is important for the national interest in the area of national defence, national security and international relations. Chapter three of the LPCI defines the different kinds of classified information and the levels of classification. According to Article 25 of the LPCI, state secret shall be the information, determined in the list[165] of Appendix No. 1, the unregulated access to which would create danger or would damage the interests of the Republic of Bulgaria, connected with the national security, the defence, the foreign policy or the protection of the constitutionally established order.

431. There are three levels of classification of the information: confidential, secret and top secret, as defined by international standards depending on the seriousness of the potential damage their disclosure might bring to national security (Article 28 of the LPCI).

432. In addition to state secret, we find the notion of official secret[166] in Article 26, paragraph 1 of the LPCI, which stipulates that official secret shall be the information, created or preserved by the state bodies or the bodies of the local government, which is not state secret, the unregulated access to which would influence unfavourably the interests of the state or would hamper other legally protected interest.

433. The current definitions contained in the two articles are similarly problematic because they remain vague on what exactly the official secret is. As for state secret, this makes it difficult to define the boundary between the right of information and its limitation.

434. Finally, the notion of trade secret can be advanced to protect commercial transactions. The provisions concerning access to trade-related information are contained in Article 11 of the Law on Commercial Register (LCR). It stipulates that any person has the right to freely access the information concerning the date of registration, the company name, the location and address, as well as the documents on the basis of which the entries, expunctions and disclosures have been made.

164. According to Art. 27 of the LPCI 'foreign classified information shall be the classified information, conceded by another state or international organization by force of international agreement, to which the Republic of Bulgaria is a party'. This definition subjects the Bulgarian information regime to the information disclosure standards of third countries, regardless of whether those provisions respect the international or the constitutional standards of the country.
165. The problem of the elaborated list is that the items listed in this document are sufficiently broad to cover practically any document a public body might hold.
166. The information, classified as official secret, shall be marked with secrecy grading 'for official use'.

435. In 2010, representatives from different business organizations proposed some modifications to Article 11 of the LCR concerning access to information by introducing a registration fee. Free access is granted only for information concerning the company name, date of registration, headquarters and management address. Any additional information, such as who is who in the company, the constitutive documents and the subsequent amendments, etc., can be obtained only against payment. According to the authors of the amendments, a paying access should ensure traceability and control over those who seek information or check the Commercial Register. According to them, there was a contradiction between the LCR and protection of personal data. In their views, it was unacceptable that a document containing the signatures of the managers or the contracts themselves could be the subject of publicity, as this may facilitate fraud. The amended LCR entered into force on 1 January 2011.

436. According to the AIPF, the LCR was fully consistent with the EU legislation in its previous form. The public character of the Commercial Register data ensures the protection from fraud of the citizens and merchants themselves, as publicity creates a secure and transparent environment for conducting business. The full visibility of data from the Commercial Register is the only way for citizens and traders to be sure of whom they give money to in a business transaction, in whom they invest, etc. The AIPF considers that the amendments clearly restrict the right of everyone to seek information, a right guaranteed by Article 41, paragraph 1 of the Constitution. The new texts have no analogue in the EU law.[167] The only consequence of these provisions may well be a reduction in the transparency of the business sphere and possible links between businesses, politicians and public figures.

437. As previously discussed, if the public body has the document to which access is demanded and if none of the conditions for access refusal is met, the public body in question should process the request and make the document available to the applicant. The LAPI imposes sanctions for civil servants who fail to respond within the specified time limit without exculpatory reasons (Article 42 of the LAPI). In that way, in order to reduce the non-justified refusals,[168] the Bulgarian National Assembly passed amendments to the LAPI on 7 June 2007. The amendments increase sanctions for public servants who fail to comply with the law or do not execute a Court decision. In addition, all administrative structures are obliged to appoint public servants responsible for the provision of public information. The requestors of the public information, on their side, are not required to prove their legal interest in obtaining this specific information. Any contrary requirement would have entertained the culture of secrecy and would have violated the operative Bulgarian Constitution.

167. Council Directive 68/151/EES, amended by Directive 2003/58/EC of the European Parliament and of the Council of 15 Jul. 2003, as regards disclosure requirements in respect of certain types of companies.
168. According to the AIP, most of the refusal were oral, unfounded refusals or silence.

438. In case of refusal to grant access, there exist no internal appeal mechanisms, nor is there an independent body dealing with such appeals. The only possibility for the requestors is to take their appeals to the Court. Clearly, this procedure is expensive and time-consuming.

439. As a matter of fact, and despite promising trends, the administration still often uses written requests for information as a sanction on journalists. Because in cases where the state authorities refuse to grant access to the requested information, the decision can be appealed before the administrative Courts or before the SAC only, this long procedure is very convenient for the public authorities as it is obviously unacceptable for the journalists.

440. The most frequent denials to the journalists for accessing information are justified, by the argument 'state secret' or 'a trade secret'. This worrying fact follows from the unclear definition in the law of the notion of state and trade secret. An increasing number of journalists are using the possibility that the law provides and brings the non-justified refusals to the Court.[169] Even though this may not help them in their everyday work, it can have a positive effect. The increased number of requests and lawsuits are educating the public administration and creating discipline towards the access to information rights. Thus, besides the problems stated so far concerning the access to information for journalists in Bulgaria, overall, there is today a positive tendency towards openness and transparency.

441. The Constitutional Court also targets the right of being able to access public information. In 1996, the Court gave a detailed interpretation of the provisions of Article 41 of the Constitution in the above-mentioned Decision No. 7 of 1996. The Court states that the right to search and receive information guaranteed in Article 41, paragraph 1 of the Constitution includes the obligation of the public authorities to provide access to information to the public, whose content is determined by legislation. It includes an obligation for the public authorities to publish official information and to provide access to the sources of the information. For the Constitutional Court, the obligation of the government to regulate access to information is directly derived from the Constitution. The Court was further precise in its decision that the right under Article 41, paragraph 1 of the Constitution is available to all, including the media. The restriction of this right requires the establishment by legislation of the circumstances related to national security or public order. This rule also applies to the grounds on which information can be denied to the citizens by public bodies or agencies in accordance with Article 41, paragraph 2 of the Constitution. The rights enshrined in this provision are private. They are related to the reasonable legal interests of the citizens, and their restriction is possible only by

169. The first case concerning the access to public information was heard on 15 Dec. 1998. The application was filed by the Environmental Association Za Zemyata against the chairman of the Energy Committee concerning a tacit refusal of access to the energy bill, as well as to conduct public debate on the bill.

the creation of a legal regulation of the situations in which the information constitutes a state (or other) secret and for which there are grounds provided by law to protect it.

§2. Access to Public Meetings

442. The access to public information also includes free access to public meetings of various bodies and institutions, such as the Municipal councils, the different Courts, the Council of Ministers and the National Assembly. Such access is associated with the ability to capture and record the places and people. The most common restriction of the right of free access to public meetings concerns meetings held behind closed doors or suspension of access to the meeting room.

443. The opportunities to participate in the meetings of the municipal councils are wider in comparison to meetings of the other public authorities. In contrast to the meetings of the state administration at the central level where the public must go through many levels and access is very difficult, if not impossible, access to the municipal council's meetings is more straightforward. At the same time, there is a particularly strong interest in the activities of the local authorities such as the municipal councils, as the results of their decisions are reflected in the first place on the people living in the specific municipalities.

444. Article 28 of the Law on Local Government and Local Administration stipulates that the meetings of the municipal councils and their commissions shall be public, except in cases where the council decides to hold its meeting behind closed doors. Furthermore, the citizens may express their views, ask questions and make statements and proposals about the competence of the municipal council, the mayor or the municipal administration. They may also expect to receive answers through the established usage and within a term determined by the regulations under Article 21, paragraph 3.

445. On the legislative side, it is possible to attend the meetings of the National Assembly. According to its rules for visits, visitors can attend the open plenary sittings of the National Assembly taking specially assigned seats. Concerning media access, only the accredited representatives of the mass media have permanent access to the building of the National Assembly of Bulgaria. The accredited representatives for these rules are: journalists, cameramen, photographers and technical staff designated by the direction of the respective media to reflect the National Assembly meetings. Each accredited media receives a specific number of passes for entrance into the National Assembly building. There is a defined quota of passes for each accredited media, which are either nominal (permanent) or rotary. Permanent accreditation is granted to electronic media (radio and TV), news agencies, as well as national magazines and newspapers (edited on weekly frequency) reporting on the overall activities of the National Assembly. The Bulgarian News Agency, which is the main source of information for the Bulgarian media and the country's governmental institutions, also has a permanent accreditation. In addition, it is possible for the media representatives who have no permanent accreditation to the National Assembly but wish to reflect a separate aspect of the work of the Parliament to be admitted to the Parliament building with a single pass.

446. As for the rules inside the Assembly building, it is possible for the journalists to film with their cameras only in places defined for this purpose, as well as in places where official and public events are held in the Assembly building. For any other places in the National Assembly, the journalists need permission given by the 'Press and Public Relations' Directorate. Moreover, during their work in the building of the National Assembly, the media representatives should respect the Constitution of the Republic of Bulgaria, the rules of organization and procedure, as well as of internal order of the National Assembly; the LRT; and the LAPI. Professional standards, norms and values defined in the Code of Ethics of the Bulgarian media and the principles of transparency, openness and democracy must also be respected.

447. According to Article 41, paragraph 1 of the rules of organization and procedure of the National Assembly, the open sittings of the National Assembly shall be broadcasted live by the BNR on a special frequency covering the entire national territory and by reportage from the BNT. Moreover, they can be broadcasted in real-time through its website. According to paragraph 4 of the same article, the plenary sittings dedicated to parliamentary control shall also be broadcasted live by BNR and BNT. Concerning the journalists, according to paragraph 3 of Article 41, the accredited and other journalists who have been provided with access may attend the open sittings of the National Assembly's standing committees. Paragraph 5 of the same article states as well that the shorthand records from the plenary sittings which are not closed and the voting records of the computerized system shall be published within seven days on the website of the National Assembly.

448. Finally, on the executive side, the opportunities to participate in meetings of the Council of Ministers are too limited. According to Article 43, paragraph 2 at a meeting of the Council of Ministers or during the examination of a particular item of the agenda, only persons invited by the Prime Minister as representatives of state institutions or other organizations may be present.

§3. Court Hearings and Documents

449. The specific rules related to access to information within the judiciary are mainly contained in the Law on Judiciary System, Civil Procedure Code, Penal Procedure Code (PPC), Administrative Procedure Code, etc. Very often the Courts publish on their Internet sites documents that contain guarantees for exchange of information between the media and the Courts. The access of the journalists to the Court hearings and documents allows the disclosure of official information in a short time, thus allowing coverage of the overall judicial activity. The access to Court hearings and documents and thus the transparency of the judiciary helps to ensure that Courts operate efficiently and effectively.

450. In general, different laws provide the public with the right to search and receive information from governmental entities, including the Courts. Trials are open to the public and the media, except as otherwise provided by law. The Codes of penal and civil procedures govern whether a trial is public or may be kept private and thus inaccessible to the public and media. The Courts can also establish their own precise rules concerning their relationships with the media.

451. Article 11 of the Civil Procedure Code (CPC) stipulates that the hearings of lawsuits shall be held at open doors, except when it is provided otherwise by law. Indeed, Article 136 of the same Code stipulates that the Courts, ex officio or at the request of one of the parties, may order the hearing or only certain actions to happen behind closed doors. The reason for this may be because the public interest or the privacy of the parties is in consideration, because the family requires it, or when a person is placed under custody. Moreover, when the case is related to commercial, industrial, inventive or tax secret and public disclosure may harm defensible interests, the hearing can also take place behind closed doors. Article 138 of the CPC specifies that when the hearing is held behind closed doors, public disclosure of its contents is prohibited.

452. Article 20 of the PPC is the analogue of Article 11 of the CPC. It stipulates that the Court hearings are public except for the cases provided in the Code. The cases when the hearings are held behind closed doors are listed in Article 263 of the PPC. According to paragraph 1, this includes the cases where this is required in order to safeguard the state secret or morality, as well as in the case of witness protection of Article 123, paragraph 2, item 2, or where this is necessary to prevent the divulgence of facts from the intimate life of citizens (paragraph 2). Paragraph 3 precises that the sentences shall be announced in public in all cases.

453. Also according to Article 409, paragraph 1 of the PPC, the Court may request the defence, the witnesses and other persons attending the hearing to declare that they will not divulge the circumstances presented in the Court hearing if the latter is constitutive of classified information.

454. Focusing on the relations between the Courts and the media, in many cases, the Courts develop media strategy and/or policies regulating the information streams between the Courts and the media. These strategies are in accordance with the statutory provisions of the Uniform media strategy of the judiciary approved by the Supreme Judicial Council, as well as the rules of professional ethics.

455. The access to Court information by the media is often done through communication with the media press services of the Courts. For example, the rules for working with the media press service of the Sofia district Court, the biggest Court in Bulgaria, are published on its Internet site. According to these rules, the press releases prepared by its press service shall always include the Court, date, time and place of the hearing, whether we have a criminal or a civil case. If the case is postponed, the reasons for this should be given.

456. In cases where there is public interest (except when the hearing is held behind closed doors or bail measures have to be determined), journalists shall receive press releases the day before the trial. If the process is not held behind closed doors, the journalists have the possibility to follow the whole case. In this case, as well as in the contrary situation, the press service shall inform the journalists only about the act issued by the Court. The journalists can contact any of the judges through the press attaché. In case of a request from a journalist for an interview with a judge, the journalist shall give his/her questions in advance. If a conference is held, the theme of the conference is announced by notice to the participants in advance, indicating the exact time and place.

457. The Administrative district Court Gabrovo also has a media strategy which guarantees the exchange of information between the media and the Court and allows for feedback from the media and citizens to the Court. Its media strategy paper also contains the rules concerning direct access of the journalists to the Courtrooms and documents, as well as the implementation and development of the media strategy.

458. As one last example, the media policy of the Administrative district Court Pleven, like the one cited above, has rules concerning direct access of journalists to the Courtrooms. For example, it marks that video or photographs in the Courtroom during the hearing shall be made only with the permission of the presiding judge of the chamber and with the consent of the parties involved. Cameras are allowed only at the beginning of the meeting, after which in the Courtroom remain only journalists without video and sound operators and photojournalists. Making sound recordings and videos in the Courtroom during the hearing after the time determined by the president of the chamber is prohibited.

459. In summary, during the Court's communications with the media, it is necessary to observe the principles of accuracy, reliability and completeness of the information, accountability and transparency, respect for the rights and the privacy of the parties, as well as the equality and fairness to all media representatives. Also, the professionalism of those working in the Courts and the media has to be respected. The press releases should be current, accurate and clear and be written in a language easily understandable by the citizens and the media.

460. The Bulgarian Constitution does not provide the public with a right to access Court records or to attend judicial proceedings. The specific rules related to access to information within the judiciary are contained in the different codes, but the access to judicial records in Bulgaria also appears to be governed largely by individual Court practices.

461. Concerning the Codes, e.g., Article 235, paragraph 5 of the CPC states that 'the Court shall announce its decision and the arguments no later than one month after the hearing, in which the consideration of the case was finished. The decision is written in the Court register, which is public and everyone is entitled free access to it'.

462. The access to Court records is governed by Court rules, i.e., the manner in which journalists and citizens may access such records varies according to the Court. Normally, to have access to the documents, the journalists or the citizens need a written permission from the judge-rapporteur or the chairman of the Court. To access a particular case, they have to fill in a standard application. It must be said that Bulgaria made efforts to make judicial documents available on the Internet, which has greatly expanded access to judicial information. For example, the Administrative district Court Varna has a web portal for access to information about Court cases. On this site, everyone can find information about the content of litigation in the system 'Court records'. This portal provides access to information concerning the necessary conditions and different options on how to access information about Court cases. This access is however restricted to lawyers, party to the case or persons registered as users of the web portal.

Chapter 6. Press Council

463. Media self-regulation[170] consists of establishing the minimum principles on the ethics, rights and duties of the media to ensure their pertinence, plurality and editorial freedom while preserving the personal rights of other people and/or entities.[171] The media self-regulation structure and framework are not universal and strongly depend on various local (national and historical) factors such as the democratic and media tradition, the culture, administration and government of the country. Beyond these specificities, media self-regulation relies either on a code of ethics, a regulatory (supervising) body or, like in Bulgaria, on both.

464. This chapter will examine the two Bulgarian Codes of Ethics and the organizations responsible for ensuring their application, namely the National Council for Journalistic Ethics (NCJE) and the Bulgarian Media Union (BMU).

§1. Two Codes of Ethics

465. The journalistic Code of Ethics defines the functions, duties and rights of the journalists. It establishes minimum standards and guidelines expressly related to the work of the journalists, such as: the right to be independent and impartial, the protection of privacy and other personal rights, the preservation of editorial freedom and freedom of speech, the diversity of points of view and opinions. This applies to both, the original Code of Ethics adopted in 2004, and the alternative one that was proposed ten years later, in 2014. In what follows, we discuss both Codes.

I. The 2004 Code of Ethics

466. The Bulgarian journalistic ethics code was adopted on 25 November 2004[172] by two hundred national and regional outlets, including major national newspapers, magazines, and the biggest private radio and television stations. The public service broadcasters BNT, BNR and BTA, metropolitan, regional and local newspapers and electronic editions were also involved. The Code applies to both the electronic media and the press and was prepared by a team including Bulgarian and foreign experts in the framework of a project financed by the PHARE EU programme.[173] Eight months after the creation of the Code, the implementing body, the

170. One should stress that the self-regulation is different from self-censorship.
171. M. Haraszi, *The Media Self-Regulation Guidebook* 12 (OSCE 2008).
172. No less than ten versions of code of ethics were prepared by different organizations between 1990 and 2002 but none of them became effective. Before being proposed for signature, the Code was discussed at several general assemblies of media representatives and sent for comments to more than 300 persons and organizations. Media groups like the Union of the Publishers in Bulgaria, the ABBRO, the Bulgarian Media Coalition, the UBJ, the Faculty of Journalism and Mass Communication and the Sofia University actively participated in this process.
173. The code is drafted within the framework of the PHARE project 'Technical Support for Improving the Professional Standards for Bulgarian Journalism'.

NCJE, was incorporated into it. In particular, the mission of the NCJE is to interpret and apply the Code of Ethics of the Bulgarian media, as well as to resolve disputes between the media and their audience.

467. Beyond the right to information and freedom of expression, the Code states that the media should provide society with reliable information and make clear the distinction between facts and comments. Media also have to respect the protection of personal dignity and private lives and must demonstrate special responsibility to respect the rights of children (including their right to be heard). The rights of both suspects and victims should also be respected when informing about crimes or cruelty. Furthermore, discrimination on the grounds of race, gender, religion or ethnicity is prohibited. Finally, in the case of public disputes, each side should have the possibility to express its position.

468. The Code is based on the principle of editorial independence from political and economic influences. The media should clearly separate editorial content from paid publications, advertisements and sponsored columns. The right of the journalists to refuse assignments or to be identified as the author of materials which violate the principles and recommendations of the Code of Ethics should be respected. All signatories to the Code of Ethics of the Bulgarian media must ensure compliance in practice.

469. Violation of the terms of this Code may be justified in the case where it is proved unequivocally that the violation was made in the public interest. The Code stresses that the notion of *public interest* should not be confused with the notion of *interesting for the public*. According to the Code, information is of public interest only when it serves to protect the health, safety and security of people, to prevent and detect crimes and abuse of power or to protect society from the danger of being seriously misled.[174]

II. The 2014 Code of Ethics

470. Ten years after the adoption of the 2004 Code of Ethics of the Bulgarian media, on 18 December 2013, at a ceremony attended by the chief editors of various national and regional media, publishers, journalists, intellectuals, a second Code of Ethics was signed.[175] A month later it was published on the site of its initiator – the BMU.

471. Numerous discussions were held on this subject as the signing of a second Code of Ethics could only lead to a division among the media. On 21 January 2014, the Association of European Journalists – Bulgaria (AEJ)[176] issued an opinion

174. *See* http://www.mediacenterbg.org/wp-content/uploads/2012/01/ethical-code-bg-final.pdf.
175. *See* http://bmu.bg/bg/code-of-conduct. (available on June 2018).
176. *See* http://www.aej-bulgaria.org/eng/.

against it, considering this second Code of Ethics of the Bulgarian media as an attempt to privatize the media self-regulation.

472. In June 2014, the Union of Bulgarian Journalists (UBJ) and Friedrich Ebert Stiftung[177] organized a forum on the topic 'The media – with an active and universal ethical code' where representatives of different media, the chairman of the Association of Bulgarian Broadcasters (ABBRO), a CEM representative, members of the Managing Board and Ethics Committee of UBJ shared their thoughts on the topic. During the discussion, a report of the Ethics Committee of the UBJ on the creation of that second Code of Ethics, presented by the journalist Maria Netsova, was of great interest. The journalist stressed that both codes do not differ significantly as they are based on the same basic principles and standards of journalistic ethics.[178] According to her the main problem of this alternative Code of Ethics was that it was drafted in the dark, without discussion in the public space. She added '*We shared our belief that the alternative Code of Ethics appeared due to the deep division of the Bulgarian media.*'

473. The new alternative Code of Ethics emphasizes the authorship of the materials, with a separate chapter, which even if not new in essence, is entirely devoted to 'copyright and related rights protection'. A separate chapter is also inserted for the 'right of reply', which requests a stricter requirement for the presence of the two parties' views. If some information is false, or non-objective, the affected party will have a right to reply in the same media.

474. It is important also to note that the spirit of the second Code is different. While the 2004 Code of Ethics says 'we will not publish', 'we will avoid', 'we will respect', 'we believe', etc., in the 2014 Code of Ethics we can read 'the media follows', 'the media are responsible', 'the media are obliged', 'the media should', etc. In the first case, the emphasis is on the free role and choice of the journalist while the second suggests more compliance with norms and rules.

§2. The National Council for Journalistic Ethics

475. While some countries in Europe have long established press councils (e.g., Germany, Netherlands and Scandinavian countries), press councils have, in other places, never existed or have been abandoned (e.g., Austria, France and Portugal). In other countries like Cyprus (established in May 1997), and especially in south-east Europe (in Bosnia and Herzegovina, Kosovo and Montenegro established in 2000, 2006 and 2012, respectively), press councils have recently been founded.

476. This is also the case in Bulgaria. Indeed, in order to enforce the respect of the journalistic principles expressed in the 2004 Code of Ethics, the NCJE was

177. *See* http://www.fes-bulgaria.org/bg/.
178. *See* http://www.sbj-bg.eu/index.php?t=23373.

established in 2005. Its mission is to ensure media's self-regulation with the duty to resolve disputes between the media and their audience (readers, viewers and listeners).

477. According to Article 4, paragraph 1 of its statutes, the NCJE is defined as a non-profit legal entity, a foundation, carrying out public benefit service. In compliance with paragraph 2 of the same article, the NCJE cannot be converted into a foundation acting for a private benefit.

478. The co-founders of the NCJE are the Association of the Bulgarian Radio and Television Operators, the UPB, the UBJ, the Bulgarian Media Coalition and the Media Development Center.

479. In order to accomplish its main objectives, the NCJE had two permanent separate bodies: the Ethics Commission for Electronic Media (ECEM) and the Ethics Commission for Print Media (ECPM).[179] Any citizen who feels personally affected by a journalistic publication and considers that the code has not been respected by the media might refer to the corresponding commission.[180]

480. In contrast with most countries in Europe where only one commission acts as the self-regulation body, Bulgaria had, until recently, two commissions.[181] According to Asia Kawrakowa, a member of the ECEM, the creation of two different commissions was imposed from the substantial differences which exist in the work of print and electronic media. In her opinion, the ECPM's workload was more important than that of ECEM as there is no regulation regarding the press. There was great interest, including from the part of the citizens, to regulate the press activity by means of the Code of Ethics. For the electronic media, there is the LRT and CEM so the ECEM has a more complementary function.

I. Functions and Membership

481. Both commissions, the ECEM and the ECPM were operating under the rules of the NCJE, and according to Article 34 of their statutes, they took their decisions in accordance with the procedural rules and by interpreting and applying the rules of the 2004 Code of Ethics. They analysed the cases and through their interpretation made recommendations to improve the journalistic work. When they were aware of shortcomings in the field of freedom of expression and information, they

179. The two commissions and the NCJE were members of the Alliance of Independent Press Councils of Europe – R. Smilova, D. Smilov & G. Ganev, *Media Policies and Regulatory Practices* 28 (Mediadem – European Research Project 2010).

180. The problem was that the sanctions of the commissions could not be imposed and, as a consequence, the citizens preferred to use the civil or penalty procedures if their rights have been abused.

181. Since December 2014, there is only one Commission, the Journalism Ethics Commission, which will be discussed later.

recommended to the Board of Founders measures for their removal. Finally, while the Commissions operated separately, they may had common meetings when necessary.[182]

482. The NCJE supported the ECEM and the ECPM in monitoring the compliance of the media with the 2004 Code of Ethics and in mediating disputes within the media. The NCJE and the Commissions worked to protect the right of the audience to be comprehensively and accurately informed by the establishment of journalistic standards. The creation of this system of media self-regulation through the application of the Code of Ethics was to allow resolving disputes between the media and the audience,[183] thus raising the prestige of the media. The NCJE and its Commissions also stimulated public debate on journalistic ethics and worked at strengthening the freedom of expression and protection of journalists and their sources. Furthermore, they support the training of Bulgarian journalists in the application of ethical rules and norms.

483. Both the ECEM and ECPM had twelve members: four of them practising journalists and elected by the journalists, four representing the media owners (publishers or broadcasters) and the other four were independent experts and media personalities who had contributed to the freedom of speech in Bulgaria and who represent the audience. It should be stressed that all groups were equally represented and that the way members were appointed was very democratic.

484. What was special for the two Commissions, however, was that the members of both ECEM and ECPM were volunteers occupying another position and that they were meeting only when the ECEM and/or ECPM had to meet to discuss complaints.

485. During their two mandates, both Commissions took decisions on hundreds of specific complaints and adopted dozens of principal recommendations for compliance with the 2004 Code of Ethics.

486. In December 2014, ten years after the adoption of its Code of Ethics, members of the ECEM and ECPM, the Board of Founders of the NCJE, as well as a working group of journalists and media experts analysed the experience gained over the last ten years and discussed whether the changes in the media environment call for changes to the self-regulation system of the media. As a result of these discussions, the Board of Founders of the NCJE considered that it would be more effective for all complaints to be reviewed by a single Commission with wider media and

182. According to Art. 23 of the Statutes when there is a dispute between print and electronic media, the matter puts fundamental questions concerning both media and its joint examination is necessary in order to establish a uniform practice; a proposal for amendment of the Code of Ethics of the Bulgarian media was made. The joint meeting of the two commissions shall be convened at the initiative of one of them and taken at its meeting.
183. Everyone who feels affected by a particular material which is printed or broadcast could submit a complaint to the respective commission. Still, for material published in Internet it is not clear which Commission will examine the complaint.

professional representation. It was thus decided to merge the two Commissions to a single twelve-member Commission – the Journalism Ethics Commission. This new Journalism Ethics Commission is to deal with complaints about violations committed by printed, electronic and Internet media.[184]

487. An invitation to nominate members of the new Journalism Ethics Commission was sent out to more than 500 media, media organizations and journalistic societies.

488. The members of the Journalism Ethics Commission were elected by the Board of Founders of NCJE for a three-year mandate, which includes representatives of some of the most influential media organizations in Bulgaria: the ABBRO, the Bulgarian Union of Publishers, and the Media Development Centre.

489. Thus, on 21 January 2015, the twelve new members of the Journalism Ethics Commission in Bulgaria began their work.

490. According to Article 1(1) of its Rules of Procedure, in case of complaints filed before the Journalism Ethics Commission, it shall meet in a regular session not less than once a month.

II. Independence

491. The Press councils are assigned media councils which seek to promote freedom of expression, ensure the highest standards of the media, settle disputes or handle complaints.[185] In that regard, there are two crucial aspects of well-functioning Press Council. First, it should consist not only of different equally represented members but also of independent members in order to defend the press freedom. Furthermore, its members must be independent not only from industry but also from state interference in case of state funding.[186]

492. For that reason, the countries which recently transformed themselves into democracies face more challenges in establishing a well-functioning press council. To do so, it is indeed essential to have a fair and transparent process of nomination and appointment of the members, as well as full financial transparency and independence from sponsors or political pressure. Small media markets and weak economies, which are characteristic of these new democracies, may however result in the collision of media with politics and economic circles. As a consequence,

184. *See* http://www.aej-bulgaria.org/eng/p.php?post=2046.
185. *See* http://www.unesco.org/new/en/communication-and-information/freedom-of-expression/professional-journalistic-standards-and-code-of-ethics/key-concepts.
186. *See* L. Fielden, *Regulating the Press: A Comparative Study of International Press Councils*, Reuters Institute for the Study of Journalism (2012); available at https://reutersinstitute.politics.ox.ac.uk/our-research/regulating-press-comparative-study-international-press-councils.

media especially public service media may be subjected to external pressures. This – and the close link between political and economic circles – represents a threat to media independence.[187]

493. In these new democracies, obstacles also arise from the lack of experience and tradition in self-regulation. In addition to political differences among journalists, this often results in poor dialogue and solidarity between journalists, thus preventing them from defending their common interest.

494. The statutes of the former ECEM and ECPM clearly stated that members were serving in their personal capacity and did not represent their media outlets or organizations and because of that could not receive instructions from them. Membership in the commissions was incompatible with membership in the Board of Founders. The members of both commissions had a two-year mandate, and the duration of their membership was also limited to two consecutive terms.

Article 14(1) of the NCJE Statutes stipulates that members of the Journalism Ethics Commission are independent in their actions and cannot receive instructions from other persons.

III. Sanctions

495. According to Article 17 of the common Statutes of the former ECEM and ECPM, in case of violation of the 2004 Code of Ethics and after all other means for reaching an agreement (i.e., mediation at every stage of the proceedings) were exhausted, the relevant Commission proposed to the media which has printed/broadcasted the contested material to print/broadcast a correction, to provide the right to an answer or to submit an apology in an appropriate way.

496. In the case where there was no implementation of the recommendation by the media within one week, the commission issued a warning for a reprimand.

497. Finally, if the media did not comply with the recommendation after the warning, the relevant Commission publicly reprimands the media by expressing its disapproval of the form or content of the contested material.

498. The publishers and the operators who had signed the 2004 Code of Ethics, therefore, had to publish or broadcast the decisions of the relevant ethics commissions that imposed the reprimand. However, the ethic Commissions could not publish a decision if this was necessary to protect the applicant and could exempt the media from the obligation to publish this decision.

187. *See* Haraszi, *The Media Self-regulation Guidebook*, *supra* n. 173, 66.

499. The commissions' decisions were mandatory for the media[188] and in case they did not comply with them within the deadline, the CEM was, according to the LRT,[189] able to impose monetary sanctions. Obviously, this was possible only for the electronic media, since the CEM had no jurisdiction over the print media. Furthermore, the ECEM and ECPM did not consider programmes or publications made more than two months before the date of the complaint. Neither could the ECEM and ECPM consider complaints against media which did not sign the 2004 Code of Ethics, anonymous reports or cases that were subject to legal proceedings.

500. All of this is now valid for the Journalism Ethics Commission. According to Article 18(1) of the NCJE Statutes, publishers and operators affiliated with the 2004 Code of Ethics shall publish in their publications or broadcast in their programmes, in an appropriate manner, information about the decisions and voluntarily provide the Ethical Journalism Committee with copies of publications in their publications or programmes broadcast in their programmes which are the subject of a complaint addressed by it.

501. In case the concerned media fails to comply with the recommendation, and after a warning for a reprimand, the Journalism Ethics Commission shall publicly condemn the relevant media, expressing its disapproval of the form or content of the contested material (reprimand) (Article 17 of the Journalism Ethics Commission rules of procedure).

502. Similarly, the Journalism Ethics Commission may not publish a decision if this is necessary to protect the person concerned (Article 21(2)) of its Rules of Procedure.

503. As mentioned before, the CEM may, according to the LRT,[190] impose monetary sanctions on electronic media.

§3. The Bulgarian Media Union

504. The BMU,[191] was initiated as an independent, voluntary, public and nongovernmental organization of the print and electronic media, was created in 2012

---

188. It should be noted that the 2004 Code of Ethics is not an official legal document, and in this case, the Commissions did not make juridical decisions. The decision of the Commissions does not prevent the complaining side to go the Court.
189. According to Art. 126g of the LRT, penalty sanctions from EUR 1,000 to 2,500 may be imposed to a media service provider who fails to comply with a decision of the Ethical Commission of the Foundation NCJE and/or the association 'National Council for Self-Regulation'. In case of a repeat offence, the penalty sanction is doubled. As explained in the text, the reference in the article is made to the ECEM.
190. *Ibid.* The reference in the article is obviously made to the Journalism Ethics Commission in regard to electronic media.
191. All information provided below about the BMU was up-to-date in 2018. As of 2024, the authors could not find evidence of an ongoing activity of the BMU or any recent information on its current status.

following disagreements among publishers in Bulgaria and their large outflow from the existing UPB.[192]

505. Its initial members included thirty-five newspapers and Internet publishers, all unsatisfied with the change in the management of the existing UPB. Electronic media and advertising agencies as well as all Bulgarian editions abroad were invited to join the BMU.[193]

506. The new union announced that a new Code of Ethics was to be adopted as a condition for the admission of new members. This new Code of Ethics was to stipulate that the members who would be part of the union had to provide true and accurate information.

507. Thus, at its Annual General Meeting on 24 October 2014, the BMU adopted a decision approving the composition of its Ethics Committee that will observe the principles and norms of the organization's self-regulatory mechanism – the Professional Code of Ethics of the BMU adopted at the end of 2013 and published on the BMU site in January 2014. With the election of the Ethics Committee, the BMU aims to protect the public interests for true and objective information, to help raise the professional standards of Bulgarian journalism, and to support the training of young journalists in the print and electronic media.

508. The decisional body of the BMU is composed of a Chief Executive Officer, a Managing Board and an Auditing Board, composed respectively of eleven and five members, including their chairmen.

I. Functions and Membership of the Ethics Committee

509. The Ethics Committee is a collegiate body without managing functions with a three-year term of office which shall apply the 2014 Code of Ethics of the Bulgarian media. The Committee consists of ten members divided into three quotas of three persons each – a quota of the journalists, an independent quota and a quota of the owners, plus an additional person elected by the General Meeting of the BMU. The chairman is elected among the Ethics Committee members with a qualified majority.

510. The three members of the journalist quota shall be full-time journalists from the media – members of the BMU and the media which have joined the 2014 Code of Ethics. Their nominations and elections are done by the guild of journalists.[194]

192. *See* http://sib.bg/en/.
193. Beginning 2018 BMU counts seventy-one members.
194. For more details *see* Art. 5 of the Regulation on the implementation of the Code of professional ethics.

511. The three members of the independent quota shall be persons of high public standing, with recognized professional qualities related to the media, law, protection of human rights, freedom of speech, etc., but shall not be employed by media, advertising agencies or distribution companies under an employment, service or consultancy contract.[195]

512. The three members of the owners' quota shall be persons nominated by the owners or managers of the respective media.[196]

513. The main task of the Ethics Committee is to analyse the reasonableness of the submitted complaints and to adopt acts on their conformity to the norms of the 2014 Code of Ethics.

514. All complaints, alerts or other materials are recorded in an electronic register, which contains the name of the complainant, the name of the respondent party, subject of the complaint, text of the 2014 Code of Ethics which was allegedly breached, as well as any other relevant information.

515. The BMU shall also record all information, circumstances and actions that have been undertaken in relation to the complaint, as well as the decisions made.[197]

II. Independence

516. As for the NCJE, the members of the BMU Ethics Committee shall be independent. According to Article 14 of the Regulation on the implementation of the 2014 Code of Ethics, the members of the Ethics Committee shall perform their duties on their own conscience and shall not allow attempts of external influence or conflicts of interest. In case a conflict of interest arises the member shall withdraw from his/her position.

III. Sanctions

517. If the Ethics Committee decides that a complaint is admissible and establishes a breach of the 2014 Code of Ethics, it requires the respondent party to provide a right of reply or to offer an apology to the aggrieved party in an appropriate way. In case of non respect of the decision by the respondent party to provide right of reply or to offer an apology, the Ethics Committee can publicly censure the respective media and task it to publish or broadcast this decision.

---

195. Article 6 of the Regulation on the implementation of the Code of professional ethics.
196. Article 7 of the Regulation on the implementation of the Code of professional ethics.
197. For more information on the terms and ways of submitting complaints, the proceedings and the work rules *see* Arts 10, 11 and 13 of the Regulation on the implementation of the Code of professional ethics.

518. According to Article 21 of the Regulation on the implementation of the 2014 Code of Ethics, the acts of the Ethics Committee are obligatory for all members of the BMU and for all media which have accepted and signed the 2014 Code of Ethics. In the event that the respondent party fails to fulfil an effective act, the Ethics Committee shall make this fact public. This shall be done with a press release and by including the decision in the monthly bulletin of the Ethics Committee.

Part III. Regulation of Audiovisual Media (Broadcasting)

Chapter 1. Public Service Broadcasting

519. The LRT in its Article 6 determines the types of media service providers as public and commercial. Therefore, Bulgaria has introduced the dual system of functioning of electronic media.

§1. The Concept and Mission of Public Service Broadcasting

520. The mission of public service broadcasting is not explicitly stated in the LRT. Instead, it describes a list of tasks and functions, which public service media providers have been assigned to fulfil. Public service providers shall:

- provide for broadcasting political, economic, cultural, scientific, educational and other socially significant information;
- provide access to national and global cultural values and popularize scientific and technical achievements through broadcasting Bulgarian and foreign educational and cultural programmes for all age groups;
- provide, through their programme policy, protection of the national interests, the all-human cultural values, the national science, the education and culture to all Bulgarian citizens regardless of their ethnic belonging;
- encourage the creation of works of Bulgarian authors; and
- promote the Bulgarian performing art.

521. In Bulgaria, there are several public service radio stations such as Classic FM (having specialized musical profile), Deutsche Welle (multi-thematic profile) and Alma Mater (multi-thematic profile). It should be noted that many of the public service radio stations ceased to exist in recent years. The local radio station of BBC terminated its activity in 2005. Very recently, on 15 December 2009, Radio France Internationale was deregistered by the CEM. Public service televisions are the Military TV Channel and ROMA which are broadcast on the territory of the whole country and the regional film channel Vreme and Dunavtsi.

522. A central place in the organization of the public service broadcasting in Bulgaria is assigned to BNR and BNT. They are determined as national public providers[198] of radio services and audiovisual media services, respectively. The LRT confers on them, in addition to the aforementioned tasks and functions valid for all public service media providers, the following specific functions:[199]

- To provide media services for all citizens of the Republic of Bulgaria.
  This function reveals the mission of the national public service providers to provide media services not only to Bulgarian citizens who reside on the territory of the Republic of Bulgaria but also to those of them living and working abroad. In a broader context, a part of the mission behind this function could be also defined as a contribution to the retention of the bond of Bulgarian citizens who happened to reside abroad with the country of their citizenship.
- To contribute to the development and popularization of the Bulgarian culture and Bulgarian language, as well as the culture and the language of the citizens in compliance with their ethnic belonging.
  This function shows the important role of the national public service providers as cultural institutions which are called upon to present to the public and promote works of art of Bulgarian authors as well as to encourage the creation of such works in the field of culture. Furthermore, a similar function shall be exercised with respect to the culture and the language of citizens of different ethnic belonging and for whom the Bulgarian language is not a mother tongue.
- To provide through their media services access to the national and European cultural heritage.
  This function shows the role of the media in the promotion of European culture and cooperation among nations in Europe having a common historical heritage.
- To include in their programmes broadcasts which inform, educate and entertain.
  The inclusion of this function stressed the importance of provision of high-quality broadcasts and the various objectives they are called upon to pursue.
- To apply the new information technologies.
  This function shows the importance of the application of the most recent technological innovations in the field of information technologies for the development of communication in modern society.
- To reflect the various ideas and convictions of the society by pluralism of the points of view in each and every news and current publicist broadcast of political and economic subjects.
  This function highlights the fundamental principle of the independence of public media, i.e., the provision of pluralism of points of view.
- To contribute to the mutual understanding and tolerance between people.

198. By 'national' in this context is meant the territorial scope of the telecommunication networks and services. This may be derived from the opinion of the Constitutional Court expressed in its Decision No. 6 of 19 Sep. 2000 under constitutional case No. 8/2000. Therein, the Constitutional Court indicates that 'national' shall refer to territory and not to the significance of the particular objects or services. In the latter case the term 'national significance' should be used.

199. Article 6, para. 3 of the LRT.

This function supposes encouragement of the dialogue between conflicting groups in the society by BNT and BNR and avoidance of any broadcasts that might provoke social intolerance.
- To provide citizens the possibility to become familiar with the official position of the state on important issues of public life.

523. The compliance of the provision, which lays down the last function, with the Constitution was questioned before the Constitutional Court, which commented on that issue in its Decision No. 10 of 25 June 1999. According to the initiators of the challenge, the so-stated obligation of BNR and BNT infringes the principle of political pluralism, freedom of expression, the prohibition of censure and the right of information laid down in Article 11, paragraphs 1, 39, 40 and 41 of the Constitution.

524. The Court noted that the idea behind the challenged obligation of BNR and BNT was the guaranteeing of the constitutional right of citizens to receive information. All citizens have the right to know the official position of the state in important matters of public life. The position of the state is expressed through the state bodies on various occasions. Pursuant to the Court's analysis, the right to information would be infringed if the electronic media had no obligation to provide all citizens with the possibility to receive information regarding the official position of the state about important issues. The Court further reviewed the contested obligation vis-à-vis the obligation of the BNR and BNT to reflect the various ideas and convictions of the society by pluralism of the points of view in each and every news and current publicist broadcast of political and economic subject. It noted that the official position of the state may be expressed solely by its official state bodies and not by the opposition. The latter may express its opinions concerning the official position of the state and criticize it through the live broadcasts on the BNR and BNT of some of the sessions of the Parliament and the parliamentary control which is always broadcast by the electronic media live. All sessions of the Parliament are broadcast by the BNR at a certain frequency covering the territory of the whole country.

525. The opposition has the possibility to express opinions also via private electronic media. In compliance with the contested provision of Article 7, section 8 (after the amendments of the normative act in 2010, the provision found its expression in Article 6, paragraph 3, section 8) of the LRT with the Constitution could not be derived on the basis of potential disproportion with Article 51 of the LRT either. The said article obliges the BNR and BNT to provide immediately and free of charge upon request their programme time for official messages of state bodies' representatives in cases of disasters or direct threats to life, security and health of the population or individual persons. The Constitutional Court regarded the provision of Article 51 as special vis-à-vis the general rule of the contested provision and applicable only in the presence of the specified circumstances. The Constitutional Court outlined that the BNR and BNT not only are public service providers but also serve as national information institutions. Exactly the obligations of the BNR and BNT as such institutions are set in the challenged provision; however, this text does not affect the freedom of the electronic media to determine its independent editorial policy and does not impose any limitations on the appearance of the opposition.

526. At the end of its analysis, the Constitutional Court presented another serious argument upholding the compliance of the contested provision with the Constitution. It rejected the allegation that the official position of the state is the position of the governing majority. The acceptance of the above allegation in the opinion of the Constitutional judges would mean denial of fundamental principles of the constitutional law. The contested Article 7, section 8 of the LRT does not infringe on the right of citizens to express an opinion and disclose it and does not introduce censure with respect to the BNR and BNT broadcasts. The Constitutional Court concluded that the challenged provision does not reject and rather ensures the right of citizens to receive information concerning the official position of the state on important issues of public life without preventing them from searching and disclosing the said information. Consequently, the challenge was not granted.

527. Apart from the so exhaustively described tasks and functions, the LRT does not clarify what exactly is the mission of BNT and BNR as national public media service providers.

528. Chapter 3 of the LRT deals with the status, programmes, management and financing of BNR and BNT.

§2. The Organization of Public Service Broadcasting

I. Legal Status of BNR and BNT

529. BNR and BNT are legal entities having their seat in the capital Sofia. They are dependent on the state in several aspects. First, their property, which has been granted to them prior to the entrance into force of the LRT, remained in state ownership and the two national public service providers are entitled to carry out only its operational management.[200] BNR and BNT may own or hire on a contractual basis the electronic communication networks and/or facilities for terrestrial analogous radio broadcasting necessary for the broadcasting of the radio and TV programmes of BNR and BNT. However, the financing of the latter is entirely provided by the state from the state budget. Further, the state is obliged to undertake all necessary measures in order to guarantee the broadcasting of the programmes of the BNR and BNT on the whole territory of the country while implementing its policy in the field of electronic communications.[201] The state shall fulfil the said obligation through the CEM which shall license BNR and BNT for broadcasting of their programmes

200. Article 42 of the LRT.
201. Article 44 of the LRT.

through electronic communication networks for terrestrial digital radio broadcasting.[202] The state also undertakes the respective measures for guaranteeing the digital equipment necessary for the creation of programmes in compliance with the applicable digital technologies.[203]

II. Management Bodies

530. Article 55 of the LRT specifies the management bodies of the BNR and BNT. Such management bodies shall be the Management Board of the BNR and the General Director of the BNR. The Management Board of the BNT and the General Director of the BNT are the management bodies of the BNT, respectively. In order to be eligible to occupy the positions of General Directors with the BNR and BNT, the respective candidates must meet the requirements set with regard to members of the CEM.[204] The mandate of the General Directors of the two media is three years, and they cannot be elected to the same positions for more than two consecutive mandates (Article 66 of the LRT).

531. In 2016, the Bulgarian Parliament voted to change Article 66 of the LRT. A new paragraph 4 was added stating that in the case where, at the expiration of the mandate of the General Director of the BNT, respectively of the BNR, the election of a new candidate failed, they shall continue to exercise their powers until the new General Director enters into function.

532. Moreover, according to Article 60, paragraph 1 of the LRT in case Article 66, paragraph 4 of the LRT applies, the members of the Management Boards of BNT and BNR, shall exercise their powers until the new boards of directors from CEM have been approved. This modification followed a one-year delay in the process of electing a new BNR General Director of the competition in 2016. However, this is a major loom as it allows for an indefinite extension of the current BNR and BNT General Directors mandates.

533. Bulgaria is not among the countries, in which the Parliament exercises functions related to the management of the public service providers. The General Director is elected and dismissed by the regulatory body, which is the CEM on the grounds enumerated in the LRT. The remaining four members of the management board are approved by the CEM following the proposal of the General Director. The decisions of the CEM regarding the election and dismissal of General Directors of the BNR and BNT have been very often subject to legal challenges before the SAC.

534. In 2001, the General Director of the BNT Lilyana Popova was dismissed by the CEM because of the then-inserted amendment in the LRT requiring five years of practise in television for the candidates for General Director of the BNT. At the

202. Article 45, para. 3 of the LRT.
203. Article 45, para. 4 of the LRT.
204. *See* Part V, Ch. 1, para. 776.

time of the amendment, Popova was lacking such records. According to the CEM, which at that time had just succeeded the NCRT and constituted a new regulatory body, the changed requirements had led to incompatibility and, therefore, the dismissal of Popova was justified. This way, the CEM construed the newly adopted provision as having a retroactive effect. The SAC found infringement of the law because a normative act becomes effective *ex nunc*. The amendment of the legislation has no effect with regard to rights which have been validly acquired in accordance with the legal rules in force before its occurrence. Consequently, the SAC cancelled the decision as unlawful.

535. In the case *Dimitar Tsonev v. CEM*, the appellant questioned the lawfulness of the election of the General Director Kiril Gotsev by virtue of Decision No. 15-00-52 of 4 March 2002 of the CEM. The appellant participated in the competition and appealed the decision on various grounds such as lack of motives, failure of the newly elected General Director to meet the LRT requirements for the position, lack of publicity, transparency and impartiality of the CEM members throughout the procedure as well as procedural violations. The appeal was dismissed.

536. The mandate of the General Director of the BNR or the BNT, respectively, may be prematurely terminated on the same grounds justifying a similar termination of the CEM members' mandate as well as in case of gross or systematic breaches committed by other persons of the provisions laying down the principles of the activity of the radio and TV operators.[205] The mandate of the General Director Kiril Gotsev was so terminated, and he appealed before the SAC. The termination was justified with the presence of three penal orders to the BNT issued by the CEM. One of them imposed monetary sanctions for the breach of the principle for the protection of the personal inviolability of citizens and two concerned infringement of the obligation for provision of a right to reply. The Court granted the appeal because of the failure of the CEM to notify the appellant regarding the pending procedure aiming at the premature termination of his mandate as a General Director of the BNT thus depriving him of his legally guaranteed possibility to protect himself from the accusations for lack of professional merits and morality as well as on other grounds.

537. The SAC decision commented also on the concept of a gross breach used in the LRT by referring to Decision No. 10 of the Constitutional Court dated 25 June 1999, in which the constitutional judges concluded that the evaluation of the gravity of the breach shall be made on a case-by-case basis. The absence of evidence for the conduct of such evaluation in the attached documentation was also among the reasons for the success of the appeal.

538. The CEM availed itself of its right to appeal the decision before a five-member panel of the SAC, which ultimately succeeded. The panel found that the breaches of the BNT, which resulted in the three penal orders, have been significant

205. Article 67 of the LRT.

and, according to the panel's members, the CEM was obliged to terminate the mandate of the General Director prematurely. In light of the above, even the absence of notification and discussions of the potential objections of the General Director was justified because CEM did not dispose of any other possibility. The panel concluded that the breaches could be undoubtedly said to be gross regardless of the lack of definition of that concept in the LRT and, therefore, the termination of the mandate was justified.

§3. The Financing of Public Service Broadcasting

539. The LRT obliges the BNR and the BNT to prepare, operate, conclude and account independent budgets. The following revenues may be received in the budget of BNR and BNT: (i) financing from the fund 'Radio and Television'; (ii) subsidy from the state budget; (iii) own income from commercials and sponsorship; (iv) revenue from additional activities related to the radio and television activity; (v) donations and inheritance; and (vi) interest and other income related to the radio and television activity.[206]

540. The subsidy from the state budget shall be: (i) for preparation, creation and broadcasting national and regional programmes; the subsidy shall be determined on the basis of normative per hour of programme approved by the Council of Ministers; and (ii) expedient subsidy for long-term material assets according to a list annually approved by the Ministry of Finance.

541. The BNR and the BNT receive state subsidies on the basis of a draft of the budget, which is prepared by them, approved by the CEM and submitted to the Parliament for discussions and inclusion in the Draft Law on the State Budget for the respective calendar year.[207]

542. The establishment of the fund for Radio and Television was contemplated at the time of the enactment of the LRT in 1998; however, it has still not started functioning. The Transitional and Final Provisions of the LRT provide for the financing of the BNR and BNT through subsidy from the state budget until 31 December 2018.[208] As of 1 January 2019, the state subsidy for the BNR and BNT is supposed to be entirely substituted by financing through the fund Radio and Television.

543. On the basis of the above, Bulgarian media law allows the dual funding of the national public service broadcasters, i.e., commercial and public financing

206. Article 70 of the LRT.
207. N. Ognyanova, *Bulgarian Media Policy and Law: How Much Europeanization*, 2 Central European Journal of Communication, 27–41 (2009).
208. It was initially provided that the financing of the BNR and BNT would be provided from the state budget until 31 Dec. 2012. Over the last years, these provisions have encountered several amendments related to the postponement of the contemplated shift in the financing.

whereas the public financing from the state budget is to be gradually substituted by financing from the fund Radio and Television.

544. The fund Radio and Television shall be established under the CEM to finance the radio and TV activity.[209] Therefore, in Bulgaria, such funds are provided for establishment with the regulatory body.

545. The resources of the fund 'Radio and Television' shall be accumulated from: (i) monthly fees for receiving radio and television programmes; (ii) licensing or registration fees collected by the CEM; (iii) interests on the funds accumulated therein; (iv) donations and wills; and (v) other sources determined by the law.[210]

546. The LRT provides that for financing the public service broadcasting, a monthly fee shall be paid on the basis of every registered electric gauge.[211] The amount of the monthly fee is 0.6% of the minimum salary for the country determined by the Council of Ministers for every registered electric gauge.[212] Companies and individuals carrying out trade activity, as well as the state and municipal organizations shall pay a monthly fee amounting to 2.5% of the minimum salary for the country determined by the Council of Ministers for every registered electric gauge.[213] The monthly licensing fees shall be paid together with the due amounts for electric power by the respective order through the desks of the electric supply enterprises of the National Electric Company.[214] No fees shall be paid for an electric gauge for three-phase electricity registered for industrial purposes. Persons who do not possess radio and TV receivers or do not receive radio and television broadcasts may be released from payment of fees after declaring this fact by a declaration filed with the respective office.[215] Citizens with impaired hearing or sight with II degree of disability are also released from payment of such fees.[216] Fees are further not paid for using receivers and devices by health institutions, kindergartens and homes, educational, social and cultural institutions according to a list proposed by the respective ministries and administrative bodies and approved by the CEM, as well as if the receivers and the devices are used as monitors.

547. The compliance with the Constitution of the monthly fees for receiving radio and TV programmes, their amount and method of collection were questioned in proceedings before the Constitutional Court. The challenge was based on the argument that fees in the context of Article 60, paragraph 1 of the Constitution may be paid only in consideration for services received and, therefore, the obligation of all citizens to pay fees on the basis of the possession of electric gauge contradicts

209. Article 98 of the LRT.
210. Article 102, para. 1 of the LRT.
211. Article 93, para. 1 of the LRT.
212. Article 94, para. 1 of the LRT.
213. Article 94, para. 2 of the LRT.
214. Article 95 of the LRT.
215. Article 93, paras 2 and 3 of the LRT.
216. Article 96 of the LRT.

the Constitution.[217] In order to justify the rejection of the challenge, the Court accepted that in the case at hand the fee is not a price in consideration for a service but state receivable serving for accumulation of resources in the fund Radio and Television. The Court took into account that such fees constituted the single possible mechanism for the financial independence of the BNR and BNT from the state budget and their respective transformation from state to public service media. The Court also noted that the method for collection of the fees on the basis of the registered electric gauges with the exception of the gauges for industrial use had been already applied in other countries having similar conditions to those in Bulgaria. The possibility for release of certain citizens, who have filed a declaration, from payment of fees was perceived by the Court to be enough for the avoidance of social injustice. The adoption of other models such as payment in accordance with the number of radio receivers and TV sets was considered to be inadequate in view of the development of new technologies and the possibility of receipt of radio and TV programmes by means of computers, mobile phones and other technical way, which will render the registration of all receiving devices practically impossible.

548. However, regardless of the arguments stated by the Constitutional Court in support of the method for collection chosen by the legislator, no effective mechanism for collection of the fees for receiving radio and TV programmes provided for in the LRT has been introduced. Among all possible reasons, the privatization in the energy sector should be noted as opposed to the previously existing monopolist position of the National Electric Company in that market. The newly established energy-supplying companies were restricted in the exercise of economic activity. This means that those kinds of fees are currently not relevant for the formation of the budgets of the BNR and BNT. This way, the main source of revenues for the two media remains the state subsidy. This system of financing has invoked for a long period of time questions about the actual independence of the two national public service providers, which, in terms of financing may be still defined as state and not public.

549. The licensing fees collected by the CEM are similarly not relevant for the financing of the BNR and BNT because they are used for the financing of the CEM. The licensing and registration fees, collected by the CEM are intended to cover its administrative expenses for the activities connected with the licensing, registration and supervision of the activity for observing the conditions provided in the licences and the conditions under which the registration has been made.[218]

550. Further to the financing of the two national public service providers, the fund Radio and Television has been meant to finance the CEM, projects of national importance connected with the introduction and use of new technologies in the radio and TV activity, significant cultural and educational projects; projects designated to extend the broadcasting of radio and TV programmes in terms of population and/or

217. Decision No. 10 of 25 Jun. 1999 of the Constitutional Court of Bulgaria under const. file No. 36/98.
218. Article 102, para. 2 of the LRT.

territory; the management of the fund; and the National Electric Company in consideration for the collection of the fees for receiving of radio and TV programmes.[219]

551. In Bulgaria, since the very beginning of the legal regulation of the advertising activity broadcasting of commercials on the BNT and BNR has been restricted. The total duration of the commercials for each individual programme cannot exceed fifteen minutes per day and night and four minutes per hour for BNT and for the BNR the restriction is six minutes per hour.[220] The BNT is entitled to use up to one-third of the total volume of the commercial time for the day and night within 19.00–22.00 hours.[221] The aforementioned restrictions do not apply to commercials included in programmes at the time of broadcasting art, cultural and sports activities with national and international importance.[222] In the programmes of the regional centres of BNR and BNT intended for regional broadcasting, the general duration of the commercials shall not exceed six minutes per hour.[223] It should be noted that the restriction for the BNT is more rigid than the restriction imposed on the BNR. Currently, the BNT is trying to lobby for the abolishment of all restrictions concerning broadcasting of commercials whereas the commercial operators insist on total prohibition of such broadcasting by the BNT due to the use of public resources.

219. Article 103 of the LRT.
220. Article 90, para. 1 of the LRT.
221. Article 90, para. 2 of the LRT.
222. Article 90, para. 4 of the LRT.
223. Article 90, para. 3 of the LRT.

Chapter 2. Private Broadcasting

§1. Different Categories of Private Broadcasters

552. As was mentioned above, the LRT divides two types of media service providers: *public* and *commercial*. Furthermore, the provision of Article 3, paragraph 1 of the LRT points out that the media services can be *linear* and *non-linear*. Thus, another classification could be made out by dividing the media services providers into such that provide linear media services (in this case commercial linear media service providers) and such that provide non-linear media services (commercial non-linear media service providers).

553. *Linear* media services are those media services which are provided for simultaneous viewing or listening of programmes on the basis of a programme schedule. The simultaneous viewing or listening includes quasi-simultaneous viewing or listening because of the variations in the short time lag which occurs between the transmission and the reception of the broadcast due to technical reasons inherent to the transmission process.

554. *Non-linear (on-demand)* media services are such media services which are provided by a media service provider for viewing or listening to programmes chosen by the users at any time and at their individual request on the basis of a catalogue of programmes selected by the media service provider. Pursuant to Article 125g of the LRT, such media providers shall notify CEM about their willingness to provide on-demand media services by submitting a notification completed in a standard form.

§2. Licensing Requirements

555. In Decision No. 33 of 8 December 1998, the Constitutional Court while construing the provisions of Article 18, paragraph 3 of the Constitution granting to the state sovereign rights over the radio frequency specter concluded that *the intervention of the state in the allocation of the radio frequency specter is inevitable.* Article 18, paragraph 5 of the Constitution referred to provisions of concessions regarding the objects and granting of licences for the activities under the previous paragraphs, including the radio frequency specter under paragraph 3. In Decision No. 18 of 30 June 1998, the Constitutional Court concluded that considering the specifics of the sovereign rights of the state over the radio frequency specter they could be exercised either through provision of concession or by granting licences and the particular regime should be determined by the respective law.

556. The LRT upon its enactment in 1998 provided for a licensing regime with respect to the content of the services, which would be provided through the specter. At the same time, the then-effective Law on Telecommunications provided for licensing of telecommunications networks and use of the radio frequency specter. Therefore, initially, Bulgarian law introduced two independent licensing regimes exercised by two different bodies – the media regulator, at that time the NCRT, and the Commission for Regulation of Communications.

557. In 2001, the LRT introduced a registration regime for the creation and broadcasting of radio and TV content in cases when such content is broadcast via other technical means and not by the use of the radio frequency specter. Further, the LRT provided for the so-called bound licensing of the radio and TV operators as broadcasters of programmes pursuant to the LRT and in their capacity as telecommunication operators under the Law on Telecommunications. The bound licensing provided the opportunity for every operator who had obtained a licence for radio and TV activity following certain procedures with the leading role of the CEM to receive also a telecommunication licence. Therefore, one person could not hold a programme licence without also having a telecommunication one.

558. Both, the introduction of the registration regime and the bound licensing were challenged before the Constitutional Court.

559. The initiators of the challenge alleged that the existence of two regimes for the creation and broadcasting of radio and TV programmes, i.e., two different regimes in terms of content and burden for one and the same activity, contradicted Article 19, paragraph 2 of the Constitution, saying that the law creates and guarantees to all citizens and legal entities equal legal conditions for economic activity and prevents the misuse of monopolist position, unfair competition and protects the consumer.

560. In 2001, the Constitutional Court was requested to decide on the alleged unconstitutionality of certain provisions in the Law on the Amendment and Supplement of the LRT allegedly providing for two different legal regimes governing the ostensibly identical activity of creation and broadcasting of radio and TV programmes, namely licensing regime and registration regime. Article 19, paragraph 2 of the Constitution guarantees to all natural persons and legal entities equal legal conditions for economic activity, which, according to the fifty members of the Parliament who made the request, would be violated by the existence of the said two regimes. In its Decision No. 1 of 26 March 2002, the Constitutional Court noted that the Law on the Amendment and Supplement of the LRT opted for the method of registration only with respect to the broadcasting of programmes via technical means other than the terrestrial. Instead of finding incompliance with the Constitution, the Court rather considered such registration regime as a positive development qualifying it as *a step towards deregulation of the media activity*. Thanks to this new regime the operators who are willing to exercise radio and TV activity would be facilitated by the option to avail themselves of the procedure, which is much easier than the licensing. Furthermore, registration is not limited in terms of scope and period of validity because no use of the limited frequency resource is necessary in case of broadcasting via technical means other than terrestrial. The range of the persons who may search, receive and diffuse information in line with Article 41 of the Constitution will also expand as a result of the introduction of the registration regime according to the analyses of the Constitutional Court. Therefore, the regime was in harmony with the right of free economic initiative as proclaimed by the Constitution. The presence of objective conditions precedent necessitating licensing of terrestrial radio and TV broadcasting must not have as a consequence the introduction of an analogical regime also for the other operators creating programmes for broadcasting by other technical means. According to the Court, the presence of equal legal conditions for pursuing economic activity correlates with the right of a free choice of how the activity is to be exercised – as a terrestrial operator or as a registered operator. Therefore, the difference in the two regimes is not a condition precedent for the choice but rather a result thereof.

561. The initiators of the challenge contested also the compliance with the Constitution of the provisions in the Law on the Amendment and Supplement of the LRT concerning the bound licensing, i.e., the requirement for each operator to obtain two licences under the LRT and the Law on Telecommunications. According to them, the Constitution is breached because the provisions placed in unequal position the two sectors (analogous and digital) of the electronic media market and deprived the consumers of the possibility to use DTT. This way, the development of the electronic media has been blocked.

562. The Constitutional Court found that the absence of legal regulation of the various fields of economic activity could be linked to judgment for expediency and, hence, with the objection of a particular act of governance or omission but not considered a ground for incompliance with the Constitution. This way, the Court refused to analyse whether the Law on the Amendment and Supplement of the LRT provided for regulation of the digital means for terrestrial broadcasting.

563. The constitutional judge Gotsev expressed his dissenting opinion with respect to the decision of the Constitutional Court. He opined that the dual regime for the creation of programmes established unequal positions for some economic actors vis-à-vis other actors. Furthermore, this had the same effect also with respect to the consumers of the respective programmes. With the issuance of a licence imposing certain rules, with which the content providers acting on the basis of registration are not obliged to comply, the consumers would have different products dependent on the fact whether the producer of the programme has a licence or is only registered. The difference also creates different working conditions for the persons who produce programmes although, in principle, one radio or TV programme is created in equal conditions notwithstanding its method of transmission – terrestrial or not.

564. Judge Gotsev noted that the LRT prior to the amendment provided for separate licensing of the content and the broadcasting. This way not every operator was necessary to create also a programme. There could be economic actors who only transmit and do not create programmes. Gotsev observed that the bound licensing is inapplicable to the digital industry, because there one broadcaster may provide services with respect to a lot of programmes. This way inequality is created between the analogous and digital industry. The procedure of bound licensing was inapplicable, according to Gotsev, to the applicants for digital television and radio because one operator has the technical possibility to broadcast more than one programme.

565. The dissenting opinion of judge Gotsev proved to be justified in view of the difficulties encountered in the process of licensing in the years following the 2001 amendments. As of the time of writing this country monograph, two national telecommunication licences for terrestrial broadcasting of TV programmes, namely, bTV and Nova TV and one national telecommunication licence for terrestrial broadcasting of radio programmes, namely, Darik Radio, have been granted. For a long time, the process of licensing has been blocked because of the uncertainty of whether licensing for analogous frequencies is necessary in view of the forthcoming digitalization of the radio frequency specter. Ultimately, the regime for bound licensing with respect to terrestrial analogous broadcasting has been retained with some changes and an entirely new regime for the licensing of the radio and TV activity for the creation of programmes intended for broadcasting through electronic communication networks for terrestrial digital radio transmission has been introduced as a separate section in the LRT in 2009.

566. The currently effective LRT imposes some restrictions on the potential candidates for licences. Pursuant to Article 105, paragraph 4 thereof the following persons are not entitled to apply for issuance of licence: (i) legal entities, to which a permit for carrying out insurance activity has been denied or withdrawn; (ii) legal entities, in which the legal entities specified in (i) or the shareholders therein hold shares; (iii) natural persons – sole traders and legal entities who are not able to prove their ownership over their property or capital pursuant to Article 6 of the Law on the Measures against the Money Laundering; (iv) legal entities, in which the natural persons – sole traders and the legal entities specified in (iii) or the shareholders therein hold shares; (v) natural persons – sole traders and legal entities, which in the recent five years preceding the application for licence have been declared insolvent or are in procedure for declaring insolvent or in liquidation; (vi) legal entities, in which persons included in the list under Article 3, paragraph 1 of the Law on Information regarding the Unserviced Credit Hold Shares; and (vii) sole traders and legal entities which in the last year, preceding the application for licence has been rejected for the same kind of licensed activity or their licence issued in accordance with the LRT has been withdrawn.

567. From the entry into force of the LRT until the most recent amendments in 2010, legal entities having partners or shareholders, who are also partners or shareholders in legal entities having in their registered scope of activity 'advertising activity' or carrying out advertising activity, as well as the natural persons – sole traders having in their registered scope of activity 'advertising activity' or carrying out advertising activity, have been similarly prohibited for applying for issuance of licence. However, in 2010 the prohibition with respect to this specific category of persons was removed.

568. Under the currently effective regime for licensing of radio and TV activity by using available and/or new electronic communication networks for terrestrial analogous radio transmission, a licence must be issued following the conduct of the competition. The procedure for conduct of competition shall be commenced upon request of an interested person or the initiative of the CEM. In the request to the CEM, the person may indicate the desired point for broadcasting and territorial scope. The CEM in the fourteen-day time limit following the filing of the request shall request from the CRC information about the technical parameters necessary for terrestrial analogous radio transmission of radio and TV programmes in the particular town or village, region or for the whole territory of the Republic of Bulgaria, including the free radio frequencies, the admissible capacities of broadcasting, the possible points of broadcasting, as well as other necessary technical information. The CRC shall present to the CEM its decision on the request within three months, and when international coordination of the radio frequencies and radio frequency bands is necessary as well as the technical characteristics of the radio facilities, which shall be used – within eight months, observing the requirements for the efficient use of the radio frequency spectrum. In case of availability of free radio frequency specter, the CRC shall enclose to the decision a draft licence for the use of individually specified limited resource – radio frequency specter.[224]

569. Within fourteen days of receiving the reply, the CEM shall take a decision for opening competition or competitions in compliance with the available free radio frequency spectrum. The LRT contains certain requirements to which the competition papers must comply. The competition shall be held not earlier than thirty days from the promulgation of the decision in the State Gazette. If several competitions are announced in compliance with the available radio frequency spectrum, they shall be held simultaneously. When in a three-month period following the receipt of the reply of the CRC the CEM does not take a decision for the opening of competition or competitions in accordance with the available free radio frequency specter, the CRC may, after consultations with the CEM and in compliance with the state policy for planning and allocation of the radio frequency specter, propose a review of the objectives, for which the limited resource has been provided.[225]

570. The CEM shall appoint a chairman and members of an expert commission for holding the competition which shall obligatorily include members of the CEM and the CRC. Participants in the commission can also be experts from other interested administrative bodies and organizations. The chairman of the CEM shall issue an order for the appointment of the expert commission. The members of the commission shall sign a declaration for confidentiality of the information having become known to them in the process of the competition. The CEM on the basis of the competition documents, evaluation criteria, the report of the expert commission and the assessment for the most complete fulfilment of the competition requirement shall classify the candidates and shall take decisions for issuance of licence for radio or television activity and of individual licence for use of individually specified

224. Article 116 of the LRT.
225. Article 116a of the LRT.

resource for performance of electronic communications via available and/or new electronic communication networks for terrestrial analogous radio transmission from the CRC with respect to the candidate classified on the first place.

571. Licence for radio and television activity for the territory of the Republic of Bulgaria shall not be issued to a person or persons related thereto in the context of the Law on Commerce who hold licences of the same kind for radio and television activity with regional or local range unless they renounce it. The latter provision is not applicable to BNR and BNT, which are allowed to have national and regional programmes, and, also, in the cases of terrestrial digital radio broadcasting. Within three days from the ènactment of the decision for the issuance of licence, the CEM shall inform the CRC. Within ten days the CEM shall issue licence for radio and/or television activity, and the CRC shall issue licence for use of individually specified limited resource – radio frequency specter for the performance of electronic communications through available and/or new electronic communication networks for terrestrial analogous radio broadcasting.[226]

572. If within ten days from the decision of the CEM the approved candidate gives up on the issuance of the two licences, they shall be offered to the participant rated second. The procedure shall be terminated in case of refusal by the second candidate.[227]

573. The licence for radio and TV activity for the creation of programmes intended to be broadcasted through electronic communication networks for terrestrial digital radio broadcasting shall entitle the undertaking, to which a licence by the CRC for the use of individually specified limited resource – radio frequency specter for the performance of electronic communications through such networks on a territory designated in the licence is issued, to broadcast programmes. The programmes must be licensed and be in kind and profile specified by the CEM or coordinated with the CEM following the procedures described below.[228]

574. The procedure for the issuance of licence for programmes broadcast through electronic communication networks for terrestrial digital radio broadcasting shall be commenced upon a request by an interested person or following the initiative of the CEM or the CRC. The CEM announces the procedure on its webpage on the Internet and in the State Gazette and, also, indicates the term and the venue for filing of applications. The candidates are requested to include with their application form evidence of their capabilities for the creation of qualitative production as well as a draft of a business plan for the performance of the activity.

575. Within seven days from the expiry of the term, the chairman of the CEM shall designate an expert commission, in which three members of the CEM and two members of the CRC must be included. The members of the expert commission

226. Article 116c of the LRT.
227. Article 116d of the LRT.
228. Article 116e of the LRT.

shall review the applications on the basis of criteria such as: (i) originality and variety of the programme; (ii) possibilities for creation and provision of own production; (iii) level of readiness and stages for complete (twenty-four hours) broadcasting of the programme; and (iv) proven experience as a radio or TV operator. The expert commission shall propose to the CEM to issue or refuse the issuance of licence with respect to each of the candidates. In case of adoption of the decision for issuance or refusal for issuance of licence, the CEM shall be governed by the principles of: (i) guaranteeing the right of information of the citizens of the Republic of Bulgaria; (ii) creation of favourable conditions for a variety of the media environment and pluralism; and (iii) preservation of the national identity. The number of licences shall not be limited. The CEM shall rule within thirty days from the designation of the expert commission with the decision for issuance or refusal for issuance of licence and within ten days from the adoption of the decision, in case it is positive, the CEM shall issue licences for TV activity.[229]

576. With a decision accompanied by reasons, the CEM shall determine the kind and the profile of the licensed Bulgarian TV programmes or radio programmes, which must be carried on the networks for terrestrial digital radio broadcasting. The number of such programmes cannot be more than two programmes for each electronic communication network.[230] The undertaking which has obtained a licence under the procedure set in the LEC shall propose within one month following its issuance to the CEM the kind and the profile of the licensed radio and/or TV programmes, which it shall broadcast through electronic communication networks for terrestrial digital radio broadcasting. Within one month following the filing of the proposal, the CEM shall conduct consultations with the undertaking by taking into account the proposed kind and profile of the programmes and observing the principles of guaranteeing the right of information of the citizens of the Republic of Bulgaria, creation of favourable conditions for a variety of the media environment and pluralism and the preservation of the national identity.

577. Within seven days from the expiry of the aforementioned term, the CEM shall coordinate the kind and profile of the licensed radio and TV programmes, which shall be broadcast by adopting a decision with reasons. The failure of the CEM to decide within the said seven days shall be considered acceptance of the proposed kind and profiles of the programmes.[231]

578. An undertaking having a licence issued by the CRC for the use of an individually specified limited resource – radio frequency specter – is not allowed to be a radio and TV operator.[232]

229. Article 116f of the LRT.
230. Article 116g of the LRT.
231. Article 116h of the LRT.
232. Article 116i of the LRT.

I. Withdrawal and Renewal of Licenses

579. Licence shall be withdrawn in case of gross infringements of the principles of the radio and TV activity; in case of broadcasting of programmes with unsettled copy and related rights in advance; in case of denied access to important event by an operator having an exclusive right of broadcasting of such event; in case of incompliance with the rules for the promotion of European works; and in case of declaration of untruthful facts in the application procedure.[233]

580. The withdrawal of the licence shall be done by the CEM through the issuance of a decision with reasons following a written warning stating a certain period for remedy of the breach and failure of the operator to do so within the stated time limit. The withdrawal shall always take place automatically in case of imposition of two monetary sanctions with respect to one and the same breach. The decision for withdrawal shall designate a time period, within which the persons would not be allowed to apply for issuance of a new licence. The said period cannot be shorter than two years.[234] In case of withdrawal of licence for radio and TV activity through the use of available and/or new electronic communication network for terrestrial analogous radio broadcasting, the CEM is obliged to notify the CRC in order for the latter to terminate the licence issued for the use of a limited resource – radio frequency specter.[235] Upon the withdrawal of the licence, the holder thereof is obliged to terminate its radio and TV activity.[236]

581. The licence may be renewed on the basis of a request for continuation of the term of validity of the licence, which has to be filed not later than six months prior to the expiry of the current term of validity of the licence. The CEM is obliged to review the request and within a term of three months before the expiry of the term of validity of the licence to take a decision and notify the licence holder in writing about it. In case of renewal of licence for radio and TV activity through the use of available and/or new electronic communication network for terrestrial analogous radio broadcasting, the CEM shall notify the CRC, which within ten days shall prolong the term of the licence issued by the CRC for the use of a limited resource – radio frequency specter.[237]

II. Registration of Radio and TV Operators

582. Operators who intend to create radio and TV programmes to be broadcasted by means other than through the use of the radio frequency specter or via electronic communication networks for terrestrial digital broadcasting are subject to registration. They are obliged to respect the principles listed in Article 10 of the

233. Article 122 of the LRT.
234. Article 123 of the LRT.
235. Article 123a of the LRT.
236. Article 124 of the LRT.
237. Article 125 of the LRT.

LRT, namely: (i) guaranteeing the freedom of expression; (ii) guaranteeing the right to receive information; (iii) keeping the secret of the source of information; (iv) protection of the personal inviolability of citizens; (v) non-admission of broadcasts suggesting intolerance among citizens; (vi) non-admission of broadcasts contradicting the good morals especially if containing pornography, praising or exculpating cruelty or violence or inciting hatred based on racial, sexual, religious or national nature; (vii) guaranteeing a right to reply in the programmes; (viii) guaranteeing the copy and the related rights in the broadcasts and programmes; and (ix) preservation of the purity of Bulgarian language.

583. Further, such radio and TV operators must observe the following requirements: (i) respect of human dignity; (ii) provision of the ratio within the annual programme time, designated for European production as well as for works created by independent producers; (iii) protection of children; (iv) respect of the copy and related rights under the effective legislation; and (v) provision of information to the CEM.

584. The operators who are willing to register shall file an application before the CEM with certain documents attached thereto. In fourteen days the CEM shall issue a Decision. No, and limits related to the broadcasting of the programme can be imposed. In certain cases, the CEM may deny registration such as: (i) if the applicant belongs to one of the categories of persons who are prohibited from applying for issuance of a licence as enumerated supra; (ii) the provided programme project, programme concept, programme profile or programme scheme contradict the provisions of the law; and (iii) in case of irregularities in the application documents if not removed in the due course.

585. Upon the decision for registration, the applicant shall receive a certificate containing: (i) the company name and the seat of the radio and TV operator; (ii) the name of the programme and the method of its broadcasting; (iii) the type of the operator – public service provider or commercial operator; (iv) the programme profile; and (v) the day of the commencement of the broadcasting of the programme. The registered operator is obliged to notify the CEM regarding the conditions, the place and the method of broadcasting, the programme time and each and every change therein within fourteen days from its occurrence. Registrations are not limited in time.[238]

586. The CEM is obliged to deregister an operator in case of infringements of the principles and the requirements, which such operator has been obliged to observe as well as in case of occurrence of some of the circumstances which prevent such operators from applying for licence. The CEM may deregister an operator also if: (i) the registered programme has not been broadcast for a period longer than twelve consecutive months following the entry in the registry or at any time after the registration; (ii) in case of contradiction arising between the programme project, programme concept, programme profile or programme scheme and the law;

238. Article 125a.

and (iii) the registered operator has failed to notify the CEM regarding the conditions, the place and the method of broadcasting, the programme time and each and every change therein within fourteen days from its occurrence. In the said cases, the registration shall be deleted if, after a warning giving a thirty-day period for remedy of the circumstances, which has provided grounds for deregistration, the operator has not removed them.

Chapter 3. Programme Standards

587. For the past ten years, the media industry in Bulgaria has shown dynamism and progress, which could be seen mainly in the commercial TV channels. The development of the private electronic media and the democratization of the country since 1989 helped develop a very diverse programme content of the private electronic media. The appearance of market competition between the different operators forced them to always look for newer genres and to expand their programmes. But the programmes in their diversity have to fulfil certain standards. The programme obligations are enshrined in the LRT in the Articles 10–19.

§1. Definition and Obligations

588. The LRT in its paragraph 1, item 3[239] of its additional provisions defines the programme as a system of all elements that creates and distributes the operator and which carries certain content, distributed in an hour schedule.[240] The LRT determines the programme[241] obligations, which can be classified into three different categories: (i) basic principles applicable to all broadcasters; (ii) principles applicable to public service broadcasters; and (iii) programme requirements for BNT and BNR.

589. Basic programme principles applicable to all broadcasters concern the fact that media service broadcasters are responsible for the content of their programmes and should, consequently, prevent the creation of programmes inciting national, political, ethnic, religious and racial intolerance, praising or exculpating cruelty or violence, or programmes which may threaten the physical, mental, moral or social development of children (Article 17, paragraphs 1, 2 and 3 of the LRT). Paragraph 6 of the same article relates to impartiality and stipulates that facts in the news must be distinguished from commentaries. Article 32, paragraph 3 of the LRT foresees access of the public to events of significant public interest. Article 82, paragraph 1

239. In its previous wording, the LRT defined the programme as a system of all elements that creates and distributes the operator *through a signal of a definite frequency* and which is a bearer of certain content, distributed in an hour schedule. Such wording was not taking into consideration the other ways of broadcasting, such as the cable or the satellite broadcasting and thus the disseminated by them content was outside the legal definition of programme. Furthermore, para. 1, item 1 of the additional provisions of the LRT stipulates that 'broadcasting' is the original transmission or broadcasting, regardless of the technology used, of a radio or television programme intended for reception from the viewers or listeners. It includes the exchange (retransmission) of programmes between operators to be accepted by the audience. It does not include electronic communications services for individual use.

240. There are eight-hour schedules: early morning (6:00 to 9:00), morning (9:00 to 12:00), noon (12:00 to 14:00), early afternoon (14:00 to 16:00), afternoon (16:00 to 18:00), early evening (18:00 to 20:00), evening (20:00 to 23:00) and night (23:00 to 6:00). The latest hour schedule is normally used for the replay of already broadcasted programmes during the day.

241. Depending on the scope of their dissemination, the programmes can be national, regional and local (Art. 110, para. 5 of the LRT). The national programmes are transmitted throughout the country. The regional programmes are broadcast within a specified region including more than one built-up area, opposite to the local programmes, which are intended for the residents of a specific built-up area.

states that sponsored advertising cannot influence the content of the programme and independence of the media service broadcaster or total prohibition of sponsorship messages in a specific type of programme (Article 82, paragraphs 3 and 4).[242]

590. Article 6 of the LRT contains the programme obligation of the public radio and television broadcasters. It also contains the programme obligations of BNT and BNR. Regarding the commercial broadcasters, their programme obligations are defined only in their broadcast licences, issued by the CEM.

§2. IMPARTIALITY

591. The main activity of the media is to inform the public. If this is true for every kind of programme, news, in whatever form they are presented, must be reported with accuracy and impartiality. According to Article 17, paragraph 6 of the LRT, the news as information facts should be distinguished from the comments to them. Of course, opinionated journalism is possible in 'personal view' transmissions, which present a particular view or perspective and are acknowledged to do so. For example, in a political transmission, the political allegiance of such a person must be made clear to the audience.

592. Journalists should respect and protect the principles of impartiality and equal treatment to all subjects of social, political and economic life. In the so-long discussed LRT, consensus on how much media power must be constrained was difficult to reach. Too much media freedom and lack of responsibility could have threatened the consolidation of the new democracy in Bulgaria. In that regard 'reasonably' free media were encouraged. The term 'reasonably' being highly subjective, may easily allow for various forms of censorship.[243] The respect of the abovementioned principles is provided only in paragraph 36, item 1 of the Final Provisions of the Law amending the LRT which stipulates that an operator, which was granted permission for use of individually assigned frequency spectrum for the provision of electronic communications, should respect the principles of objectivity, impartiality, non-discrimination and equality. Concerning the journalists, these principles are supposed to be respected by the media which signed the Code of Ethics.

593. The media function in Bulgaria meets different problems. It has been suggested that impartiality is sometimes understood as a total lack of journalistic position or that the media is perceived as being a part of any authority and not as the voice of the diverse interests of civil society. In that regard, some media present the facts but are not conducive to discussion and do not give objective and impartial author comments or review analysis. Some journalists may be tempted to chase the

242. R. Nikolova, in R. Tcholakov, et al., *Media Law: Dictionary of the Main Concepts* 352–353 (Trud 2005).
243. J. Pope, *Independent and Free Media* 6 (Transparency International).

scoop, not the deepening of the problem.[244] Moreover, as was already said in the introduction to this work, very often the media in Bulgaria are controlled by individual interest groups, which are used as a tool for achieving private interests. The main issues for discussion are not always visible from both sides with enough information, explanations and access to real facts.[245]

§3. Cultural Diversity

594. In the context of globalization and technological developments, media broadcasters try to offer more programmes with wider content. The EU tries to protect and make the best of its cultural diversity in the context of globalization by creating media policies. In this part, we will have a quick overview of the EU, most importantly, audiovisual legislation and the Bulgarian legislation which respects the EU principles of cultural development. The EU legislation regulates the television media but the EU countries, including Bulgaria, apply these principles also to the radio.

I. Cultural Diversity in the Programmes at the EU Level

595. In order to promote cultural diversity at its level, the EU approach is twofold. First, it relies on directives which Bulgaria as a Member State must transpose in its national law so that EU standards apply to its audiovisual services. Also, various European programmes are available.

596. Article 151, paragraph 1 of the Treaty establishing the EU stipulates that the Community shall contribute to the flowering of the cultures of the Member States while respecting their national and regional diversity and at the same time bringing the common cultural heritage to the fore. According to paragraph 2 of the same article, the Community shall encourage the cooperation between Member States and, if necessary, support and supplement their action in areas such as the non-commercial cultural exchange and artistic and literary creation, including in the audiovisual sector.

597. Moreover, the TWF requires the Member States to ensure the coordination of their national legislation in order to ensure that:

- there are no obstacles to the free movement of television programmes on their territory (Article 2);
- television channels, where practicable, reserve at least half their broadcasting time for the production of European works (Article 5);

244. *See* http://temanews.com/index.php?p=tema&iid=255&aid=6170.
245. *See* http://www.media-journal.info/?p=item&aid=218; http://www.dnevnik.bg/bulgaria/2013/01/03/1977877_jurnalistite_v_bulgariia_si_nalagat_avtocenzura/.

- minors are protected against violent or pornographic programmes or any other programmes which are likely to impair their physical, mental or moral development by scheduling them late at night and/or by limiting access through a technical measure (Article 22);
- any individual or legal entity, unfairly criticized in a television broadcast has the right to reply (Article 23); and
- the maximum transmission of advertising and teleshopping broadcasting could not exceed a given period measured in minutes per hour or per day (Article 18).

598. Finally, the measures contained in this directive, such as cultural diversity, should be respected and correctly applied by broadcasters under their jurisdiction. Member States will provide the Commission with a report on the application of the proportions reserved for European works and independent productions in this Directive (Preamble).

599. In order to better protect the right of information of the European citizens, in June 1997 the European Parliament and the Council adopted a new TWF which aims to update the initial rules concerning the pursuit of television broadcasting activities. The main topics concerned by the new Directive 97/36/EC were events of major importance for society, such as international sports events, teleshopping and protection of minors.

600. In December 2007, the Commission presented the new Audiovisual Media Service Directive (AVMSD)[246] which amended the TWF and whose main purpose was to take into account the technological and market developments in the European audiovisual sector. The AVMSD has to cover both traditional television broadcasting and new on-demand services like on-demand films and news. The Directive also contributes to media and information pluralism, cultural and linguistic diversity, as well as freedom of speech.

601. It should be mentioned also that the EU has created support programmes for the European audiovisual industry – the Media Programmes. They are often called 'the other instrument' besides the above-mentioned directives. We could mention the Media 2007 programme (2007–2013),[247] which objectives are to strive

246. It should be noted that it is not clear from the AVMSD whether the Member States should include in their reports on promotion and distribution of EU works, the percentage of their own production, or select a clearer and differenced method distinguishing their own production from the European one. In that regard most of the Member States also include their own productions. In contrast, the LRT provides two clearly distinct legal definitions – for European production and for Bulgarian audiovisual works. The concept of Bulgarian audiovisual works has obviously a more limited scope, the main criteria being the relationship between the work itself and Bulgaria or Bulgarian citizenship.

247. The EU MEDIA Programme was started in January 2001 and was aimed to improve the competitiveness of the European audiovisual industry. Bulgaria became a member of the Media programme before joining the EU. In 2002, the country signed a memorandum of understanding with the EU and has joined the programme with Decision No. 514 of the Council of Ministers on 26 Jul. 2002.

for a stronger European audiovisual sector and to increase the circulation of European audiovisual works inside and outside the EU; the MEDIA Mundus programme (2011–2013) which aim is to bring more culturally diverse products to European and international markets; and the Media Literacy programme, which relates to all media, including television and film, radio and recorded music, print media, Internet and new digital communication technologies. The aim of this programme is to help European citizens to better understand the media and have critical approach towards media contents. Here we can also mention the European Programme Culture, which has been established to enhance the cultural area shared by Europeans and based on a common cultural heritage through the development of cooperation activities among cultural operators. The Education, Audiovisual and Culture Executive Agency (EACEA) is responsible for the management of the EU Programmes 2007–2013 in the fields of education, culture and audiovisual.

II. Cultural Diversity in the Programmes in Bulgaria

602. According to Article 6, paragraph 2 of the LRT, the main function of the public providers of audiovisual media services is to provide political, economic, cultural, scientific, educational and other socially relevant information for all citizens of the Republic of Bulgaria. The Bulgarian citizens have access to national and world cultural values and scientific and technological knowledge through the dissemination of Bulgarian and foreign educational and cultural programmes and programmes for all age groups. Furthermore, the public providers provide through their programme policy protection of the national interests, the universal cultural values, national science, education and culture of all Bulgarian citizens regardless of their ethnicity.

603. Paragraph 3 of the same article refers more precisely to BNT and BNR. They facilitate the development and the popularization of the Bulgarian culture and Bulgarian language, as well as of the culture and the language of the citizens in compliance with their ethnic belonging. They include programmes that inform, educate and entertain and apply new information technologies. Furthermore, BNT and BNR should ensure through their media services access not only to national but also to the European cultural heritage. It should be noted that according to Article 20, paragraph 1 of the Law for Protection and Development of Culture, the Minister of Culture and the General Directors of BNT and BNR conclude contracts about broadcasting programmes in the field of culture, including TV movies. The contracts specify the obligations of the BNT and BNR about the creation, presentation and dissemination of the cultural values with presence of Bulgarian highly artistic production. For example, BNT created the initiative 'The Bulgarian Cinema' to present the achievements of the Bulgarian cinema. Under this initiative, the BNT presents its viewers favourite Bulgarian movies, as well as Bulgarian films produced in the recent years and which have received international recognition. Under the heading of 'BNT presents', BNT proposes the audience the Bulgarian movies released in the last two years. By the prevalence of the Bulgarian films, BNT is promoting Bulgarian culture, as the only way these films reach the people in the smaller settlements is precisely television.[248]

604. Of course, in the programme of BNT and especially in the programmes of the commercial providers of audiovisual media services, there is also a high presence of non-European films and series.

III. Variety of Programmes

605. The programmes of most television and radio broadcasters can be characterized in different categories according to their content and depending on the specific groups of viewers or listeners they aim to reach. According to paragraph 28 of the additional provisions of the LRT, by the selection of its programmes, the television or radio stations can be defined in a given programme profile. It clearly stipulates that the programme profile is a characteristic of the programme according to the specifics of its content and its direction to the audience. Depending on the specifics of the programme profile, the programme may contain information oriented transmissions (news and current affairs), cultural orientated transmissions, transmissions for educational purpose, entertainment-oriented transmissions, own or independent producers transmissions, European production, etc. Furthermore, paragraph 28 precises that on their part the radio and television broadcasters can be of general (multi-thematic) or specialized profile. The first case is when the radio and television programmes of the operators contain transmissions with informational, educational, cultural and entertaining purpose designated for the prevailing part of the society. In the other case, we have radio and television programme of specialized nature designed for a limited part of the society.[249] In case of specialized programme profile, the applicant must specify its thematic focus.

248. Report of the activity of the BNT for the period 1 Apr. 2008–30 Sep. 2008, 14–16; Declaration of the Association of the Television Producers. For the period between 2 Jan. 2011 and 31 Jul. 2011 more than half of the films broadcasted by BNT were European. Today BNT has no competition when it comes to volume broadcast in Bulgarian and European titles. In season 2010–2011 BNT produced and broadcasted the first season of the series Undercover which was a very successful project for BNT 1. It was released by the Producing Centre Studio Screen. It was one of top-rated films from the public. The BNT has shown that it was able to impose a market trend, which feature normally is dominated by the private broadcasters and by which BNT for the first time effectively competed Nova TV and bTV in this genre. The realization of the second season of the Undercover was defined as a priority in the film making programme of BNT for the upcoming television season – Report of the Activity of the BNT for the period 1 Feb. 2011–31 Jul. 2011, 4–5.

249. The specialized programme profile can be monothematic (news, sports, etc.) or mixed – cultural and educational, film and music, film and sports, etc. – R. Nikolova, in Tcholakov, et al., *Media Law: Dictionary of the Main Concepts*, 346 (Trud 2005).

606. All the programmes of a given broadcaster provided for broadcasting are contained in the programme scheme of the broadcaster. Paragraph 31 of the additional provisions of the LRT defines the programme scheme as the sum of all transmissions intended for broadcasting or already broadcasted by a given electronic media, arranged in a graphic form in days and hours for a definite period of time.

607. For the programme scheme, the broadcasters who want to participate in a procedure for licences must describe shortly the content of the main transmissions. The description should also inform about the hour of the beginning and the duration of the transmission, the day of its broadcasting, as well as its genre characteristics – films, interviews, news, etc. Each broadcaster tries to have a programme scheme,[250] which is characterized by a wide variety of genres and an excellent selection of television programmes.

608. BNT and BNR also wanted to be competitive and proposed a high range of programmes. BNT started a structural reform willing, among other things, to develop the existing TV formats and present new transmissions in order to become the television of the viewers.[251]

609. BNR has not only initiated technical and technological reforms but also focused on the development of its programmes, including the creation of new integrated programmes between the national and the regional programmes and interactive dialogue with the listeners. New musical and entertainment emissions were created in order to find a better balance between culture, education and music. In 2011, BNR started twenty-one new regional programmes. From 1 July 2009, BNR started to broadcast programmes as a member of the European radio network Euranet, funded by the European Commission. BNR has also created a Directorate called Internet and digital programmes in order to develop a multimedia programme orientated to the young audience with specialized interests in music, culture, arts and users with high-tech attitude.[252]

610. The CEM exercises the monitoring on the compliance of the programmes of the different broadcasters with the programme profile and programme characteristics, which are contained in the licences for radio and television activities.

Despite the fact that all the broadcasters try to have a wide variety of programmes in order to attract larger audience, some critics have been expressed on the similarities between the programmes of the different broadcasters. It is true that examples are not missing – similar TV films, identical TV shows like the dancing

250. According to people who are in the media sphere, to make their television programme schemes, the media rely on 50% on the public opinion research and for the rest it is a matter of sense of the people's taste. The first thing to do in the schemes are the news, the morning and evening programme blocks, and the rest of the time is filled with other transmissions. A particular attention is paid to the female audience because it is considered that women get more easily addicted to a programme.
251. Report of the activity of the BNT for the period 1 Feb. 2011–31 Jul. 2011, 3.
252. Report for the programme, technical, business and financial activity of the BNR for the period 1 Dec. 2010–31 May 2011.

shows 'Dancing stars' on bTV or 'VIP dance' on Nova TV or the shows for singers 'X-factor' on Nova TV and 'The Voice of Bulgaria' on bTV. People often wonder which show to follow because they are broadcasted on the same time on the different channels. The explanation for this is of course that the competitors seek to achieve the same results as the broadcasters who first launched the given transmission and copy literally the successful emissions and broadcast them at the same hour instead of looking for an alternative programming. As a matter of fact, the most part of the viewers do not want new Bulgarian television channels, but better quality and a larger selection of TV programmes.[253]

611. In 2004, the reality show format entered the Bulgarian media market attracting a massive and quick interest, especially with the young audience. The first show of that kind was Big Brother. Since the programmes are filled with different formats of reality shows and the Bulgarian viewer began to wonder which one to watch. The interest diminished a little bit somewhat over time, but the TV film after the news gradually disappeared replaced by the different formats of reality shows.

IV. Linguistic Requirements

612. Article 12, paragraph 1 of the LRT stipulates that the programmes must be broadcasted in the official language under the Constitution of the Republic of Bulgaria, which according to Article 3 of the Constitution is the Bulgarian. Paragraph 2 of the same article provides for the possibility that some programmes or individual transmissions can be broadcasted in a language other than Bulgarian in the cases: (i) when they are broadcasted for educational purposes; (ii) designed for Bulgarian citizens for whom Bulgarian is not the mother language; (iii) or are meant for listeners or viewers from abroad; and (iv) in case when foreign radio and television programmes are broadcasted in Bulgaria.

613. Since 2001, the programme licence of BNT states that BNT will broadcast every day in the afternoon news in Turkish aimed at the Turkish minority in Bulgaria. The news in Turkish is supposed to be watched by fifty to sixty thousand people. This decision was criticized and a subscription list against the broadcasting of news in Turkish on BNT was created. The BNT stressed that its programme licences require broadcasts in Turkish and that change in the programme licence may be made only at the request of the board of the television and this in the presence of motives that are not in breach of the LRT. The option to move them into a regional programme of the BNT is not appropriate because the news will only be available for people in this region, and, however, they will not clearly cover topics of national scope. If the news in Turkish is removed from BNT, they will need to be replaced by other programmes in Turkish, which are aimed at this minority. According to the Director of the BNT of that time, the problem is that BNT has only one programme that must meet all specifications, mentioned by the LRT. If BNT had

---

253. CEM, *Development of the Radio and Television Activity in the Republic of Bulgaria (2001–2006)*, 160.

more national programmes, such programmes would be on the second programme, as it is in many countries of Europe, and such problem had never existed. The question of the presence of Turkish news on national television was raised before the CEM, which categorically stated that the news in Turkish is not in violation of the LRT.

614. There is a radio station called ROMA, whose staff is mainly comprised of Roma people, but it airs programmes in Bulgarian.

615. Finally, one should stress that today Bulgarian journalists are more and more using foreign words, in particular English words, in the news. At first, it may seem an ordinary thing that today in one language people use words from other languages, e.g., from the neighbouring countries or the English language. The problem is that Bulgarian is a Slavic language and people from small villages, especially older people, may have some difficulties understanding the news. It is a really serious remark to make towards the journalist language today.

§4. Protection of Minors

616. The Bulgarian legislation provides standards for the protection of children from harmful television influence. They are contained in the Constitution, the Law for Child Protection (LChP), the Criminal Code, the LRT, as well as the Law on Film Industry (LFI).[254]

I. Legislative Measures

617. According to Article 2 of the LChP and as it is adopted in international law, a child is any person who is less than 18 years old. As stipulated by Article 14 of the Constitution, children are protected by the state and society. The Bulgarian legislation provides a legal definition of child protection. The meaning of the term child protection is defined in paragraph 1 of the Additional provisions of the LChP as a system of legislative, administrative and other measures guaranteeing the rights of every child.

618. The Bulgarian penal code punishes the creation, publication on whatever form it takes and the distribution of pornographic materials, including the distribution of child pornography. Precisely, Article 159, paragraph 1 of the Criminal Code stipulates that one who creates, displays, presents, transmits, distributes, sells, rents or otherwise distributes pornographic material shall be punished by imprisonment of one year and a fine of EUR 51,700 to EUR 1,550. Paragraph 2 of the same article

254. Bulgaria also ratified on 11 Apr. 1991 the Convention of the Rights of the Child of the United Nations.

focuses on the web space and stipulates that those who distribute through the Internet or in other similar ways pornographic materials shall be punished by imprisonment for up to two years and a fine of EUR 50,000 to 15,000. These provisions concern all types of media.

619. Article 11, paragraphs 1 and 2 of the LChP can also refer to media because the media, in their activity, must follow some principles to protect children. The two paragraphs stipulate that every child has the right of protection against involvement in activities adverse to his physical, mental, moral and educational development or against any physical, psychological or other forms of violence and impact, which are contrary to his/her interests, as well as against the dissemination of pornographic materials. In this line, according to Article 36 of the LFI, the distribution and/or the display of films in Bulgaria is possible after the reception of a visa to the applicant from the Bulgarian National Film Centre (NFC).

620. The Executive Agency NFC is a legal entity funded by the Ministry of Culture and implementing the state cultural policy in the field of cinema. The National Commission for Film Classification (CFC)[255] is an expert advisory body to the NFC, which according to Article 37, paragraph 4 of the LFI in term of seven days from the reception of the application of the regularly shaped demand for visa shall determine the category of the film. There are five possible categories of the films: (i) category 'A' (recommended for children) – when the film is for children and has educational character; (ii) category 'B' (no age restrictions) – when the film confirms the ideals of humanism, promotes national and world culture, or in no way is contrary to the accepted moral standards in the country and has no restrictive recommendations by the CFC; (iii) category 'C' (not recommended for children under 12) – when the film contains a few scenes of erotic content or use of alcohol, drugs or stimulants or a few scenes of violence; (iv) category 'D' (no persons under 16) – when the film contains a significant number of scenes with erotic content or use of alcohol, drugs or stimulants or a considerable number of scenes with violence; and (v) category 'X' (no persons under 18) – when the film is naturalistically erotic or particularly aggressive.

621. Films whose content is contrary to the accepted moral standards and laud or exculpate atrocity, violence or drug use, incite hatred based on race, sexuality, religion or nationality are not categorized (Article 37, paragraph 5 of the LFI). This means that such a film will not reach the audience because according to paragraph 8 of the same article, the Executive Director of the agency refuses to issue visas when the film has not been classified according to paragraph 5. These measures contained in Article 37, paragraph 5 are analogues to the measures contained in Article

255. Its members are appointed for a term of two years. The commission includes representatives of the Ministry of Culture, the Ministry of Education, Youth and Science, the National Council for Cinema, which is also an expert advisory body to the NFC, the NFC and a psychologist. This is the body which determines the category of any film to be distributed in Bulgaria.

10, paragraph 1, items 5 and 6 and Article 17, paragraph 2 of the LRT, which forbids the broadcasting of programmes which incite hatred among citizens or are contrary to morality, especially if they contain pornography, praise or exculpate cruelty or violence or incite to hatred based on race, sexuality, religion or nationality. Moreover, Article 17, paragraph 2 precises that the media service broadcasters are required to prevent the creation or distribution of programmes which threaten to harm the physical, mental, moral and/or social development of children. Similarly, Article 5, paragraph 3 of the LRT ensures the freedom of reception, as well as the retransmission of media services from other EU Member States, but paragraph 4, stipulates that paragraph 3 may temporarily not apply to programmes from another Member State of the EU if they violate Article 17, paragraph 2 of the LRT.

622. In order to protect children from unsuitable contents, the LRT foresees time limits for transmissions which may endanger their welfare. Such transmissions must be broadcasted between 23:00 and 6:00 hours and must be clearly marked at the beginning by an audio and/or audiovisual sign or with a visual symbol throughout the transmission (Article 17, paragraph 2 of the LRT).

623. Article 19d of the LRT concerns the broadcasters of on-demand media services. According to this article, they must make their services available in a way to ensure that children will not normally hear or see such media services which can seriously impair their physical, mental or moral development.

624. Children are protected not only as an audience but also as participants in the media sphere. According to Article 17a(7) of the LRT, the media service providers are not allowed to make children participate in programmes that threaten to harm their physical, mental, moral and/or social development. According to this article, the broadcasters are obliged to respect the rights of the children listed in the Law on Child Protection or in any other enactment. They should also respect the criteria for evaluation of the content developed by the CEM[256] and the State Agency for Child Protection and adopt pursuant to Article 32, paragraph 6 of the LRT.

II. Non-legislative Measures

625. Today the development of telecommunication technologies has opened up access to the widest possible range of programmes (DVB-T, DVB-C, DVB-S, DVB-H) through the offer of many commercial and public service providers, and the media exercise a larger influence over children. For that reason, it is very important to pay attention to the programmes they are offering. The broadcasters not only offer different kinds of programmes, which might be educational but also contain violence or a particular topic not appropriate for children. That is why, besides the legislative measures, there are also additional programmes or strategies which are

256. On its meeting held on 25 Oct. 2011, CEM discussed the criteria for evaluation of content that is adverse or creates risk of damage to physical, mental, moral and/or social development of children – Decision No. 234 of CEM and the State Agency for Child Protection.

aimed at reinforcing the protection of children from harmful television influence. Also, the Bulgarian Code of Ethics of the media contains rules related to child protection when the child is a participant in the media space.

626. Concerning the Code of Ethics, the media have to observe the rights of children, including their right to be heard. It will not take advantage of the inexperience and trustfulness of children and will not publish information or photos for the privacy of children unless a significant public interest requires it. Neither will the media disclose the identity of children in distress or affected by crime. Moreover, the media will avoid interviewing children without the consent of the adults responsible for them.

627. Following the amendment of the LRT to transpose Directive (EU) 2018/1808, on 1 February 2023, Bulgaria enforced the 'Code of Conduct[257] on the Measures for Assessment, Designation and Limitation of Access to Programmes that are Unfavourable or Create a Risk of Physical Harm, Mental, Moral and (or) Social Development of Children (Code of Conduct),' which regulates child safety in media and video-sharing platforms. The Code of Conduct was developed by CEM, the ABBRO, the BNR and the BNT, according to Article 17a, paragraph 3 of the LRT.[258] It was adopted by CEM Decision No. RD-05-7 of 12 January 2023. According to Article 17a, paragraph 5 of the LRT, the Code of Conduct is mandatory for all media service and video-sharing platform providers.

628. Concerning the national programmes or strategies, there are a few national programmes which establish priorities and needs. For example, the National Strategy for Child Protection (2008–2018) considers that it is necessary that public broadcasters develop specialized educational and entertainment programmes for children and devote at least a quarter of their programme time to children's programmes, broadcasted at appropriate times. Furthermore, public broadcasters should create programmes and competitions that stimulate children's creativity and evolve capacities. The strategy considers that not only the public but also all the media should be encouraged in this direction. A special framework to monitor the impact of advertising on children should be created, as well as a better system for controlling children's access to information on the Internet.

629. There are also national programmes dedicated to protecting children from harmful Internet content. For example, the National Programme for Child Protection aims to raise public and child awareness about the risks of child abuse on the Internet by informing children how to protect themselves and to establish a partnership between various state institutions, non-governmental organizations working in child protection, children's organizations and Internet providers as a basis for further joint action on these issues.

---

257. Available in Bulgarian at https://cem.bg/files/1673946952_code__17a.pdf.
258. Available in Bulgarian at https://www.abbro-bg.org/ кодексът-за-поведение-относно-меркит/.

630. There are also social media made especially for children like the portal www.az-deteto.com, which offers games, songs, stories and other reading and educational materials for children of different ages.

631. In 2005, the Bulgarian Safer Internet Hotline (web112.net) was created, co-funded by the European Commission within the framework of the Safer Internet Programme, to fight against illegal and harmful content, primarily in the fields of child pornography or violence against children by other Internet users.

III. Sanctions

632. The CEM oversees the programmes of the broadcasters for their compliance with the provisions concerning transmissions aimed at children (Article 33, item 7 of the LRT). In case of violations, the CEM is required to decide within one month on the imposition of a penalty or the withdrawal of the licence (Article 118 of the LRT). The CEM has imposed numerous monetary sanctions on a number of operators for infringing the provisions of Article 10, paragraph 1, item 6; Article 17, paragraph 2 and Article 76 of the LRT.

633. One of the most frequently cited case in the practice of CEM concerning programmes with content inappropriate for children is related to the suspension (after wide public discussion) of the wrestling shows 'Raw Force' and 'SmackDown' broadcasted by bTV before 11 p.m. According to CEM, broadcasting programmes containing violence before this time hours contravenes the law. The CEM asked the television to comply with the requirements of its licence and to terminate those broadcasts. According to bTV, the decision of the CEM is void because the council has no right to interfere in the media programmes. Thus, bTV appealed the decision before the SAC. According to the Court, the complaint was unfounded.[259] The CEM wanted bTV to comply with the requirements of the issued licence and actually legitimately exercise its powers.

634. The CEM also found a violation of the LRT in the broadcasted reality show 'Fear' on Nova TV. A 13-year-old child accidentally hung himself while playing on the playground in imitation of a popular TV show. In this show, participants overcome stages with varying degrees of difficulty associated with physical exertion and dangerous stunts. Days after the incident, the CEM came with the position that the television format violates the LRT and has to be moved to a later hour. Finally, the CEM indicated that the transmission will continue to be broadcasted without hour change. The only change will be an additional signalling 'Recommended Parental Control' and repeated voice warnings during the game.

635. According to Article 126, paragraph 4 of the LRT concerning the administrative liability provisions for violation of Article 17, paragraph 2; Article 17a;

259. Decision No. 6284 of Supreme Administrative Court of 28 Jun. 2002.

Article 19, paragraph 1; Article 75, paragraphs 7 and 9 and Article 77 the media service providers shall be liable to sanction from EUR 7,500 to 15,000.

§5. Human Dignity

636. Human rights and human dignity are inextricably linked. Human rights can be linked either to the respect of the private sphere of the person or to the respect of the person as a human being. Ensuring this respect is, first and foremost, the task of the Constitution. The Bulgarian Constitution contains a set of constitutionally protected rights. Similarly, these same rights are also protected in the LRT because the media should do the balancing between these rights and the public interest.

I. Constitutional Protection of Human Rights

637. At the beginning of the Constitution, precisely in Article 6, it is said that all persons are born free and equal in dignity and rights. It requires that there shall be no privileges or restriction of rights on the grounds of race, national or social origin, ethnic identity, sex, religion, education, opinion, political affiliation, personal, social or property status. The Constitution clearly states that all citizens shall be equal before the law.

638. Concerning the respect of the private sphere of the person, the privacy of citizens shall be inviolable and in that regard, everyone shall be entitled to protection against any unlawful interference in their private or family affairs and against encroachments on their honour, dignity and reputation (Article 32, paragraph 1). Furthermore, paragraph 2 stipulates that no one shall be followed, photographed, filmed, recorded or subjected to any other similar activity without his knowledge or despite his express disapproval, except when such actions are permitted by law. It can be precised that Articles 33 and 34 of the Constitution respectively provide for the inviolability of the home and the confidentiality of the correspondence. The aim of this set of constitutionally protected rights is the protection of the intimate sphere of every person.

II. The LRT and the Human Rights

639. The LRT also provides for the protection of the private life of the individuals. Article 16, paragraph 1 states that the media service providers cannot create and broadcast programmes containing information related to the privacy of the citizens without their consent. The definition of private life is contained in paragraph 1, item 21 of the Additional provisions of the LRT according to which for this law private life is the life of a person in family, health and sexual aspects. By contrast, the media service providers may include in their broadcasts information about the private lives of people, who exercise powers of state authorities or whose decisions have an impact on society and in that regard is of public interest. The public figures should expect to be observed and photographed, which of course does not mean that they do not have the right to have private life and privacy. The difficulty here is to find a balanced presentation of the facts. In particular, one has to define which are the media revelations or investigations that violate privacy but satisfy the strong public interest and the facts, and which are media revelations or investigations that violate privacy and which are interesting for a significant part of society but are not of public interest.[260] For that reason, the moral judgment of the journalist is very important. However, the so-called paparazzi journalism stays out of this ethical dilemma.

640. However, today emerged transmission formats in which deeply personal and intimate questions are exported to the media by the people themselves.[261] These kind of TV shows, which destroy the taboos of privacy and private life are developing, and Bulgaria is not an exception to this new phenomenon.

641. Moreover, Article 6, paragraph 2, item 3 and paragraph 3, item 7 promote mutual understanding and tolerance in human relations and defend universal cultural values, as well as assess the protection of national interests, science, education and culture of all Bulgarian citizens regardless of their ethnicity. These positive obligations concern the public media providers.

642. However, Article 10 and Article 17 of the LRT contain negative obligations for the respect of human dignity. According to these two articles, the media service providers must prevent the broadcasting of transmissions, which incite hatred based on race, sex, religion or nationality (Article 10, paragraph 1, item 6) or prompt national, political, ethnic, religious and racial intolerance (Article 17, paragraph 2). According to Article 5, paragraph 5, item 1 in case of incitement to hatred based on race, sex, religion or nationality and violations of human dignity of individuals, the freedom of reception and retransmission of media services from other countries – Members of the EU – may temporarily not be applied concerning the media services on demand.

643. Moreover, the Council of Europe, of which Bulgaria is a member, in its Recommendation (97) 20 of the Committee of Ministers to Member States on Hate Speech sets the principles which apply to hate speech, in particular when disseminated through the media. According to this recommendation, the term hate speech shall be understood as covering all forms of expression which spread, incite, promote or justify racial hatred, xenophobia, anti-Semitism or other forms of hatred based on intolerance, including: intolerance expressed by aggressive nationalism and ethnocentrism, discrimination and hostility against minorities, migrants and people of immigrant origin.

644. Also concerning hate speech, it is important to mention Alpha the European Court of Human Rights case *Jersild v. Denmark* decided in 1994, as it is very

260. V. Tabakova, *The Freedom of Expression and Journalistic Ethics* 52 (University Press Saint Kliment Ohridski 2008).
261. For example, 'Big Brother', or the Bulgarian transmissions 'Sea of love' and 'You Have Mail'.

important for the practice of European journalists. The Court protected the freedom of media coverage of debates on racism, xenophobia, religious intolerance, etc. In this particular case, the journalist Mr Jens Olaf Jersild, who had conducted and edited a TV interview with members of a group of young people, calling themselves 'the Greenjackets', who made abusive and derogatory remarks about immigrants and ethnic groups in Denmark during the interview, has also been prosecuted for broadcasting it. The Court decided that Denmark violated Article 10 of ECHR (freedom of expression), stressing that 'the punishment of a journalist for assisting in the dissemination of statements made by another person in an interview would seriously hamper the contribution of the press to discussion of matters of public interest and should not be envisaged unless there are particularly strong reasons for doing so' (paragraph 34). In the opinion of the Court, it is 'moreover undisputed that the purpose of the applicant in compiling the broadcast in question was not racist' (paragraph 36). For the Court, the purpose or intent of Jersild was not to promote racism but, on the contrary, to expose and analyse it.

645. Ignoring such kind of problems is not and should not be the solution. Journalists have the freedom of expression but should be careful how they present the news, not to be influenced by social divisions including class, race, ethnicity, gender, age and sexuality. What was said is important for the Bulgarian media concerning the media approach to the coverage of the Roma people.[262] The difficult situation of the Roma concerning not only their integration into the labour process, and their problems with education, housing, health and poverty but also criminality starts to provoke social tensions between Bulgarians and Roma.[263] The media approach to how they will cover minority issues is very important in order not to create ethnic hierarchies and stereotypes.[264]

262. National strategy of the Republic of Bulgaria for the integration of Roma (2012–2020), 17.
263. *See* http://www.fes.bg/files/custom/calendar/2007/03/Romite_v_Bulgaria_Doklad.pdf.
264. *See* http://www.mediapool.bg.

Chapter 4. Political Broadcasting

646. As was mentioned above, the media are called the fourth power because they are those that explain what happens to society, filter information, and seek the truth. To put it otherwise, the media can create a positive or negative image of people and put the attention of the public on anything they want to. Whether it is about television, radio, newspapers, magazines, books or the Internet, independence is a precondition for having alternative viewpoints; it determines what we see, hear and read. In that regard, the objectivity and independence of the media is also important for the politicians themselves. For that reason, there are rules for the political independence of the broadcasters, as well as for the fair representation of the political parties in election periods. We should also note that there are special rules concerning political advertising.

§1. Rules on Political Independence of Broadcasters

647. As previously discussed in the introduction, the new LRT of 1998, in its Article 5, paragraph 1 guarantees the independence of the broadcaster of media services and their activity from political and economic interference. Beyond this, paragraph 2 of the same article states that there shall be no censorship of media services in any form. But to say that is not enough, there must be means which shall guarantee that the broadcast will take place in an independent and efficient manner and these means are mentioned in other articles of the LRT.

648. According to Article 32, paragraph 1 of the LRT, the CEM elects and releases the General Directors of BNR and BNT. The fact that the CEM elects the General Directors, who on the other side propose the members of the Management Board of BNT and BNR, can be a problem for the independence of the BNT and BNR unless the CEM itself is entirely independent of any political influence. This is of the utmost importance as the CEM is the organ that supervises the activities of BNT and BNR (Article 32, paragraph 1, item 1 of the LRT), elects and dismisses the General Directors (Article 32, paragraph 1, item 2), approves the board members (Article 32, paragraph 1, item 3) and gives its opinion on the draft state subsidy to BNR and BNT (Article 32, paragraph 1, item 5). What is striking here is that CEM has a very big power over the BNT and BNR because it has the privilege to decide not only on the board members and Director but also on the budget of the two public operators regarding the subsidy from the state budget. The way the members of CEM are appointed is not safe from political interference.

649. According to Article 70, paragraph 3 of the LRT, the budgets of BNR and BNT include financial support from the fund 'Radio and Television', subsidies from the state budget, as well as other revenues such as own incomes from advertisements and sponsorship, revenues from additional activities related to the radio and television activity, donations, inheritances and interests and other incomes related to the radio and television activity. Paragraph 4 of the same article specifies that the subsidies from the state budget must be accorded for the preparation, creation and broadcasting of national and regional programmes. The subsidies are determined on the basis of normative per hour of programmes approved by the Council of Ministers.

650. The LRT is often criticized for providing such subsidies that distort the market by placing the BNT and BNR in a privileged position. In fact, this is an argument that is often used against the public media. The contra argument for this is that BNT and BNT are media with public functions and thus they have specific powers and duties. Also, they are limited in the broadcast of commercial messages and respectively in the manner of their financing. The outcome is that the state gives money but at the same time sets the legislative framework for the public media.

651. In the case of commercial media, which does not fulfil a public function, flexibility in decision-making is slightly larger.

652. In order to take into consideration these critics of the LRT regarding the place of public service broadcasting and its financing, it was decided that a new bill amending the LRT should be elaborated. The new media law had to seek balance and transparency between the media, and from the very beginning of its elaboration, the opinions of the experts in the media area must be taken into consideration. Besides, the chairman of the CEM proposed that the new media law regulate all types of media, including print and online editions. The representatives of the print media, however, declared themselves against this law, as, according to them such an intervention of a regulatory body as CEM may throw a shadow of censorship and would not improve the quality of journalism. This new law or the concepts for it had to be submitted for discussion in the National Assembly at the latest in November 2010.

653. There are three most important changes. First, these amendments consider the technological neutrality of the content. With the end of analogue broadcasting and the development of the technologies, various ways of transmission for the same content became available and it would have been useless to have different rules applying to these various ways. In that regard, the words 'via satellite' in paragraph 3 of Article 44 of the LRT concerning the broadcasting of the programmes of BNT and BNR were deleted. Second, a part of the money set in the fund 'Radio and Television' will finance projects of private media, but only if they are of exceptional public interest.

654. Concerning commercial broadcasters, Article 5, paragraph 1 of the LRT is the basis for guaranteeing their political and economic independence, but the situation is different in some aspects. The commercial broadcasters are free to choose their directors and management boards. As was pointed out in this country monograph, in the case of commercial broadcasters the main risk is that private economic powers can exert influence over their content, which of course does not rule out the possibility of political dependence of these broadcasters.

§2. Fair Representation in Election Periods

655. The election periods are very important periods both for the politicians and for the public because during this period the politicians can present their point of view and methods for governing the country and the voters need adequate and full information in order to make their choice. The media coverage of the election periods in Bulgaria is done through different programme formats. It can take the form of opening and final addresses or videos where the candidates of the different political parties and coalitions present to the voters their programmes. It can also take the form of a news brief where are presented the election activities of the candidates such as meetings, concerts and debates where the candidates of different political parties and the presenter of the emission are debating on predefined topics. The election periods can also be covered in the news and the current affairs programmes, which are not specialized election programmes. Another characteristic of the election periods in the media is the existence of political advertisement, which concerns both the electronic and the print media. In that regard, the coverage of the election period in the print media is done through publications. In any case, the media should be impartial and fair in the coverage of the election periods.[265]

656. The procedures for the conduct of the elections and the election campaigns in the media are governed by the Election Code of the country. Since March 2014, Bulgaria has had a new Election Code that creates new rules for coverage of the election campaign and explicitly specifies which media are taken into account by the law – public and commercial electronic media, print media and online news services. Moreover, the new 'media' amendments in the new Election Code introduce free-of-charge videos and debates. The election campaign period begins on the day following the date of the end of the period for registration of the candidates. According to Article 175 of the new Election Code, the election campaign starts thirty days before the election day.

657. All participants in the elections – candidates and political parties, coalitions of parties, nomination committees and independent registered candidates – are entitled to equal access to sources of information which are necessary for the campaign (Article 176 of the Code). All of them, as well as their official supporters and every citizen, have the freedom of expression and agitation in oral and written form during election meetings, as well as through media service providers (Article 181). The election campaign is conducted in Bulgarian language.

658. The requirements for the programmes of the public media during election periods remain in the new Election Code more strict and precise than the requirements for the private media. These requirements mainly concern BNT and BNR but some of them also concern private broadcasters and are compulsory for both types

265. Recommendation No. R (99) 15 on Measures Concerning Media Coverage of Election Campaigns and Recommendation CM/Rec (2007) 15 on measures concerning media coverage of election campaigns both of the Committee of Ministers of the Council of Europe to Member States, available on the website of the Council of the European Union (https://www.coe.int/en/web/portal/home).

of media. The coverage of the election campaigns by all radio and TV broadcasters begins thirty days before the election day and finishes the day before the election day. In case where the rights or the reputation of a candidate is offended in his absence during a programme broadcasted by a media, he has the right to reply in accordance with Article 18 of the LRT, which applies equally to the public and private media.[266]

659. It should be noted that there is special obligation for the inclusion in the election campaign period of clear and understandable messages that the vote-buying represents a crime. According to Article 183 of the new Election Code, each promotional material has to stress that buying and selling votes is a crime. The information should take no less than 10% of the face area of the campaign materials and be located in a separate box. In the audio and audiovisual materials this information is contained as a clear and understandable message.

660. During the election campaign, radio and television broadcasters must not allow the broadcasting of programmes that contain hate speech. They must call participants to lead the campaign in a good manner, with mutual ethics, tolerance and respect for others' opinions.

661. According to Article 189, paragraph 1 of the Election Code, the election campaign is covered in the programmes of the BNT and BNR in the form of videos, debates and other forms agreed under paragraph 4 of the same article. The BNT and BNR are required not only to cover the election campaigns but they are also limited to do it within a defined time limit. Their programmes cannot be used for election campaigns beyond the time provided for the forms under paragraph 1 of the Election Code (paragraph 2 of Article 189). The BNT and BNR are obliged to respect the principles of equality and objectivity in covering the events of the candidates, registered by the political parties, the coalitions of parties and the initiative committees in their information emissions. The teams, forms and themes of the debates shall be determined by joint agreement between the General Directors of BNT and BNR and the empowered representatives of the parties, coalitions of parties and initiative committees. The agreement has to be approved by the Central Election Commission (CEC) no later than thirty-one days before the election day and sent immediately to the National Audit Office (paragraph 4 of Article 189).

662. Besides the above-mentioned rules of conduct, Article 191 prohibits making political suggestions in the commercial advertising on BNT and BNR for the benefit or detriment of one or another participant in the election campaign in the commercial advertising.

---

266. The concerned person or organ has seven days from the date of the programme broadcasting to make a written request to the operator. The request must indicate the challenged statements and the date and time of the transmission. The operator must include the response in the next broadcasting of the same programme or in an equivalent one, twenty-four hours after receiving the complaint, with no modification or reduction of the text. The duration of the response may not exceed the duration of the disputed part of the show.

663. Article 192 defines the rules concerning the order of presentation of the candidates of the registered political parties, coalitions of parties and nomination committees in the various forms of the campaign. According to paragraph 1 of the same article, the order is chosen by lot by the CEC for each form individually. The lot takes place in the presence of the candidates or empowered representatives of the different political parties, coalitions of parties and nomination committees and representatives of the BNT and BNR. The CEC has to announce its decision no later than thirty-one days before the election day.

664. The election campaign in the programmes of BNT and BNR begins and ends with video clips of the political parties, coalitions of parties and nomination committees, with a duration of up to forty seconds that are broadcasted for free. In the case of elections for president and vice president, the BNT and BNR election campaign programmes begin and end with addresses of the candidate of three minutes each broadcasted for free. In case of a second round for the elections of president and vice president, candidates have the right to make ten-minute addresses, again freely broadcasted. Their order of appearance is determined by the CEC and the time of broadcasting of the clips is determined by agreement between the General Directors of BNT and BNR and the empowered representatives of the political parties, coalitions of parties and nomination committees (Article 193).

665. In addition to the free-of-charge covering of the election campaign, paid forms can also be used for political coverage. The law does not specify the type of paid forms – most often it comes to political advertising clips, its aim is to influence the voters upon a matter which is currently the subject of political debate or to present the political programmes and to promote the respective candidate or party. (Article 194). The news in brief presenting the activity of the party or the candidate is also often used. According to paragraph 2 of this Article, the duration of the paid forms, the time and the number of their broadcasting are determined by agreement as in the previously mentioned cases. The audio and audiovisual materials included in the paid forms are provided by authorized representatives of the parties, coalitions and nomination committees and registered candidates, or are made by teams of the BNT and BNR under the same conditions and prices, defined by their directors. The rates and conditions are to be sent to the National Audit Office and the CEC.

According to Article 179 in case of broadcasting, publishing and distribution of paid forms of coverage of the election campaign, the media service providers have to keep such forms separate by optical, acoustic or spatial means and indicate in an appropriate manner that the item is paid. This article contains the general conduct rule of the election campaign and refers not only to BNT and BNR and their regional centre but also to the commercial and print media and online news services.

666. Article 177 prohibits the broadcasting and publication of anonymous materials related to the election campaign.

667. BNT and BNR provide the parties, coalitions, nomination committees and registered candidates with free-of-charge debates on previously agreed topics for a total duration of not less than 240 minutes and equally distributed time among the participants (Article 195). In the case of elections for president and vice president, in the period between the two rounds, the candidates can conduct free disputes lasting at least 60 minutes.

668. The regional radio and television centres of BNT and BNR are also used by the parties, coalitions of parties and nomination committees during the election broadcasts in the manner provided under the programmes of the two media. They should allow for no less than sixty minutes free-of-charge broadcasting time for debates between the candidates and the representatives of the different political parties, coalitions of parties and nomination committees. The order of participation in the disputes is determined by the regional or municipal election commissions by lot no later than thirty-one days before the election day. The teams, forms and conditions for the realization of the programmes, as well as the topics of the disputes are determined jointly by the heads of the regional radio and television centres and the representatives of the parties, coalitions of parties and initiative committees (Article 196).

669. The broadcasting of the election campaigns in the programmes of BNT and BNR and their regional centres beyond is not free. The parties, coalitions of parties and nomination committees have to pay fees, which are fixed by the Council of Ministers,[267] no later than forty days before the election day. The payment is made before the broadcasting of the election campaign (Article 197).

670. There were only two cases according to the previous Election Code (Article 147, paragraph 2) in which the registered participants in the elections can have free participation – in the presidential runoff the candidates have the right to address the voters on the final day of the campaign between the two rounds in ten minutes (Article 142, paragraph 3) and hold a dispute within an hour (Article 145, paragraph 5).

671. Bearing this in mind, one could wonder whether or not if the candidates do not pay, the public media will not cover the campaign and how this will allow the respect of the principles of equality and objectivity in covering the events of the candidates as required Article 139, paragraph 3 of the Election Code. The fact that the election campaign on the two-state broadcasters is fully paid was enshrined in the Election Code and was largely criticized. Public radio and television should be the ones that have to present the participants in the fullest, fair and equal way in the election period and help thus the voters make the most informed and adequate choice. Instead, they were collecting money from the candidates for their participation in the debates and thus they admit only those who are able to pay. The media

267. The Decree No. 217 of the Council of Ministers determined the tariff under which the parties, coalitions of parties and initiative committees pay for the 2011 election broadcasts on BNT and BNR and their regional centres.

focus their attention only on certain candidates and entities because of purely financial interests, and it is practically impossible to present marginal points of view, which drastically limits the opportunities for debate and hence the development of the social environment and political system.

672. These contradictions in the Election Code were immediately reported by international observers during the election period in 2011. Furthermore, according to Part II, point 4 'Free airtime for political parties/candidates on public broadcast media' of the Recommendation R (99) 15 of the Committee of Ministers to Member States concerning the media coverage of election campaigns of the Council of Europe,[268] to which Bulgaria is a member, the Member States may examine the advisability of including in their regulatory frameworks provisions whereby free airtime is made available to political parties/candidates on public broadcasting services in electoral time. Wherever such airtime is granted, this should be done in a fair and non-discriminatory manner, on the basis of transparent and objective criteria.

673. In addition to the requirements provided by the legislation, for the elections of 2011, the BNT invited representatives of all parties, coalitions of political parties and nomination committees registered to participate in the elections to sign the agreement on how the campaign will be covered in the programmes of BNT.

674. The private media, other than BNT, BNR and their regional centres, may use paid and free-of-charge forms to cover the election campaign of the parties, coalitions and nomination committees. The commercial electronic media should propose identical terms and rates to all registered candidates. The terms and procedure for the allotment of time for coverage of the election campaign, as well as the rate schedules, have to be made public on the Internet site of the respective media not later than forty days before the voting day (Article 198). For the free-of-charge forms, the state will provide funds to the private media. These funds will be only for the parties and candidates without subsidies. Nevertheless, this text remains controversial, because the EU prohibits the funding of private entities with state funds even if the idea is to help people to make informed choices.

The terms, procedure and rate have to be transmitted to the Bulgarian National Audit Office and CEC for the media with a national coverage and to the district election commission, i.e., the municipal election commission for the media operating within a regional or a local range, no later than the opening of the election campaign.

In the previous Election Code, the private media were under a less stringent regime. While it contained a dozen articles related to BNT and BNR, there was only one article concerning the rules on granting of time by the other electronic media. There was only one condition that the private media should respect and this was the financial equality among the candidates.

268. Adopted by the Committee of Ministers on 9 Sep. 1999 at the 678th meeting of the Ministers' Deputies.

675. The condition that the coverage of all political parties is done under the same conditions and prices is mandatory in order to limit/prevent the risk that the paid media campaign will threaten the principle of equality by creating an indirect financial censure.[269]

676. There are only a few requirements and restrictions on the behaviour of the print media and online news services during the election periods. According to Article 187, they have to provide the same conditions and prices for all registered elections parties, coalitions and nomination committees, which have to be made public on their website no later than forty days before the election day and are immediately sent to the National Audit Office and the CEC. The payment is made in advance.

677. In case where the rights or the reputation of a candidate was offended, the editor of the concerned printed edition has to publish the reply in the first number of the edition, after the reception of the reply, and at the same place and the same print as the contested publication. The reply must be published without charge, it may have at maximum the same volume as the contested material and it has to be published without any accompanying comments (Article 188).

678. Since the majority of the election publications in the print media appear as paid advertisements, the question one can ask is whether the right of reply should be published without charge when it is the reply to a paid advertisement. The legislator is silent on that point, but the logic is that in order to guarantee this important right of reply, the media have to publish the reply without charge, even in this case.[270]

679. In case of violation of the procedure for conducting the election campaign from the media broadcasters, Article 200 of the new Election Code provides that the candidates or those who represent them or their empowered persons can make a complaint within twenty-four hours after the broadcasting of the transmission to:

- the CEC for broadcasters with a national scope, as well as when the offence is committed in more than one electoral district;
- the district election commission, i.e., the municipal election commission, corresponding to the residence of the broadcaster when he has a licence or registration of a regional or local scope.

680. Furthermore, when the complaint is made before a commission which has no competency, it shall immediately forward the complaint to the competent commission, and the applicant should be notified. As a rule, the competent election commission has twenty-four hours to consider the complaint, but if the complaint is made on the election day it must be considered immediately. Upon breach of the procedure for the conduct of the election campaign by media service providers, the

269. S. Dimitrova, in Tcholakov, et al., *Media Law: Dictionary of the Main Concepts*, 322 (Trud 2005).
270. *Ibid.*, 324.

competent election commission may also take action against the offenders on its own initiative. The decision issued by the CEC is subject to appeal before the SAC.

681. Moreover, Article 33, paragraph 3 of the LRT provides that the CEM, as a specialized independent body, supervises the broadcasters regarding the coverage of the elections for central and local authorities, as well as for the election of the Bulgarian members of the European Parliament. The CEM and particularly its chairman have already pointed out the existence of flawed practices or legislative gaps, more precisely concerning the political advertising during election periods by the media.

§3. News and Current Affairs Programmes

682. There are no special requirements concerning the news and current affairs programmes neither in the LRT nor in the new Election Code. The broadcasters must as always respect the basic professional standards such as pluralism in opinions and viewpoints, equality and impartiality along with other general principles such as the interdiction of broadcasting programmes that contain hate speech, etc. It is prohibited to include in the news and current affairs programmes political publicity. The principles, which have to be respected during election periods, are contained in the CEM opinion of 18 May 2009 concerning the coverage of the election campaign of radio and television broadcasters for the election of members of the European Parliament from Bulgaria. According to point 5 of the opinion, during election campaigns, radio and television broadcasters should not be allowed in the news and current affairs programmes to show preferential treatment to state and local authorities.

§4. Political Advertising

683. Neither the LRT nor the previously adopted Election Code considers paid political advertising. Moreover, the Election Code does not even have a separate article, which explicitly and clearly states that the coverage of the election campaign is a paid service. In that regard, in its opinion of 18 May 2009, CEM drew its attention to political advertising.

684. According to CEM, during the election campaign, radio and television broadcasters must differentiate paid political advertising from the advertising blocks that contain commercial advertising, and this must be done with the appropriate indication. It states that time restrictions on the advertising contained in Article 86, paragraphs 1 and 4 of the LRT apply only to commercial advertising.

685. This requirement, however, does not solve all the problems related to political advertising. In 2011 with the presidential and local elections, the chairman of the CEM proposed that the term political advertising should be defined in a law. The CEM considers that political advertising must be clearly labelled as such and have all the characteristics, including restrictions on space and time in the programme, in order to distinguish political advertising from real journalism, as the content has different qualities. In the present situation, voters cannot always make a difference when they watch or listen to paid political advertising or political chronicles, and thus they are unable to make informed choices.

In the new Election Code of March 2014, the term 'political advertising' is still not defined. It should be noted, however, that during the elections held in 2014, political advertising was done with appropriate indications and was visible and separable from commercial publicity or emissions of a political nature.

On 27 February 2024, the European Parliament agreed on a regulation on transparency and targeting of political advertising[271] designed to promote informed decisions by voters within a more secure environment during elections. Under the new rules, political advertising will have to be clearly labelled. Citizens, authorities and journalists will be able to easily obtain information on whether they are being targeted with an ad, who is paying for it, how much is being paid, and to which elections or referendum it is linked.

Political advertising is defined in the Regulation as: 'the preparation, placement; promotion, publication, delivery or dissemination, by any means, of a message, normally provided for remuneration or through in-house activities or as part of a political advertising campaign:

- by, for or on behalf of a political actor, unless it is of a purely private or a purely commercial nature; or
- which is liable and designed to influence the outcome of an election or referendum, a voting behaviour or a legislative or regulatory process at Union, national, regional or local level'.

With this Regulation, the EU has moved into a sensitive space that has been reserved for the EU Member States. The Regulation will have distinct implications for the EU Member States that already have definitions of political advertising and a national regulatory framework and the EU Member States that do not have specific legislative rules on political advertising, such as Bulgaria.

The European Parliament and the European Council must now formally adopt the resolution and eighteen months following its entrance into force, Bulgaria will have to ensure compliance with the Regulation rules.

The new EU Regulation standardizes political advertising rules, aiming to harmonize varying national laws. This move is pivotal for increasing electoral transparency and fighting misinformation, demonstrating the EU's dedication to protecting democracy in the digital era.

271. https://www.consilium.europa.eu/en/press/press-releases/2023/11/07/transparency-and-targeting-of-political-advertising-eu-co-legislators-strike-deal-on-new-regulation/.

Chapter 5. Advertising Rules

686. Mass media has always been a natural means of communication for companies to advertise their products and influence a large audience. Over the last decades, advertising methods have improved and eventually have shaped the consumerist world we live in. Today television is a commercial enterprise, which finances itself by commercial messages. Advertising helps the media to pay their costs. Media are now governed by the laws of the market; advertising is a mandatory part of their existence and for that reason needs to be regulated in order to protect the audience.

§1. Different Forms of Commercial Communications

687. The various forms of commercial communications are contained in Chapter 4 of the LRT including Articles 72–92. Commercial messages can be audiovisual messages with images, with or without sound or audio messages designed to promote, directly or indirectly, goods, services or reputation of a natural or legal person engaged in business, or to assist in the promotion of a cause or idea, or to set up some other effect desired by the advertiser, accompanying or included in a programme against payment or other similar remuneration or to provide self-promotion (Article 73 of the LRT).

688. Article 74 of the LRT defines four forms of commercial messages. According to its first paragraph, advertising is a form of commercial message, accompanying or included in audiovisual or radio transmission against payment or similar remuneration or for self-promotion of a public or private entity or individual in connection with trade, business, craft or profession, aimed to promote the supply of goods and services, including immovable property, rights and obligations, or to advance a cause or idea, or some other effect desired by the advertiser against a fee.

689. According to paragraph 2 of the same article, sponsorship is a form of commercial message consisting of the contribution of a natural or legal person, who is not engaged in providing media services or creating audio or audiovisual works, to the financing of the media services or transmissions in order to promote its name, brand, reputation, business or products.

690. Paragraph 3 then defines teleshopping as a form of commercial message, which is a direct offer to the public for the provision of goods or services, including immovable property, rights and obligations in audiovisual or radio transmissions against a fee.

691. In its last paragraph 4, Article 74 finally defines product placement as a form of commercial message, which consists of the inclusion or reference to a product, service or trademark in the transmission itself against payment or similar consideration. The product placement is typically found in films or TV shows.

692. The LRT contains different provisions regarding all those forms of commercial messages.

§2. Restrictions on Content

693. As a general rule, advertising must not mislead, harm or offend.[272] These broad principles apply regardless of the product being advertised. Besides this general rule, there are specific rules for certain products such as alcoholic drinks, tobacco products, and health and beauty-related products.

694. According to Article 75, paragraph 1, commercial messages must be clearly identified as such – hidden commercial messages are prohibited. By hidden commercial messages, one here implies any situation where words, sound or pictures are used to promote goods, services, name, trademark or activities of a producer of goods or provider of services in transmissions which are not formally acknowledged as advertisement (in particular when it is done for remuneration or similar consideration (Article 75, paragraph 2 of the LRT)). In that regard, commercial messages must not use techniques which act on the subconscious. Such techniques are indirect methods that are not designated as commercial messages and are not recognized as such by the audience but can form a subconscious psychological reaction and attitude in the audience towards the presented goods and services (Article 75, paragraph 4 of the LRT).

695. Article 75 of the LRT also prohibits all commercial messages which can affect human dignity, include or promote any discrimination based on gender, race or ethnic origin, nationality, religion or beliefs, disability, age or sexual orientation, encourage conduct that endangers health or safety, encourage behaviour seriously prejudicial to the environment (Article 75, paragraph 5 of the LRT).

696. Commercial messages must not create physical or moral harm to children. Neither can they directly exhort them to purchase or hire a product or service by exploiting their inexperience or credulity, nor directly encourage them to persuade their parents or others to buy advertised products or services (Article 75, paragraph 9 of the LRT).

I. Tobacco and Related Products

697. Article 75 also prohibits all forms of commercial messages for cigarettes or any other tobacco products in radio and television transmissions. According to

272. Article 33 of the LPC; and National rules for Ethical advertising and commercial communication in Bulgaria: https://www.nss-bg.org/en/the-code/.

Article 35 of the Law for Tobacco and Tobacco Products, advertising of tobacco and tobacco products is prohibited.[273]

698. The advertising of tobacco and tobacco products in the press and other print media or through information society services is allowed only for publications that are: (i) intended exclusively for professionals in the field of production and trade of tobacco and tobacco products; and (ii) printed or published in a third country and are not intended for the EU internal market or for the Member States of the EEA.[274] Any other tobacco advertising is prohibited.

699. It is also prohibited for entities whose main activity is the manufacture or trade in tobacco and tobacco products to sponsor radio and television programmes or any events or activities taking place in several countries members of the EU or of the EEA, or activities which in any other way have transboundary effects.

II. Alcohol

700. There are also special requirements concerning alcohol advertising. In 2004, members of the Committee on Health of the National Assembly decided to ban direct advertising of alcoholic drinks and cigarettes for all media.[275] The motive for the restrictions was to limit the consumption of alcohol. This restriction came into force on 1 January 2005 and there are fines of BGN 5,000 (approximately EUR 2,584) for the first non-respect and up to EUR 5,168 in case of the second and each subsequent offence. In contrast to direct advertising, indirect advertising means that in the advertising can be shown only the label but not the bottle and someone drinking from it. According to paragraph 7 of Article 75 of the LRT, the advertising for alcoholic drinks[276] must not be aimed specifically at children and must not encourage immoderate consumption of such drinks. Moreover, also according to Article 55 of the Health Law, the direct advertising of spirits[277] is prohibited.[278] This article provides that the indirect advertising of spirits, as well as the advertising of wine

273. Except for company premises where manufactured tobacco or tobacco products are produced or establishments dealing with tobacco and tobacco products, the use of a trademark when in the advertising persons less than 18 years are participating and it is not intended or directed to them or in places or events where access to persons under 18 is prohibited.
274. Iceland, Liechtenstein and Norway.
275. However, there are no restrictions for the clips on beer and wine.
276. The alcoholic drinks include spirits, wine and beer (para. 17 of the Additional provisions of the Health Law).
277. Spirits is a liquid intended for human consumption that contains at least 15 volume per cent of ethyl alcohol (para. 18 of the Additional provisions of the Health Law).
278. According to para. 19 of the Additional provisions of the Health Law, the direct advertising means any form of commercial message aimed to promote alcoholic drinks and/or their consumption by using the drinks themselves or activities associated with their consumption, production and distribution. However, the indirect advertising means any form of commercial message that uses the name or the brand of alcoholic drinks, as well as the company or the brand of a manufacturer of alcoholic beverages on products and goods that are not alcoholic drinks (para. 20 of the Additional provisions of the Health Law).

and beer is authorized if it is not directed to persons under the age of 18 or broadcasted in transmissions or published in publications intended for them. In addition, persons under the age of 18 cannot participate in such advertising (Article 55 of the Health Law and Article 88 of the LRT). Both, the above-mentioned articles of the LRT and the Health Law precise that this kind of advertising could not connect the use of alcoholic drinks with sports and physical performance or driving or contain claims about health, social or sexual benefits, or present abstinence or moderation in a negative light. Neither can advertising emphasis on high alcoholic content as being a positive quality of the drinks (Article 55 of the Health Law and Article 88 of the LRT). The indirect advertising of spirits is possible only after 20:00 hours. Due to these restrictions, more and more companies started to advertise on digital screens in public transport, railway stations and airports and according to marketing experts, advertising of alcohol in unusual places will increase. But the control there is in the hands of the Ministry of Health.

III. Medicinal Products

701. The advertising of medicinal products is also subject to some special requirements. Chapter 11 of the Law on Medicinal Products for Human (LMRHU) regulates the advertising of the medicinal products. Advertising intended for the public of medicinal products available without prescription is allowed (Article 247 of the LMRHU and Article 87 of the LRT). Commercial messages for medicinal products which are available only by prescription are prohibited, except for the cases under Article 248 of the LMRHU. According to Article 244, paragraph 1 of the LMRHU, the advertising of medicinal products is any form of information, presentation, promotion or proposals which aim to stimulate the prescription, sale or use of the product. This kind of advertising includes the advertising intended for the population or the health professionals, visits of medical sales representatives to medical specialists, provision of samples of medicinal products, sponsorship of promotional meetings and scientific congresses attended by medical professionals, including the assumption of their travel and stay in the country where the event takes place.

702. However, the text on the packaging and leaflet of medicinal products approved in the authorization procedure for use, the correspondence concerning a specific issue or problem related to a medicinal product, the information and instructions with regard to changes in packaging, warnings about adverse reactions as part of general measures for the safety of the product, trade catalogues and price lists (on the condition they do not include data regarding promotional nature of the product), statements related to human health or diseases when they are not directly or indirectly referred to the treatment, prevention or diagnosis with medicinal products and vaccination campaigns conducted by the Ministry of Health (when the related materials do not contain data for a specific product) are not considered advertising.

703. The advertising of the medicinal products must be directed only to its correct use, present objectively its therapeutic indications (without exaggerating the possibilities for treatment, prevention or diagnosis). As a general rule, advertising cannot contain misleading information. This rule is valid also here, but in addition, the advertisement cannot contain any proposal and/or promise of gift and/or any other benefit. The medical specialists or any person presenting himself as exercising a medical profession cannot directly or indirectly advertise medicinal products in the print and/or electronic media, as well as in Internet (Article 246 of the LMRHU).

704. The projects for medicinal products advertisement are approved by the Bulgarian Drug Agency (BDA) where an Expert Commission on medicines advertising is created. The Commission includes physicians as well as specialists with experience in advertising. In case of inconformity with the requirements of the LMRHU, the BDA must issue within seven days from the date of application written instructions for removal of the concerned advertisements. If the applicant fails to comply with the instructions within a month from the date of notification, the authorization procedure shall be terminated (Article 251 of the LMRHU). The Executive Director of the BDA authorizes the advertisement or gives a motivated refusal. The refusal of the Executive Director may be appealed under the Administrative Code.

IV. Commercial Messages and Child Protection

705. According to Article 73 of the LRT, the commercial messages are audiovisual images with or without sound (television) or audio messages (radio) designed to promote directly or indirectly goods, services or reputation of a physical or legal person engaged in business. They shall promote a cause or idea or provoke some other effects desired by the advertiser and are accompanying or included in a programme in return of payment or other similar remuneration or aim to provide self-promotion. The commercial messages can be advertisements, sponsorship, radio and television market and product placement.

706. It should be clarified that here, when we talk about commercial messages, the focus is mainly on advertisements because it is this form of the commercial messages that is more aimed at children. One reason is that children often watch more TV than their parents and at the same time they have strong influence on the purchase of goods in the household. But that is not all. Another reason to target children is that they are easily fooled, e.g., by using very colourful or cartoon characters, the advertisements attract and retain the attention of young children very easily. Moreover, while adults have some criteria and know what is advertising, what is its role and how to pay attention, to children it is a real recommendation, which they think they should comply with. The influence of advertising on children is reinforced by their lack of critical perception of the message of the publicity.

707. Because of these reasons, there are specific texts relevant to advertising and teleshopping, which apply to child protection. The provision of Article 75 of the LRT sets special requirements for commercial messages, aimed at children. According to paragraph 7 of this article commercial messages of alcoholic drinks must not be aimed specifically at children or encourage immoderate consumption of such drinks. Concerning the commercial messages of cigarettes and other tobacco products, they are prohibited. According to paragraph 9 of the same article commercial messages addressed to minors shall not endanger children physically or morally and shall not bring children directly to purchase or hire a product or service by taking advantage of their lack of inexperience or trustfulness. The commercial messages shall not either directly encourage children to persuade their parents or others to buy the advertised products or services. Moreover, it shall not be taken advantage of the special trust children place in their parents, teachers or other persons; showing of children in dangerous situations is also prohibited.

708. However, Article 77 of the LRT forbids commercial breaks which contain pornography or incite violence and disrespect for human dignity, as well as to behaviour which violates public order and the accepted moral standards. The article prohibits advertisements with erotic content involving or aimed at children.

709. Advertisement of food and drinks inadequate or advised against consumption by children (candy, chips, popcorn, drinks, chocolates, etc.) has recently attracted the attention of the legislator. In 2010, the new paragraph 1 of Article 76 stipulates that media service operators shall enlist in their Code of Ethics rules concerning the commercial messages accompanying or included in children transmissions related to food and drinks containing nutrients and substances with a nutritional or physiological effect, in particular fat, trans fatty acids, salt/sodium and sugar. Excessive intakes of such products in diet are indeed not recommended. This new paragraph was motivated by higher children obesity. When children watch TV they are under the influence of the advertisements of various high-calorie and high-sugar foods and snacks, and these advertisements have particularly big effect on the young audience.

§3. Time and Frequency Restrictions

710. In its chapter 'Advertising and Teleshopping in Television Programs', the LRT contains the provisions regarding time and frequency of the advertising broadcasting, as well as requirements regarding special categories of programmes which cannot be interrupted. Hidden commercial messages are prohibited, so that advertising and teleshopping shall be clearly separated from the other parts of the programme by optical and/or acoustic and/or spatial means (Article 85, paragraph 2 of the LRT).

711. According to Article 86 of the LRT, when advertising and teleshopping spots are located in a transmission, they must not violate its integrity by taking into account natural the breaks and duration. It is possible to interrupt TV movies, cinematographic works, information and children programmes[279] once for each programmed period of at least thirty minutes on the condition that the scheduled duration of the programme is larger than thirty minutes. The duration of advertising and teleshopping spots within a one-hour period may not exceed twelve minutes. This does not concern, however, the announcements made by the operator in connection with its own programmes, promotion of European films, as well as appeals to charity and community causes (Article 89 of the LRT).

712. Article 90 of the LRT precises that the total duration of advertising for each programme of BNT and BNR may not exceed fifteen minutes per day and four minutes per hour for BNT and six minutes per hour for BNR. For the regional centres of BNT and BNR, the total duration of advertising may not exceed six minutes per hour. The above-mentioned limitations do not apply to advertising included during coverage of events of art, culture and sport with national and international importance. In this case, the general provisions for duration of advertising mentioned above apply.

713. Finally, it should be pointed out that in all kind of advertising the sound is higher than for other transmissions. After more and more complaints to the CEM, it has decided to contact the Parliamentary Media Commission to start the discussion of a specific text in order to have the sound of the advertisements reduced and placed in normal limits. The LRT does not regulate this issue; it has been left as a technical parameter of the free choice of the operators. The aim of CEM is to eliminate the sense of 'noise aggression' when people watch TV.

§4. Misleading Advertising

714. Misleading advertising concerns any advertisement, which in any manner, including the way of its presentation, deceives or may deceive the persons to whom it is addressed and therefore may affect their economic behaviour (Article 33 of the LPC). The advertising is misleading when even if part of the information is factually correct, the results is or is likely to be that the person will take decision that she/he would not have taken without the ambiguous, missing or incorrect information. The ambiguous, missing or incorrect information may refer to the merchant, his identity, qualifications, the characteristics of the goods or services, such as nature, origin, mode of production, safety, health, environment, as well as to the price of the products or the services, e.g., the way the price is formed.

715. The explicit identification of misleading advertising can be difficult because of the inherent exaggeration of the product or service capabilities in all (or most) advertisements. That's why misleading advertising, in contrast to, e.g., hidden

279. In its formulation of 1998, the LRT provided in its Art. 83, para. 2 that advertising cannot interrupt national celebrations and religious services, news, political and economic commentaries and analysis, documentaries and children transmissions.

advertising, cannot be the subject of media regulation; there is not any related provision or definition in the LRT. This information is contained in the Law for Consumer Protection (LCP) in the part 'Incorrect Commercial Practices' (Article 68(b)–68(l)), as well as in the LPC in its Chapter 7 called 'Prohibition of Unfair Competition'. More precisely, the LPC contains definitions of the different types of advertising, and Article 32 clearly prohibits the misleading and unlawful comparative advertising. The comparative advertising explicitly or by implication makes reference to a competitor or competing goods or services. This type of advertising is only permitted when it is not misleading. In particular, the comparisons should relate to goods or services which meet the same needs or are intended for the same purpose, compare products with the same designation of origin, deal objectively with the features of those goods or services (which may include price), avoid confusion between traders and should not discredit, imitate or take advantage of the trademark or trade name of a competitor (Article 34 of the LPC).

§5. Sponsorship

716. A programme can be sponsored in whole or in part. This means that the sponsor can contribute for the direct or indirect financing of the whole programme or to finance part of the programme or a particular activity of its creation (e.g., providing decor, equipment and transport).

717. Sponsorship is considered in Article 82 of the LRT. This article specifies that when a transmission is sponsored, it must be clearly identified as such in an appropriate way at its beginning and/or at its end. The identification should be done by the name, logo and/or other symbol of the sponsor as a reference to its products or services. This provision is mandatory, meaning that the name and/or the trademark of the sponsor may be shown only at the beginning and/or at the end of the transmission. The content and scheduling of this transmission cannot, in any case, be influenced by the sponsor in a manner to affect the responsibility and editorial independence of the broadcaster.

718. Moreover, sponsored transmissions must not encourage the sale, purchase or rental of goods or services of the sponsor or a third party, particularly by reference to those goods or services in the transmission. Media services or transmissions cannot be sponsored by producers or traders which principal activity is the manufacture or sale of cigarettes and other tobacco products. When sponsoring media services or transmissions, the producers or traders in medicinal products or medical institutions can promote the name or image of the sponsor, but the advertising of specific medicinal products available only on prescription or treatment which shall be appointed only on prescription is not permitted. It is only possible to promote the name or the image of the sponsor. In all case, news and current affairs programmes cannot be sponsored. Also the political parties and organizations, as well as the religious ones and the legal or natural persons whose products or services are prohibited of advertising cannot be sponsors. Displaying the logo of the sponsor in children and religious programmes is forbidden.

719. The CEM authorizes the interruption for advertising of the sponsored transmissions for the advertisement of goods or services of the sponsor or of a third party, as according to the LRT, the advertising is not part of the sponsorship. Contrary understanding would lead to a general prohibition on the inclusion of advertisements in the sponsored transmissions and if it was so, the legislator would have made it explicitly formulated in the LRT. In that regard, the only condition is that the advertising interruptions in sponsored transmissions respect the rules on advertising.

§6. PRODUCT PLACEMENT

720. The term of product placement has been recently introduced in the Bulgarian LRT. It was in fact formally introduced among the authorized advertising means in the LRT with the amendments to the LRT in 2010. In that regard, it should be mentioned that in May 2012 the CEM adopted draft methodological guidelines concerning the hidden commercial messages and product placement as a form of commercial communication. The reason for this was the increasing number of hidden commercial messages and positioning of products, goods, services and brands, which lead the CEM to react in order to protect the interests of the consumers, as the provisions specified in the LRT do not contain clear criteria for the law enforcement against these forms and practices.

721. According to Article 84 of the LRT, all transmissions, including product placement, must contain appropriate identification at the beginning and end of transmission, as well as after the advertising breaks of the transmission. This requirement does not apply to transmissions, which are not produced or commissioned by the media service provider or a related person. Also, according to this article, the content of the transmissions or the arrangement of the programmes in the programme schedule must not affect the responsibility and editorial independence of the media service provider. The viewers have to be clearly informed of the existence of product placement but cannot be directly encouraged to purchase or rent the goods or services. Moreover, the products, services or brands can be shown only in certain boundaries and without unfounded emphasis. According to the CEM, such signs of unfounded emphasis of the product are pointedly positive attitudes towards the product, services or brands or the pleasure related to them; absence of pluralism and impartiality in the presentation of the products, services or brands; the frequency and duration of the insertion of the product, service or brand; their imposing by speech and/or visual accents; and the indication of address, website and/or coordinates. The rest of the document of the CEM gives detailed comments on other commercial practices where the mention of goods, services, company names, trademarks or activities of a producer in radio and television programmes is unacceptable and will be penalized.

722. Obviously, the transmissions must not contain product placement of cigarettes or tobacco or similar products, as well as companies whose main activity is the manufacture or sale of cigarettes and other tobacco products. In addition, the product placement of specific medicinal products available only on prescription or of a treatment, which is administered only on prescription, is forbidden. Finally, product placement in news, religious programmes and children programmes is prohibited (Article 83 of the LRT).

723. It should be noted that in cases where the inclusion of a product or service in a transmission is not made against a fee, but is made for the needs of the transmission, such as providing it with wardrobe, requisite, awards, etc., and related products and services are not of significant value, this cannot be considered product placement (paragraph 4 of Article 83 of the LRT). Significant value under paragraph 5 is one that exceeds five times the average value of commercial messages broadcasted in the transmission, according to the previously announced rate of the media service provider. The providers of the products or services under paragraph 4 have the right to announce in appropriate way their provision in the final captions of the transmission (paragraph 6 of Article 83 of the LRT).

Chapter 6. Right to Information

724. Both, the Bulgarian and the EU legislation[280] ensure the right of the broadcasters to have access to information on subjects of major public interest and importance or to short extracts of such events for the short news reports. Thus the right of the public to have access to information is guaranteed.

§1. Access to Major Events

725. Paragraph 1, point 8 of the Additional provisions of the LRT defines the major events as events of social, political, economic, sport or entertainment character, which affect the interests of the majority of the audience.

726. In order to reinforce the obligation of the broadcaster, who has acquired exclusive rights for events of major public interest not to deprive a significant proportion of the audience in the country of the opportunity to watch entirely or partly these events live, Article 19(b) of the LRT requires that a radio or television broadcaster, who has exclusive rights over a major event, has to provide access of other radio or television broadcasters for its informational presentation in accordance with the obligations of the Republic of Bulgaria under the applicable international agreements. This article guarantees, in fact, the access to major events for the short news reports.

727. According to Article 32, paragraph 3 of the LRT, the CEM adopts and publishes a list of events of major public importance and provides measures to protect the right of access of the audience to these events. The CEM has to exercise this right in such a way that a broadcaster under the jurisdiction of the Republic of Bulgaria, who has acquired exclusive rights for events of major public interest cannot deprive a significant proportion of the audience in the country, in the EU or in any country which signed the European Convention on Transfrontier Television, of the opportunity to watch entirely or partly these events live. When this is necessary or appropriate for the public interest, after an appropriate period of time these events should be broadcasted entirely or partly on the non-paid linear television. For the foreign audience, the broadcasting of events of important public interest has to be done according to the provisions adopted by that other state and under conditions of reciprocity.

728. Concerning the first requirement contained in Article 32, paragraph 3 of the LRT, in its Decision No. 140 of 12 July 2011, the CEM drew up a list of events which are seen as being of major interest to society. The list includes the television

280. Directive 2010/13/EU of the European Parliament and of the Council of 10 Mar. 2010 on the coordination of certain provisions laid down by law, regulation or administrative action in Member States concerning the provision of audiovisual media services (Audiovisual Media Services Directive – codified version).

coverage of national and non-national sports events of major interest as the Olympic Games, World and European Cups, and International meetings of the national volleyball and basketball men's teams.

729. Concerning the adoption of measures to protect the access of the audience to events of major public interest, the media service provider will acquire the right to broadcast the events proposed by CEM, if it broadcasts the event as linear media service on free television so that the event is accessible for at least 85% of the population. In case that the public media broadcasters that meet these requirements refuse or declare financial impossibility, the right to broadcast an event listed in the above-mentioned list can be acquired by a broadcaster who does not meet these conditions.

730. The elaboration of the list containing the events of major public interest contains three stages: written correspondence with certain institutions such as the Ministry of Culture, the Ministry of Physical Education and Sports, the National Assembly Committee for Culture and Civil Society and the National Sports Academy. Then additional consultations with the representative bodies of the sports added to the list after the first stage are held. The final stage is the publication of the draft list on the website of the CEM for public discussion.

731. The already approved list of events of major public interest has to be sent to the Ministry of Culture, to the Standing Committee on Transfrontier Television and the European Commission. The EU Member States can determine whether these events should be transmitted entirely or partially, either live or recorded for later transmission.

732. If an EU Member State does not provide the European Commission with a national list, this does not lead to sanctions against it. This will have deleterious consequences only for the audience of this state itself.

733. The list enters into force after the date of its publication in the Official Journal of the EU and is valid until the adoption of the next list.

§2. Short News Reporting

734. Access to major events for the short news reports is implemented according to the provision of Article 19(b) and 19(c) of the LRT. According to these articles radio and television broadcasters, established in the EU or in accordance with the obligations of the Republic of Bulgaria under applicable international agreements, have the right to fair, reasonable and non-discriminatory access to events of significant public interest, broadcasted on an exclusive basis by a broadcaster under the jurisdiction of the Republic of Bulgaria (paragraphs 1 and 2 of Article 19(c) of the LRT).

735. The right of access to major events for the short news reports includes two things. First, the broadcasters have the right to freely choose the short extracts they want to use. In case of audiovisual media services, the broadcasters have to note the name or include the logo of the broadcasters with exclusive rights. For the radio services, the source has also to be indicated in an appropriate way. Second, the broadcasters have the right of direct access to the event with the possibility of a record, which can be used only for the creation of a material no longer than ninety seconds. In that case, after the informational coverage of the event, the original reportage of the authors is destroyed where after the operator who has the exclusive rights is informed (paragraphs 3 and 5 of Article 19(c) of the LRT).

736. It should be noted that this right to access information is free. Exceptionally, the operator who has the exclusive rights can ask for compensations, but it shall not exceed the additional direct costs for the provision of the access (paragraph 6 of Article 19(c) of the LRT). Moreover, the short extracts are used only for current affairs programmes and news in a period no longer than twenty-four hours from the end of the event and in that regard, they can be used in the on-demand media services only if the same transmission is offered on record by that media service broadcaster (paragraph 4 of Article 19(c) of the LRT).

737. It is not allowed to broadcast the reports again unless to make thematic reference to events and overviews. The reports can be saved in the archives of the media service provider unless they were made by direct access to the event (paragraph 7 of Article 19(c) of the LRT).

738. Article 48 of the LRT should also be mentioned in that respect. Pursuant to this provision, BNT and BNR have the right to freely include in their news information and short reports on events for which another radio or television broadcaster has exclusive rights. In accordance with the Law on Copyright and the Neighbouring Rights, BNT and BNR have to clearly state the source of the information.

Chapter 7. Access to Networks and Platforms

§1. Introduction

739. Until the end of 2008 the population of Bulgaria had a free national access only to the programmes of BNT and two commercial television broadcasters – bTV and Nova TV. In order to ensure the right of citizens to access a wider content, the LRT postulates some obligations for the network operators regarding the access rights to networks. Such obligations are access to technical facilities and the obligation for network operators to transmit linear services. The LRT provides for the must-carry rules for the broadcasters whose programmes are of public importance. Paragraphs 37, 37(a) and 38 of the Final Provisions of the Law amending the LRT set out the conditions to be met by television programmes to be entitled to compulsory broadcasting through the network operators with national coverage.

§2. Must-Carry Rules

740. According to item 1 of paragraph 37 of the Final Provisions of the Law amending the LRT, an entity which has received permission for the use of individually assigned scarce resource – radio spectrum[281] must: (i) distribute the programmes of licensed radio and television broadcasters who, at the enactment of this law, possess an issued licence for radio and/or television broadcasting with national coverage; and (ii) distribute their programmes via electronic communication networks for terrestrial analogue broadcasting. Furthermore, these electronic communication networks must provide access to their programme to at least 50% of the population. According to item 2 of paragraph 37, the programmes must be distributed in uncoded form.

741. Besides the above-mentioned programmes under item 1 of paragraph 37, the entity can distribute other licensed TV programmes[282] with types and profiles which are consistent with the CEM (pursuant to Article 116(g) of the LRT). In that

281. Radio spectrum (different from the one provided for the broadcasting of the programmes of BNT and BNR) for broadcasting of electronic communications by terrestrial digital broadcasting networks with national coverage and with accordance with the first stage of the transition defined in the Plan for the introduction of DTT broadcasting (DVB-T) of the Republic of Bulgaria, adopted by the Council of Ministers.

282. According to CEM, the television programmes for which the law provides for compulsory broadcasting in the first stage are: bTV Media Group: programme bTV and bTV Action under para. 37 of the Final Provisions of the Law amending the LRT; New Broadcasting Group: the Nova TV under para. 37 of the Final Provisions of the Law amending the LRT:

- TV7: programme TV7 under para. 37(a) of the Final Provisions of the Law amending the LRT.
- Bulgaria On Air: programme Bulgaria On Air under para. 37(a), item 1 of the Final Provisions of the Law amending the LRT.
- Darik Radio: programme Darik Radio and Television under para. 37(a), item 1 of the Final Provisions of the Law amending the LRT.

regard, according to paragraph 37(a), item 1 of the Final Provisions of the Law amending the LRT, the entity which has received permission for the use of individually assigned scarce resource – radio spectrum must broadcast the programmes of the television operators who, at the time of the starting of the service, provide access to their programmes to at least 50% of the population. Paragraph 37(a), item 2 stipulates that the entity under item 1 must also broadcast two licensed programmes of each operator who has permission to use individually assigned scarce resource with a national coverage issued by the Communications Regulation Commission and whose term expires after 2010.

742. According to item 3 of paragraph 37(a), the programmes under item 2 can also be produced by persons, who are also operators, and who are also related to operators according to the Code of Commerce.

743. Paragraphs 37 and 37(a) cover the first phase of the introduction of DTT broadcasting (DVB-T). Concerning the second phase of the DVB-T, paragraph 38, items 1 and 5 of the Final Provisions of the Law amending the LRT, provide that the entity which has received permission for the use of individually assigned scarce resource – radio spectrum must distribute in uncoded form three licensed Bulgarian programmes that correspond to the type and profile of the programmes as defined by the CEM in Article 116(g)[283] of the LRT, as well as three licensed programmes of radio and television operators under paragraph 37(a), item 2 the Final Provisions of the Law amending the LRT. Here again, the programmes under item 5 can be also produced by persons related to the operators who are also operators themselves. The programmes under items 5 and 6 of paragraph 38 should correspond to the type and profile defined by the CEM in Article 116(h)[284] of the LRT.

744. The programmes licensed under the LRT are distributed on the basis of a contract between the linear media service broadcaster and the entity that holds a permit for use of individually assigned scarce resource – radio spectrum. In case where the broadcaster and the company do not agree on the terms of the broadcasting, each of them can request determination of those conditions by the CEM and the CRC, taking into account the opinion of the CPC. For programmes under paragraph 37 and paragraph 37(a), item 1 of the Final Provisions such contracts shall be signed no later than 31 January 2013. For programmes under paragraph 37(a), item 2 of the Final Provisions, the contracts have to be signed up to 30 June 2013.[285]

- Balkan Bulgarian Television: programme BBT under para. 37(a), item 1 of the Final Provisions of the Law amending the LRT.

283. The CEM by a motivated decision defines the type and profile of the Bulgarian licensed television or radio programmes, entitled to compulsory broadcasting through networks for terrestrial digital broadcasting. The number of programmes under para. 1 cannot be greater than two programmes per electronic communications network for terrestrial digital broadcasting.
284. These article concerns the programmes, which will be broadcasted through electronic communication networks for terrestrial digital broadcasting but their broadcasting is not compulsory.
285. Plan for the Introduction of Digital Terrestrial Television Broadcasting in Bulgaria, 2012.

§3. Obligations for Conditional Access Providers

745. Article 178 of the LEC provides conditional access to digital radio and television programmes. Conditional access can be a technical and/or organizational measure for the access to a protected service, made upon prior individual authorization.

746. According to the same article, protected services, provided on the basis of conditional access, are the services regarding radio and television broadcasting, the information society services, and the provision of conditional access for the services under items 1, 2 and 3. The access to a protected service is done with a conditional access device, provided by the protected service provider.

747. Paragraph 3 of Article 178 of the LEC prohibits all commercial activities involving the manufacture, distribution or marketing of smart cards and other devices which make it possible to circumvent protected access to television, radio and Internet pay services.

§4. Other Access Obligations for Network Operators

748. Since 1998 the EU started developing a policy of liberalization of the telecommunication market. In order to open the telecommunication market to competition, a European legal and regulatory framework in the field of telecommunications was created. It contains a basic package of legislation which all Member States are obliged to implement. On 26 April 2000, the Commission proposed to the European Parliament, the Council, the Economic and Social Committee and the Committee of the Regions a new regulatory framework for electronic communication infrastructure and associated services. As a result, in 2002 was introduced a new regulatory framework which consisted of five directives, as well as recommendations and guidelines of the Commission.[286]

286. Directive 2002/21/EC of the European Parliament and the Council of 7 Mar. 2002 on a common regulatory framework for electronic communications networks and services (Framework Directive), Directive 2002/19/EC of the European Parliament and the Council of 7 Mar. 2002 on access to and interconnection of electronic communications networks and associated facilities (Access Directive), Directive 2002/20/EC of the European Parliament and the Council of 7 Mar. 2002 on the authorization of electronic communications networks and services (Authorization Directive), Directive 2002/22/EC of the European Parliament and the Council of 7 Mar. 2002 on universal service and users' rights relating to electronic communications networks and services (Universal Service Directive), Directive 2002/58/EC concerning the processing of personal data and the protection of privacy in the electronic communications sector (Directive on privacy and electronic communications). This Regulatory framework set out in 2002 is supplemented by the Commission recommendation of 17 Dec. 2007 on relevant product and service markets within the electronic communications sector susceptible to *ex ante* regulation in accordance with Directive 2002/21/EC of the European Parliament and the Council on a common regulatory framework for electronic communications networks and services, an Explanatory Note accompanying the Commission Recommendation 2007/879/EC of 17 Dec. 2007 and Commission guidelines on market analysis and the assessment of significant market power under the Community regulatory framework for electronic communications networks and services. *See also* Identification, analyse and evaluation of the

749. This new European legal and regulatory framework was transposed into the Bulgarian legislation with the adoption in 2007 of the LEC, which repealed the existing hitherto TL. For example, the identification, analysis and assessment of the markets for electronic communications networks and/or services at the national level are done pursuant to the provisions of the mentioned law and the methodology on procedures for identification, analysis and evaluation of the relevant markets and the criteria for identifying the companies with significant influence on the market[287] which both complies with the general principle of the competition and the EU law. In that regard, in the Commission guidelines on market analysis and the assessment of significant market power under the Community regulatory framework for electronic communications networks and services, more precisely in point 114 of the guidelines, the Commission states that if the national regulatory authorities find after analysis that the competition in the relevant market is not effective, because an undertaking is defined as an undertaking with significant impact on the market, the authorities have to impose appropriate regulatory obligations on the concerned undertaking(s). According to Article 150, paragraph 1 of the LEC, the CRC is the competent authority which may impose appropriate measures.

market of provision of (physical) wholesale access to network infrastructure (including independent and joint unbundled access) at a determined location and of the market of provision of wholesale broadband access – annex to Decision No. 246 of 22 Feb. 2011 of the CRC.

287. Adopted by Decree No. 40 of the Council of Ministers of 28 Feb. 2008, promulgated in the State Gazette, issue 27 of 11 Mar. 2008.

Chapter 8. Standards and Interoperability

750. The description of the obligations regarding Electromagnetic Compatibility (EMC)[288] and connection of various media devices is contained mainly in the LRT and the LEC. The Ordinance on the essential requirements and conformity assessment of radio equipment and telecommunications devices, adopted by Decree No. 175 of 7 August 2002,[289] transposed the requirements of Directive 1999/5/EC of the European Parliament and the Council of 9 March 1999 on radio equipment and telecommunication terminal equipment and the mutual recognition of their conformity.

751. In the context of the communication technology development on 31 December 2004 was adopted Directive 2004/108/EC (EMC Directive) which regulates the EMC of both apparatus and fixed installations. It should be noted that Directive 2004/108/EC is based on the principles of the new approach[290] to technical harmonization and standards. This directive aims at harmonizing the provisions of the national laws of the Member States to ensure the protection of equipment against electromagnetic disturbances.[291] On 9 July 2008, a new legislative framework was adopted. The latter is the modernization of the new approach to technical harmonization. This broad package of measures is designed to remove the remaining obstacles to the free circulation of products and provides a major boost for trade in goods among the EU Member States.

752. On the basis of that framework in 2011, the Commission made a Proposal for a Directive of the European Parliament and the Council on the harmonization of the laws of Member States relating to EMC (recast). The text of the recast directive introduces, *inter alia*, harmonized definitions of terms which are commonly used throughout the EU and should, therefore, be given a consistent meaning throughout that legislation. The proposal also clarifies the obligations of manufacturers and authorized representatives and introduces obligations for importers and distributors.

753. In accordance with the EU legislation, the Bulgarian CRC sets the general obligations that have to be observed by the economic operators which have submitted a request for the provision of public electronic communication.

---

288. EMC is the branch of electrical sciences which studies the unintentional generation, propagation and reception of electromagnetic energy with reference to the unwanted effects (EMI) that such energy may induce. EMC aims to ensure that equipment items or systems will not interfere with or prevent each other's correct operation through spurious emission and absorption of EMI. EMC is sometimes referred to as EMI Control, and in practice EMC and EMI are frequently referred to as a combined term 'EMC/EMI'.
289. Last modification in 28 Jul. 2006 in the State Gazette, issue 61.
290. This new approach aims at recasting technical harmonization within the EU on a new basis by harmonizing only the essential requirements of products and by applying the general reference to standards formula and principle of mutual recognition in order to eliminate technical obstacles to the free movement of goods.
291. Electromagnetic disturbance refers to any electromagnetic phenomenon which may degrade the performance of equipment. It can be electromagnetic noise, an unwanted signal or a change in the propagation medium itself (Art. 2, item 'e' of Directive 2004/108/EC).

754. Concerning the LRT, the provisions regarding interoperability are contained in the Transitional and Final Provisions of the Law amending the LRT in 2003 and 2004. Paragraph 2 of the Transitional and Final Provisions of the Law amending the LRT in 2003 requires EMC of the transmitters. According to item 3 of paragraph 2, following the procedure of coordination with the aeronautical services about the EMC, the CRC has to define the technical conditions for broadcasting for each settlement. Following this procedure, the CRC may modify the parameters of the transmitters, including the frequency and the point of emission (paragraph 4 of the Transitional and Final Provisions of the Law amending the LRT in 2004).

755. The main provisions concerning standards and interoperability are contained in the LEC in its Chapter 10 called 'Access and Interconnection'.

756. Besides this chapter, according to Article 73 of the LEC, an operator that has submitted a notification for the implementation of public electronic communications complies with general obligations, depending on the type of electronic communications network and/or service. These general obligations are adopted by the CRC in accordance with the principles of transparency, equal treatment and proportionality. The general obligations may contain the requirements to negotiate and provide access and interconnection with the networks of other operators in order to ensure interoperability of the services with those of other operators (Article 73, paragraph 3 of the LEC).

757. Concentrating on the requirements of Chapter 10 of the LEC, an operator which provides public electronic communication networks has the right and the obligation when it is requested by another entity, to negotiate the interconnection of their networks for the provision of public electronic communication services (Article 158 of the LEC).

758. According to Article 160, paragraph 1 of the LEC, the CRC can encourage and, when necessary, impose on operators providing public electronic communications networks and/or services obligations for access and/or interconnection and interoperability of the services. The CRC can impose obligations which will guarantee the connectivity from end to end[292] of the operators that control the access to the final users or, in justified cases, the interconnectivity of their networks if this were not done. Also, in justified cases and to the necessary extent, the CRC can require the entities that control the access to the final users to make their services interoperable. Moreover, the CRC can indicate to the operators which provide public electronic communication networks to ensure the final users access to application programme interfaces or access to electronic programme guides on fair, objective and equal conditions.

759. Furthermore, according to Article 173 of the LEC, the obligation to provide access to and use of the necessary network elements and/or facilities may be

292. The 'end-to-end principle' is a classic design for computer networking.

imposed on an operator with significant market part at the discretion of the CRC in case of refusal to grant access. The imposition of terms and conditions, which prevent the existence of a sustainable competitive retail service market or are detrimental to the final users, are equivalent to a refusal and the CRC can also force the operator to provide access or to authorize the use of his network elements and/or facilities. The CRC may impose the obligation under Article 173 of the LEC by requiring the provision of certain services necessary to ensure interoperability of the network facilities from end to end for the users, including facilities for intelligent network services or roaming on mobile networks or interconnection of networks or network facilities (Article 174, paragraph 1, items 7 and 9 of the LEC).

760. It should be mentioned that section 2 of Chapter 10 of the LEC also provides for some specific obligations for access and interconnection. In that regard, the CRC may impose, maintain, amend or withdraw specific obligations on the operators with a significant part of the market to provide efficient access and/or interconnection and interoperability between the networks for the benefit of the consumers and in order to promote effective competition (Article 166, paragraph 1 of the LEC). According to paragraph 2 of the same article, these specific obligations may be transparency, equality, accounting separation, access to and use of appropriate network facilities and equipment and price controls.

761. In exceptional circumstances, the CRC can also impose functional separation and other obligations for access and/or interconnection than those set out in paragraph 2 of Article 166 of the LEC. This may occur after obtaining the consent of the European Commission (Article 166, paragraph 3).

762. Here, we should mention that operators, which provide public communications networks and/or services in another Member State of the EU and do not provide services and support networks in Bulgaria, may request access/or interconnection under this chapter without submitting a notification to the CRC (Article 165 of the LEC).

763. According to Article 164 of the LEC, the methods for accessing and/or interconnection shall be established by ordinance adopted by the CRC, which then shall be published in the State Gazette.

764. The Ordinance on the essential requirements and conformity assessment of radio equipment and telecommunication devices specifies the essential requirements for Radio and Telecommunications Terminal Equipment (RTTE),[293] the requirements for the connection of devices to the public telecommunication networks, the assessment procedures and methods for verification of the equipment

293. Paragraph 1 of the Additional provisions of the Ordinance on the Essential Requirements and Conformity Assessment of Radio Equipment and Telecommunication Devices specifies the essential requirements for RTTE. The telecommunications terminal equipment is a device that allows data flowing or element of a device intended for direct or indirect connection to the interfaces of the public telecommunication networks, namely telecommunications networks that serve entirely or partly for the provision of publicly available telecommunications services.

with the essential requirements, as well as the procedure for issuing licences to persons for evaluation of the conformity and verification of compliance with the conditions under which the authorization was issued (Article 1 of the Ordinance).

765. The essential requirements for all the RTTE regarding their safe use and the fact they do not generate unacceptable electromagnetic interferences (EMIs) are contained in Chapter 2 of the Ordinance. They have to be designed and constructed so as to make effective use of the spectrum allocated to terrestrial or satellite radio communications and of the orbital resources and to avoid harmful interference (Article 11 of the Ordinance).

766. When the RTTE meets the essential requirements, the operators of public telecommunication networks cannot refuse, on technical grounds, the connection of other operators' devices to the appropriate interfaces. However, the operators of public telecommunication networks may refuse to connect the devices when they cause serious damage to the network, create an adverse impact or interfere with the functioning of the network (Article 8 of the Ordinance).

767. The operators of public telecommunication networks have to publish accurate and detailed technical specifications of their interfaces for the connection devices to their networks. They have the obligation to update this information, which is published on the official page of the CRC (Article 9 of the Ordinance).

Part IV. Cross-Ownership Regulation

768. One of the most common forms of media concentration is the so-called cross-ownership. Cross-ownership can be defined as the single ownership of two or more related businesses (such as a newspaper and a television station) that allows the owner to control competition. The cross-ownership in the media occurs when one person or a company owns two or more communication media, in particular in the same local market.

769. It is obvious that the concentration of media ownership has an impact on the media content and is not favourable for the plurality of opinions and thus for the public interest. For that reason, there is a need for regulation. Specifically, regulation is mandatory in Bulgaria, as the country has a small media market, dominated by few major owners. There are however no restrictions on cross-ownership in Bulgaria. There exist no express legal restrictions in the LRT on a radio broadcaster owning a television channel or vice versa. In practice, there are cases of media cross-ownership in Bulgaria, and the CEM has not taken any negative view of those.

770. Despite the lack of provisions regarding cross-ownership, the LRT contains some provisions which try to limit the monopoly position on the market in order to prevent one person or company, whether they own two or more communication media, from dominating the media market.

771. According to Article 108 of the LRT, when submitting documents to obtain licences under Article 111 of the LRT, the candidates shall declare that they do not hold shares, stocks or other rights for participation in radio and television broadcasters over the allowable amount under the Bulgarian antitrust legislation, which is the LPC.

772. This formulation of the article can be criticized as these provisions put the candidates in a position to declare circumstances that they are unable to judge, which can be decided only by the CRC after a study is done using a strictly defined methodology.[294] It would be more convenient to ask the candidates to provide the necessary information to the CEM, who after consultation with the CRC, decide whether their percentage is above the one accepted by the law.[295]

294. According to Art. 27, para. 1 of the LPC, the CRC shall carry out sectoral analysis in cases where the competition in a sector, sub-sector or a region can be prevented, restricted or distorted.
295. J. Zaharieva, *Media Law: Dictionary of the Main Concepts* 206 (Trud 2005).

Part V. Supervision: Media Regulator

773. The LRT provides for special body that deals with the regulation of media services. The media regulator in Bulgaria is the CEM. The legal regulation of its organization and powers is settled in the provisions of Chapter 2 of the LRT. Another important act is the Structural Regulations of the CEM adopted by the Council in 2011 in pursuance of Article 23 of the LRT.

Chapter 1. Organization

774. The Council is a legal entity with an independent budget. Its headquarters is situated in Sofia. The Council is assisted in its activities by an administration. The structure of the latter is determined by the CEM at its own discretion depending on the financial resources allocated for the respective year.

775. CEM consists of five members. Three of them shall be elected by the National Assembly and the other two shall be appointed by the President of the Republic of Bulgaria. The candidates shall meet all the requirements laid down in the provisions of Articles 25 and 26 of the LRT. They shall:

- be Bulgarian citizens who: (i) have not been convicted of deprivation of liberty for international crimes of a general nature; (ii) have not been on the full-time staff or part-time informers of the former State Security; and (iii) are not sole traders, owners of the capital of commercial corporations, partners, Managing Directors, managerial agents or members of management and auditing bodies of commercial corporations and cooperatives;
- have a degree of higher education and possess professional experience in the following spheres: electronic media, electronic communications, journalism, law or economics; and
- enjoy public authority and professional recognition.

776. Furthermore, the LRT settles some other limitations of the subjective rights of the members in order to keep their independence and impartiality during their term of office. The prohibitive norm of Article 27, paragraph 1 of the LRT lays down an exhaustive list of restrictions. Pursuant to this provision, during their term of office the members of the Council may not: (i) occupy any other salaried position under labour agreement; (ii) hold elective office in any state or municipal bodies, in the governing bodies of any political parties and coalitions, or in any syndicates; (iii) be members of the management, auditing and supervisory bodies of any commercial corporations or cooperatives; (iv) be consultants or members of management, auditing and supervisory bodies of any media service providers, or acquire interests or shares in any such broadcasters or in any advertising agencies; (v) be consultants or members of management, auditing and supervisory bodies of any non-profit organizations which are media service providers; and (vi) receive remuneration in any form whatsoever from any media service provider except cases of providing of services under the intellectual property legislation. In cases described in (iv) and (v), the prohibition shall also apply for two, respectively one year, after the expiry of the term of office. Nevertheless, the law stipulates an obligation addressed to the employers of persons who are going to become members of CME. The employers shall grant unpaid leave of absence for the duration of the term of office to such persons if they have applied for leave. After the expiration or termination of the said term of office, any such employers shall be obligated to reinstate the persons to their former position if the latter expresses such will.

777. The mandate of the members is six years. The members of the CEM shall be re-elected every two years for the quota of the National Assembly and every three years for the quota of the President. A person cannot be a member of the CEM for more than two mandates. The mandates may not be consecutive.

778. The establishment of certain juridical facts leads to termination of the mandate. These juridical facts are set in the provisions of Article 30, paragraphs 1 and 2 of the LRT. Pursuant to these norms, the mandate of a member of the CME shall be terminated ahead of terms in cases of release of the person from his occupation or death. The release shall be made by a decision of the Council in cases of: (i) resignation; (ii) permanent actual inability of a member to fulfil his obligations for more than six months; (iii) established incompatibility with requirements set in the LRT; (iv) enactment of a sentence which imposes a punishment 'imprisonment' for deliberate crime; and (v) enforcement of the juridical act by which has been identified situation of conflict of interests pursuant to the Law for Prevention and Establishment of Conflict of Interests.

779. The members of the Council shall elect among each other a chairman for a period of one year. This election shall be held at the first meeting of the Council. The powers of the chairman are enumerated in Article 31, paragraph 2 of the LRT. Pursuant to this provision the chairman shall:

- represent the CEM;
- convene, prepare and chair the meetings of the CEM;
- sign the acts of the CEM adopted in fulfilment of this law;
- maintain the connections of the CEM with the state bodies and with the media service operators, as well as with international organizations in the field of media services;
- issue punitive decisions for violations of the provisions of the LRT;
- manage the work of the administration; and
- exercise control for the fulfilment of the adopted acts.

Chapter 2. Tasks

780. The most important task that the LRT assigns to the Council is the supervision of the activity of media services providers for the observation of the law. However, the supervision is not limitless. In order to guarantee the freedom and independence of the media providers, the norm of Article 33 of the LRT sets certain limits before the supervision. Those limits have to be respected by the Council when the latter exercises its functions. The supervision of the activities of the radio and television operators shall regard only:

- the observance of the principles under Article 10, paragraph 1;
- the observance of the requirements under Article 6, paragraphs 2 and 3;
- the reporting of the elections for state bodies and bodies of local independent government;
- the compliance with the requirements regarding commercial communications;
- the observance of the norms regarding charitable activities, sponsorship and product placement;
- the preservation of the secrets stipulated by the law in the media services;
- the observance of the requirements for the broadcasts directed to children;
- the information regarding decisions of the jurisdiction and the other state bodies in the cases stipulated by the law;
- the protection of the rights of the consumers;
- the technical quality of the broadcasts and programmes;
- the observance of the restrictions stipulated by the law, by the licences and enacted international agreements party to which is the Republic of Bulgaria; and
- the compliance with the conditions of the granted licences and carried out registrations.

781. Within the competence of CEM are also the election and the release of the General Directors of BNR and BNT, as well as the approval of the members of the management boards of the latter. CEM also determines the members of the management board of fund 'Radio and Television' and appoints its Executive Director.

782. Furthermore, CEM is entitled to:

- share opinion in working out normative acts and in concluding international agreements in the field of media services;
- share opinion on the project for subsidy from the state budget for BNR and BNT;
- take decisions on the issuance, amendment, supplement, revoking, transferring and termination of licences for radio and television activity for the creation of programmes intended for broadcasting through available and/or new electronic communications networks for terrestrial analogue radio broadcasting;
- issue obligatory instructions to media service providers for compliance with the provisions of Article 33;
- adopt decisions regarding programmes created and provided for transmission in breach of the requirements set in the LRT;

- keep a public register on the different radio and television programmes as well as on-demand media services;
- carry out registration of radio and television programmes, amend and delete existing registrations and issue certificates of registration; and
- issue individual licences for radio and television activity carried out by radio and television operators for national/regional programmes, who are entitled to be broadcasted by an undertaking with an authorization for individual scarce resource – radio frequency spectrum for broadcasting electronic communications through available and/or new terrestrial analogue radio broadcasting communication networks with national and/or regional coverage, etc.[296]

783. In fulfilment of its legal capacities, the CEM adopts regulations, decisions and declarations and shall give opinions in the cases stipulated by the law.

784. When making decisions, the CEM shall be guided by the principles of fellowship, publicity and transparency, independence in the discussions and decision-making, cooperation with state bodies, media service providers and non-governmental organizations active in the sphere of media services or in the protection of copyright and neighbouring rights and protection of the interests of viewers and listeners.

785. The decision of CEM may be appealed before the SAC in compliance with the procedure established by the Administrative Procedure Code.[297]

296. The powers of the CEM are enumerated in Art. 32, para. 1 of the LRT.
297. Promulgated in the State Gazette, issue No. 30 of 11 Apr. 2006.

Chapter 3. Sanctioning Powers

786. The CEM may impose monetary sanctions or revoke licences. Pursuant to Article 122 of the LRT, a licence shall be revoked in cases of: (i) gross violation of the principles of the radio and television activity; (ii) systematic (i.e., at least two) offences of the provisions of the LRT; and (iii) establishment of false data in the declarations that the candidates for licence for radio and television activity submit to the CEM. The Council revokes the licence for radio or television operators by motivated decision. The revoking shall be carried out upon written warning containing a definite term for removal of the offence. CEM shall revoke the licence if the person does not remove the offence within the stipulated term. The revoking shall be carried out in all cases upon imposing two monetary sanctions for one and the same offence.

787. The monetary sanctions are laid down in Chapter 7 of the LRT. They vary from EUR 1,000 to 15,000. In case of repeated violation, the sanction is double the amount. The establishment of the offences is carried out by the officials of the Council. The chairman of the Council is entitled to issue the penalty decrees. These juridical actions shall comply with the order of the Law for the Administrative Violations and Penalties.[298]

298. Promulgated in the State Gazette, issue No. 92 of 28 Nov. 1969.

Selected Bibliography

Chichovska, V. *The Political Censure in Bulgaria*. University Ed. Chernorizec Hrabar, 2003.

Daskalova, N. *The Bulgarian Media System after 1989: Restructuring in Three Directions*. EastBound, 2010.

Nikolova, E. *The Media in South-East Europe. Comparative Media Law and Policy Study*. Country Report Bulgaria, 2011.

Ognyanova, N. *Audio-Visual Policy and Legislation of the European Union*. Sofia: University Press Saint Kliment Ohridski, 2005.

Pecheva, M., et al. *The Words of the Media Transition*. Faber Ed., 2010.

Raycheva, L. 'Television, the Fragile Virtual Shelter?'. *Media Research, Croatian Journal for Journalism and the Media – Media and the Public Interest* 15 (2009): 81–102.

Raycheva, L. 'The Dynamics of the Electronic Mass Media System in Bulgaria (1989–1999)'. *The Global Network* 13 (2000): 37–57.

Smilova, R., D. Smilov & G. Ganev. *Media Policies and Regulatory Practices in a Selected Set of European Countries, the EU and the Council of Europe: The Case of Bulgaria*. Background information report, 2010, European research project.

Staneva, E., et al. *The Radio Environment 2001–2010*. Faber Ed., 2011.

Tcholakov, R. *Media Law: Dictionary of the Main Concepts*. Newspapers Group Bulgaria, Publishing House Trud, 2005, (Медийно право: речник на основните понятия, in Bulgarian).

Television across Europe: Follow up Reports 2008. Open Society Institute, 2008.

Selected Bibliography

Index

The numbers here refer to paragraph numbers.

Index

www.ingramcontent.com/pod-product-compliance
Lightning Source LLC
Chambersburg PA
CBHW071443230926
51846CB00001B/327
9789403546681